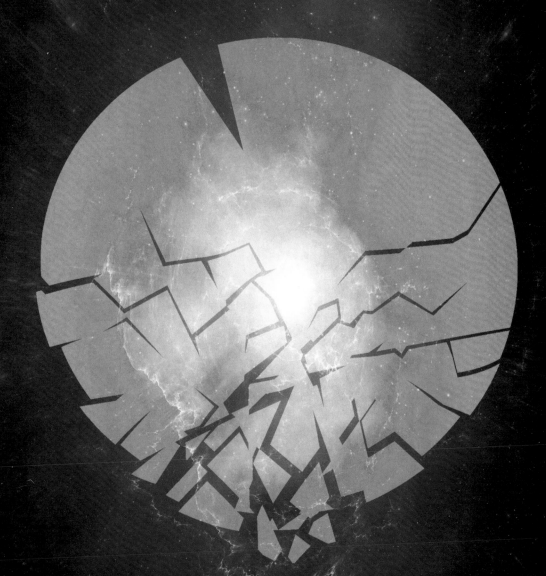

FALLEN WORLD™

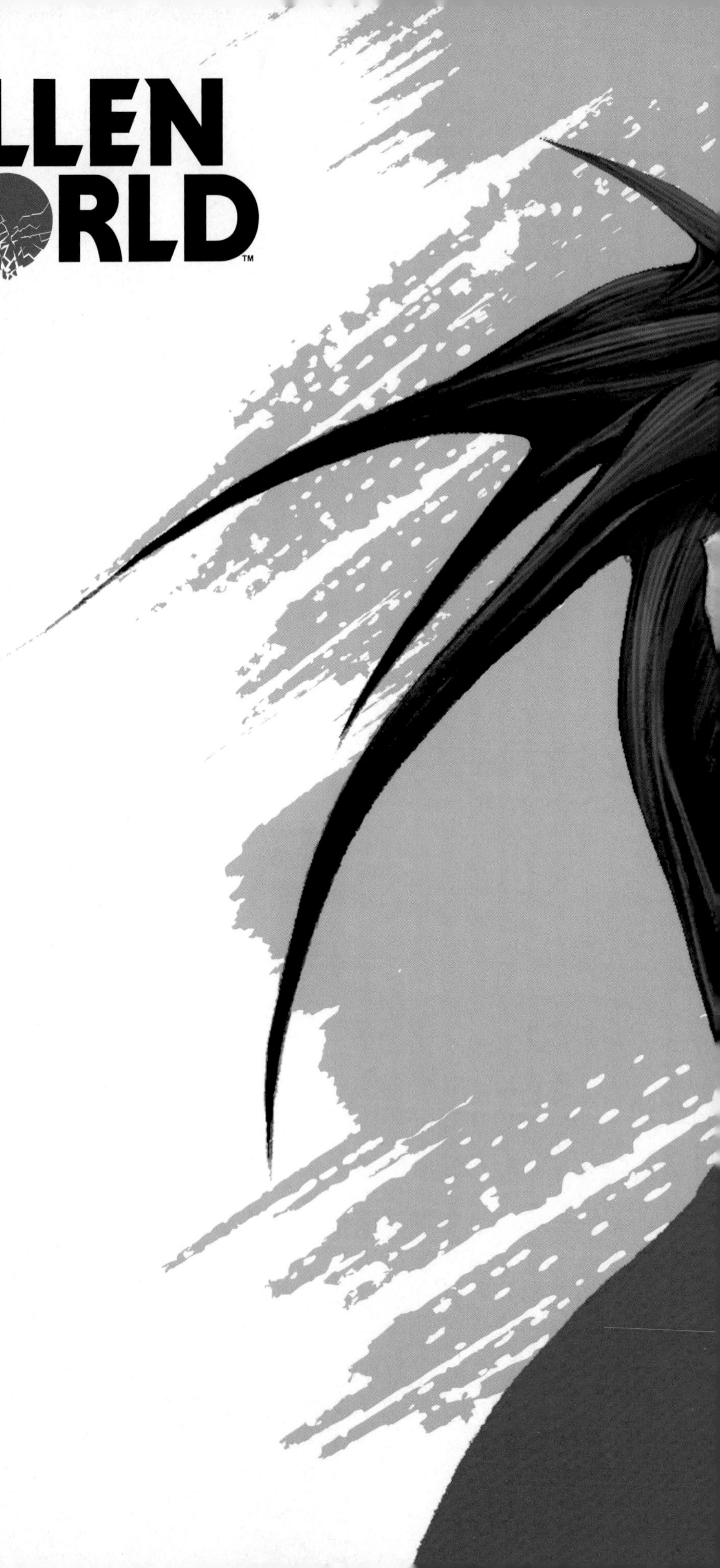

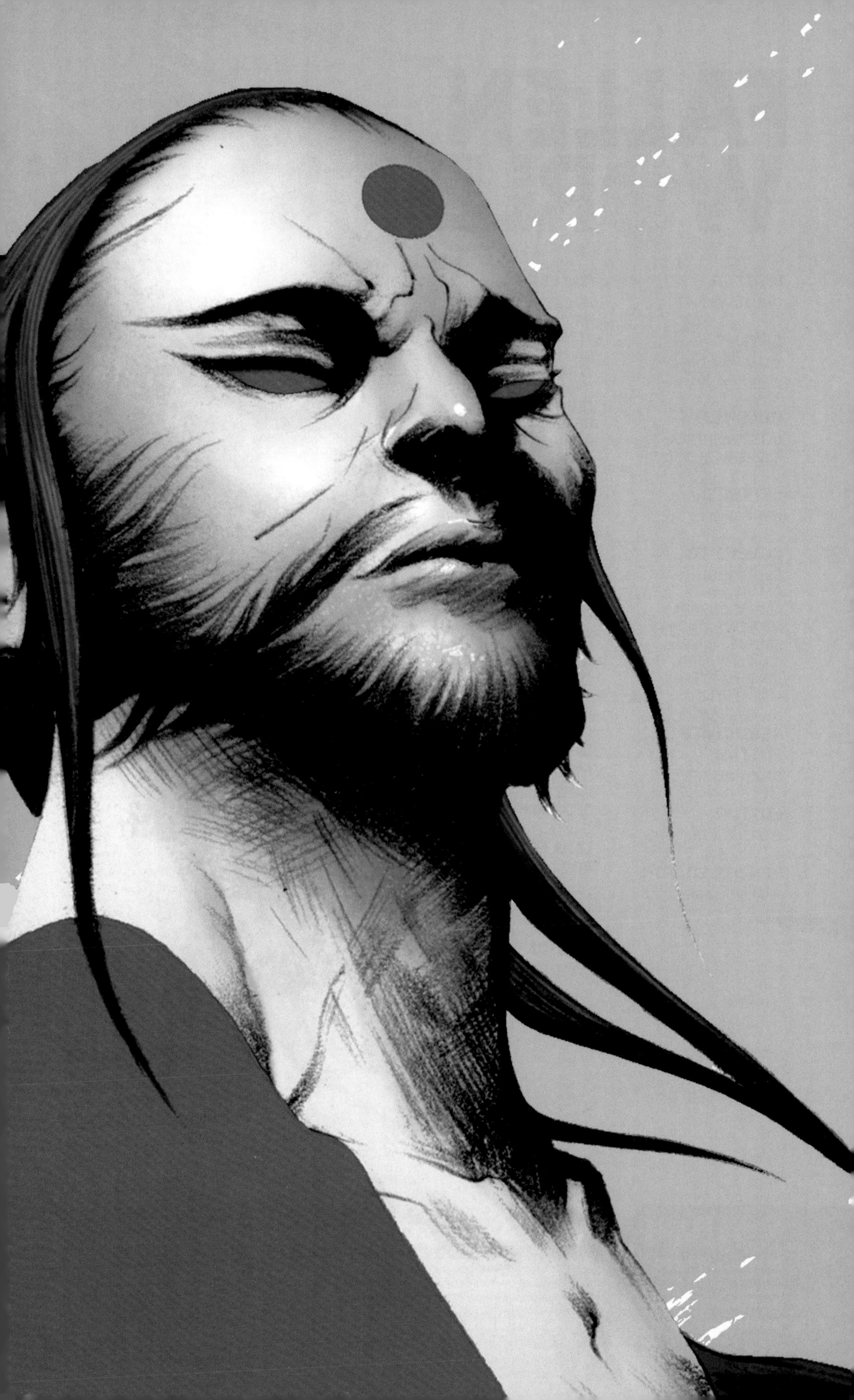

FALLEN WORLD ™

WRITER
DAN ABNETT

ARTIST
ADAM POLLINA
JUAN JOSÉ RYP

COLORISTS
ULISES ARREOLA
ANDREW DALHOUSE

LETTERER
JEFF POWELL

COVERS BY
BRETT BOOTH
DAN BROWN
ADELSO CORONA
ANDREW DALHOUSE
SANFORD GREENE
RICK LEONARDI
JONBOY MEYERS
ADAM POLLINA

ASSOCIATE EDITOR
DAVID MENCHEL

EDITOR
LYSA HAWKINS

SENIOR EDITOR
KARL BOLLERS

GALLERY
DAN ABNETT
RAÚL ALLÉN
ULISES ARREOLA
DAN BROWN
FERNANDO DAGNINO
GABE ELTAEB
STEVE FOXE
BEN HARVEY
AJ JOTHIKUMAR
RICK LEONARDI
DAVID MACK
ADAM POLLINA
JIMBO SALGADO
CASPAR WIJNGAARD

COLLECTION COVER ART
DOUG BRAITHWAITE
with DIEGO RODRIGUEZ

COLLECTION BACK COVER ART
JONBOY MEYERS

COLLECTION FRONT ART
JAE LEE
DECLAN SHALVEY

COLLECTION EDITOR
IVAN COHEN

COLLECTION DESIGNER
STEVE BLACKWELL

VALIANT®

DAN MINTZ Chairman   **FRED PIERCE** Publisher   **WALTER BLACK** VP Operations   **MATTHEW KLEIN** VP Sales & Marketing   **ROBERT MEYERS** Senior Editorial Director
TRAVIS ESCARFULLERY Director of Design & Production   **PETER STERN** Director of International Publishing & Merchandising   **LYSA HAWKINS, HEATHER ANTOS & GREG TUMBARELLO** Editors
DAVID MENCHEL Associate Editor   **DREW BAUMGARTNER** Assistant Editor   **JEFF WALKER** Production & Design Manager   **KAT O'NEILL** Sales & Live Events Manager
EMILY HECHT Digital Marketing Manager   **CONNOR HILL** Sales Operations Coordinator   **DANIELLE WARD** Sales Manager   **GREGG KATZMAN** Marketing Coordinator

Fallen World™. Published by Valiant Entertainment LLC. Office of Publication: 350 Seventh Avenue, New York, NY 10001. Compilation copyright © 2019 Valiant Entertainment LLC. All rights reserved. Contains materials originally published in single magazine form as Fallen World #1-5, and Valiant: Bloodshot FCBD 2019 Special. Copyright © 2019 Valiant Entertainment LLC. All rights reserved. All characters, their distinctive likeness and related indicia featured in this publication are trademarks of Valiant Entertainment LLC. The stories, characters, and incidents featured in this publication are entirely fictional. Valiant Entertainment does not read or accept unsolicited submissions of ideas, stories, or artwork. Printed in the U.S.A. First Printing. ISBN: 9781682153321.

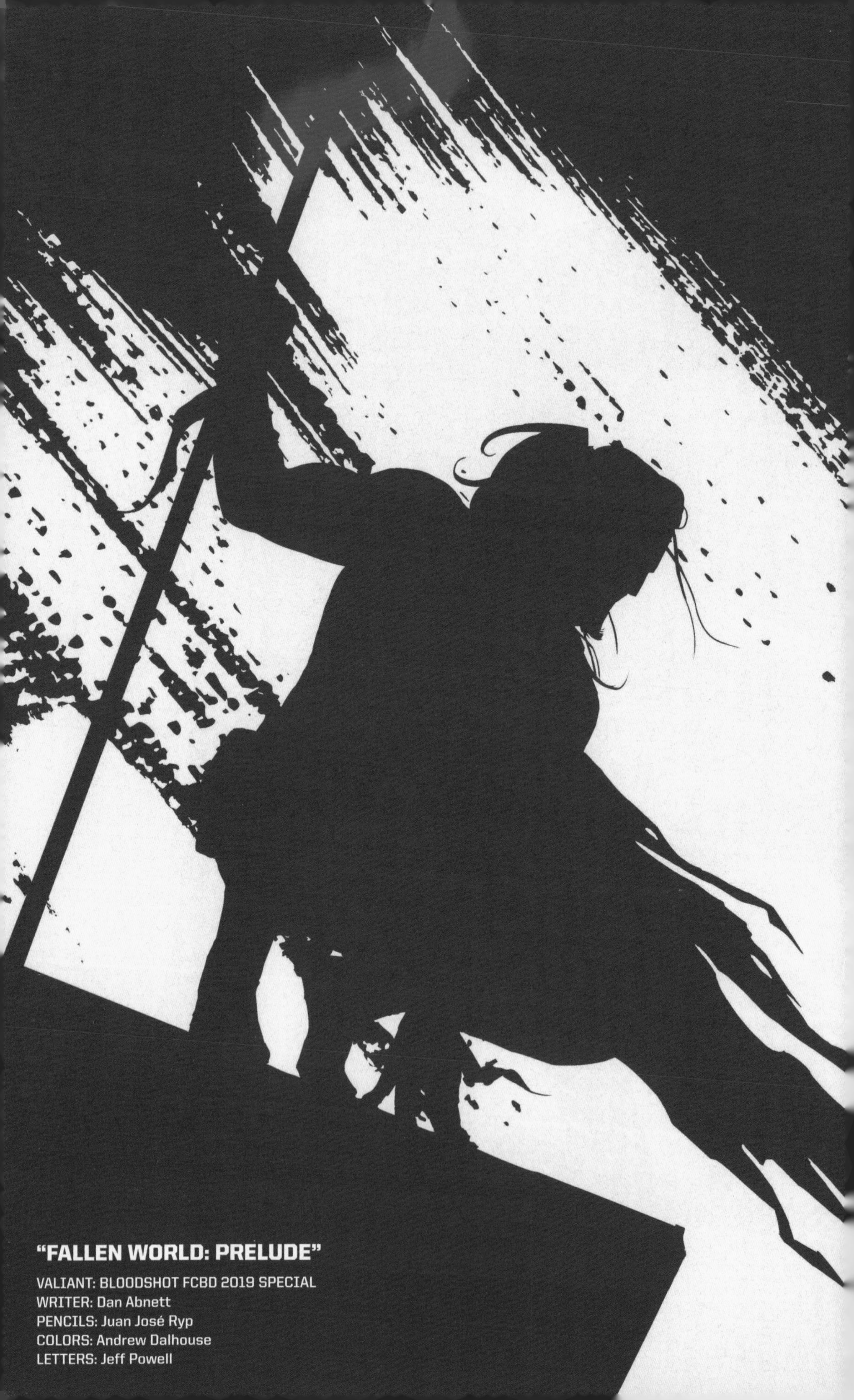

"FALLEN WORLD: PRELUDE"

VALIANT: BLOODSHOT FCBD 2019 SPECIAL
WRITER: Dan Abnett
PENCILS: Juan José Ryp
COLORS: Andrew Dalhouse
LETTERS: Jeff Powell

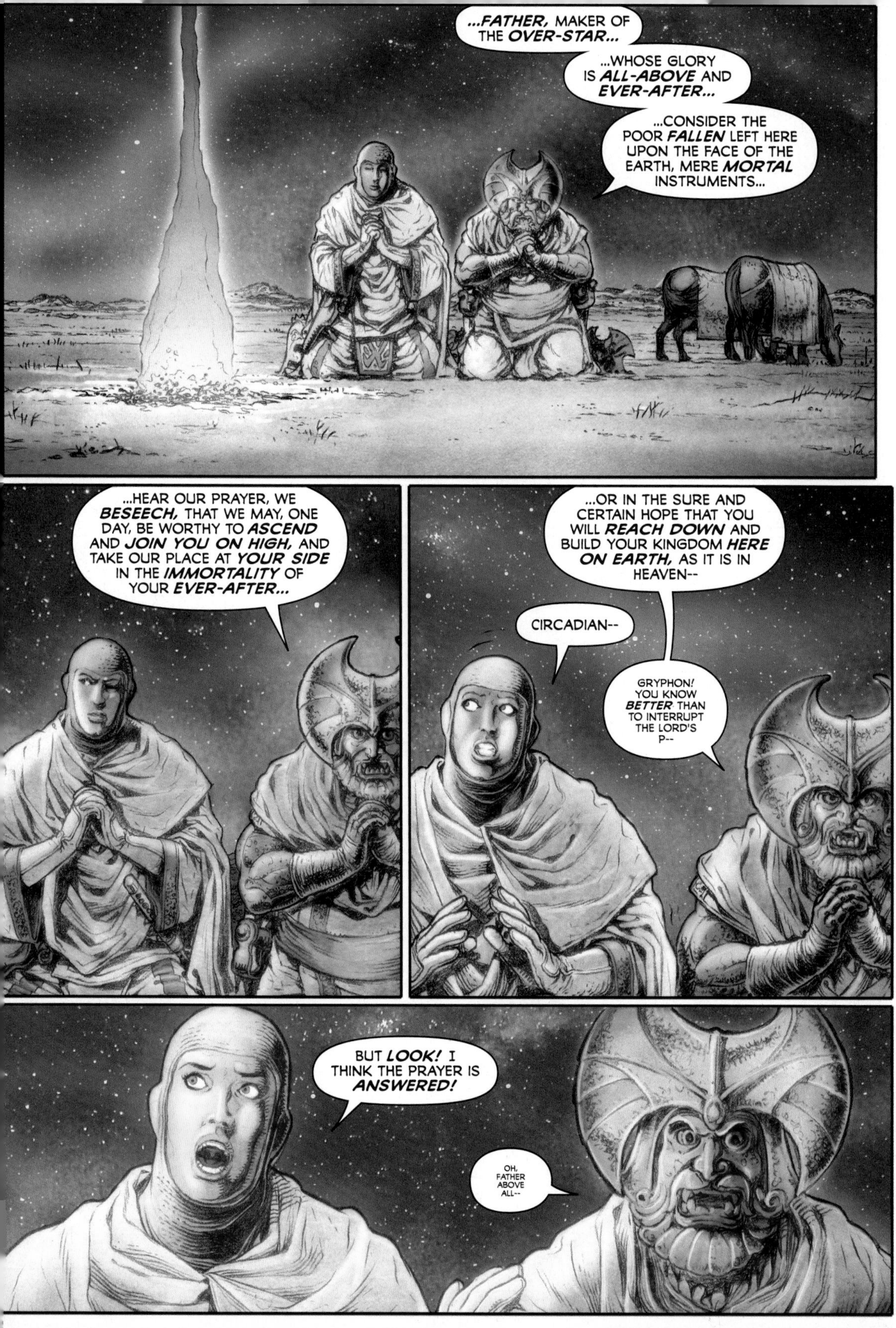
...FATHER, MAKER OF THE OVER-STAR...
...WHOSE GLORY IS ALL-ABOVE AND EVER-AFTER...
...CONSIDER THE POOR FALLEN LEFT HERE UPON THE FACE OF THE EARTH, MERE MORTAL INSTRUMENTS...
...HEAR OUR PRAYER, WE BESEECH, THAT WE MAY, ONE DAY, BE WORTHY TO ASCEND AND JOIN YOU ON HIGH, AND TAKE OUR PLACE AT YOUR SIDE IN THE IMMORTALITY OF YOUR EVER-AFTER...
...OR IN THE SURE AND CERTAIN HOPE THAT YOU WILL REACH DOWN AND BUILD YOUR KINGDOM HERE ON EARTH, AS IT IS IN HEAVEN--
CIRCADIAN--
GRYPHON! YOU KNOW BETTER THAN TO INTERRUPT THE LORD'S P--
BUT LOOK! I THINK THE PRAYER IS ANSWERED!
OH, FATHER ABOVE ALL--

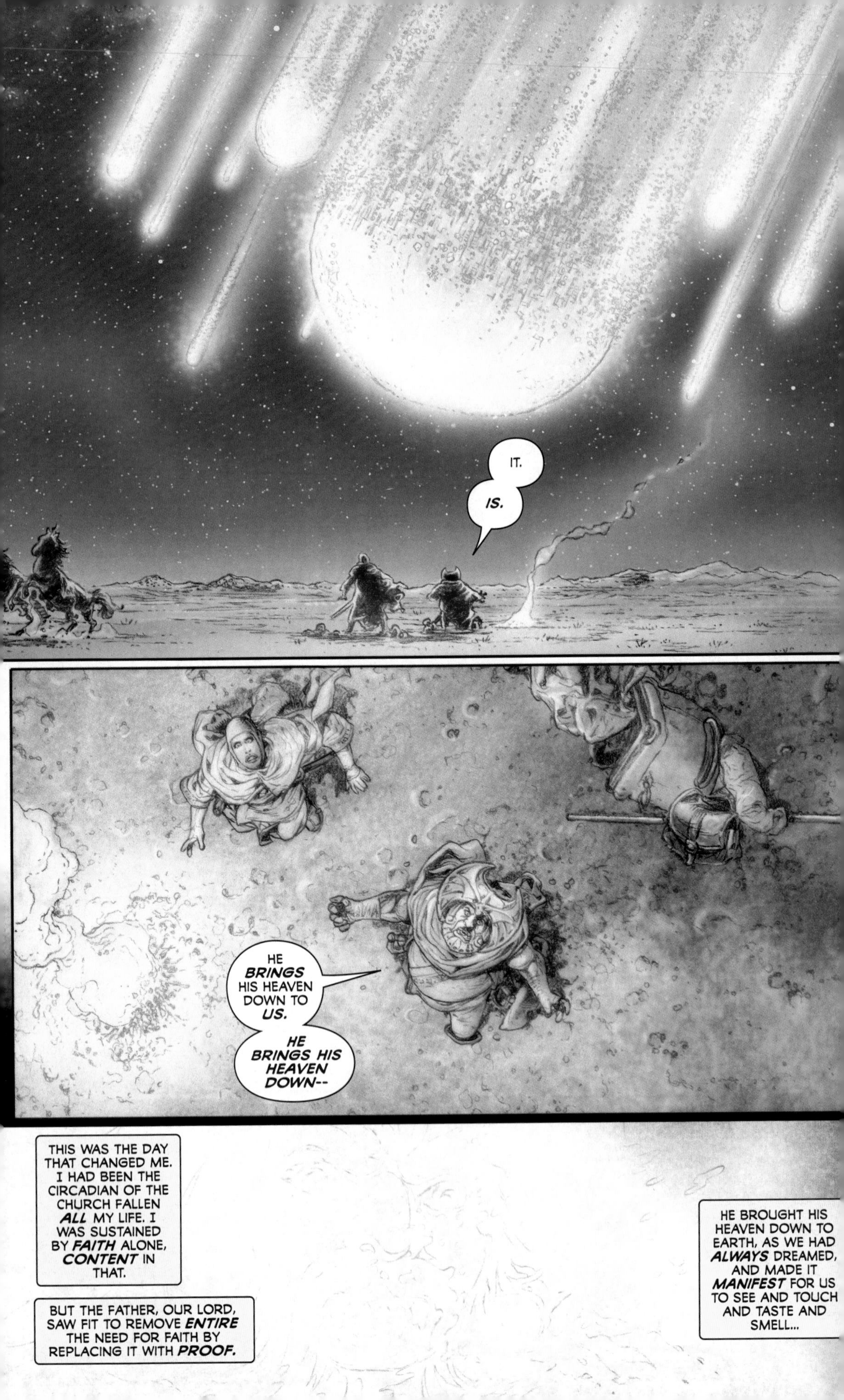

IT.
IS.
HE BRINGS HIS HEAVEN DOWN TO US.
HE BRINGS HIS HEAVEN DOWN--
THIS WAS THE DAY THAT CHANGED ME. I HAD BEEN THE CIRCADIAN OF THE CHURCH FALLEN ALL MY LIFE. I WAS SUSTAINED BY FAITH ALONE, CONTENT IN THAT.
BUT THE FATHER, OUR LORD, SAW FIT TO REMOVE ENTIRE THE NEED FOR FAITH BY REPLACING IT WITH PROOF.
HE BROUGHT HIS HEAVEN DOWN TO EARTH, AS WE HAD ALWAYS DREAMED, AND MADE IT MANIFEST FOR US TO SEE AND TOUCH AND TASTE AND SMELL...

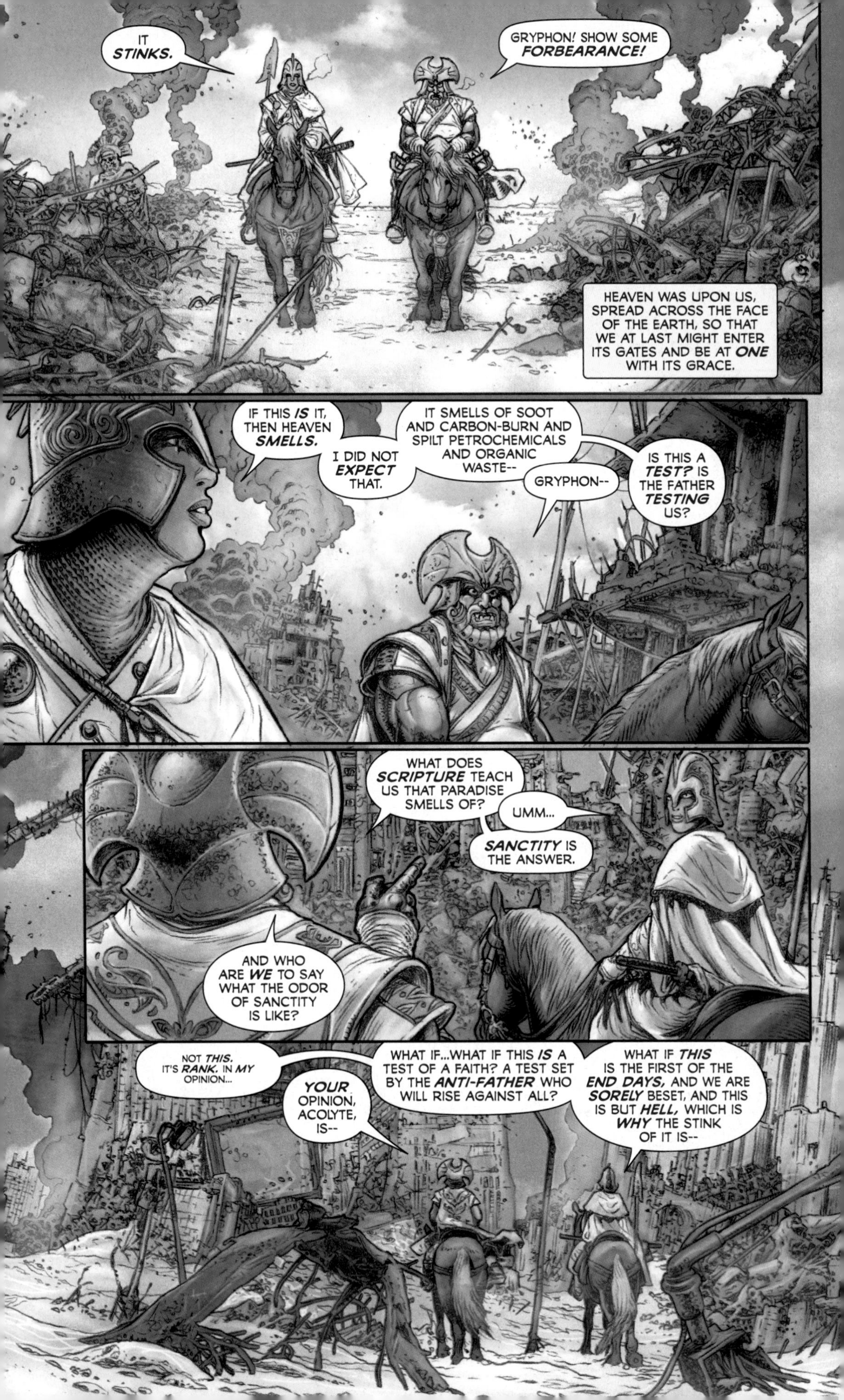
IT STINKS.
GRYPHON! SHOW SOME FORBEARANCE!
HEAVEN WAS UPON US, SPREAD ACROSS THE FACE OF THE EARTH, SO THAT WE AT LAST MIGHT ENTER ITS GATES AND BE AT ONE WITH ITS GRACE.
IF THIS IS IT, THEN HEAVEN SMELLS.
I DID NOT EXPECT THAT.
IT SMELLS OF SOOT AND CARBON-BURN AND SPILT PETROCHEMICALS AND ORGANIC WASTE--
IS THIS A TEST? IS THE FATHER TESTING US?
GRYPHON--
WHAT DOES SCRIPTURE TEACH US THAT PARADISE SMELLS OF?
UMM...
SANCTITY IS THE ANSWER.
AND WHO ARE WE TO SAY WHAT THE ODOR OF SANCTITY IS LIKE?
NOT THIS. IT'S RANK. IN MY OPINION...
YOUR OPINION, ACOLYTE, IS--
WHAT IF...WHAT IF THIS IS A TEST OF A FAITH? A TEST SET BY THE ANTI-FATHER WHO WILL RISE AGAINST ALL?
WHAT IF THIS IS THE FIRST OF THE END DAYS, AND WE ARE SORELY BESET, AND THIS IS BUT HELL, WHICH IS WHY THE STINK OF IT IS--

--OH!

BIPLANE. ANTIQUE. OLD PATTERN.

NO. AN ANGEL OF THE FATHER'S HOST, SETTING DOWN UPON--

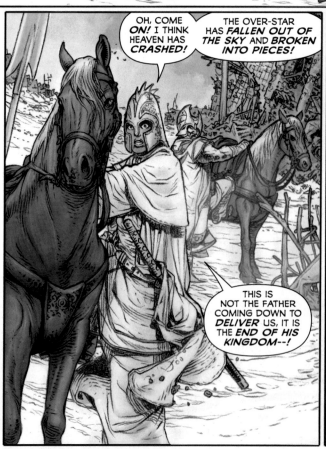

OH, COME *ON!* I THINK HEAVEN HAS *CRASHED!*

THE OVER-STAR HAS *FALLEN OUT OF THE SKY* AND *BROKEN INTO PIECES!*

THIS IS NOT THE FATHER COMING DOWN TO *DELIVER* US, IT IS THE *END OF HIS KINGDOM--!*

I'M SORRY, CIRCADIAN. THAT WAS *BLASPHEMY--*

CEASE YOUR MUSINGS, CHILD...

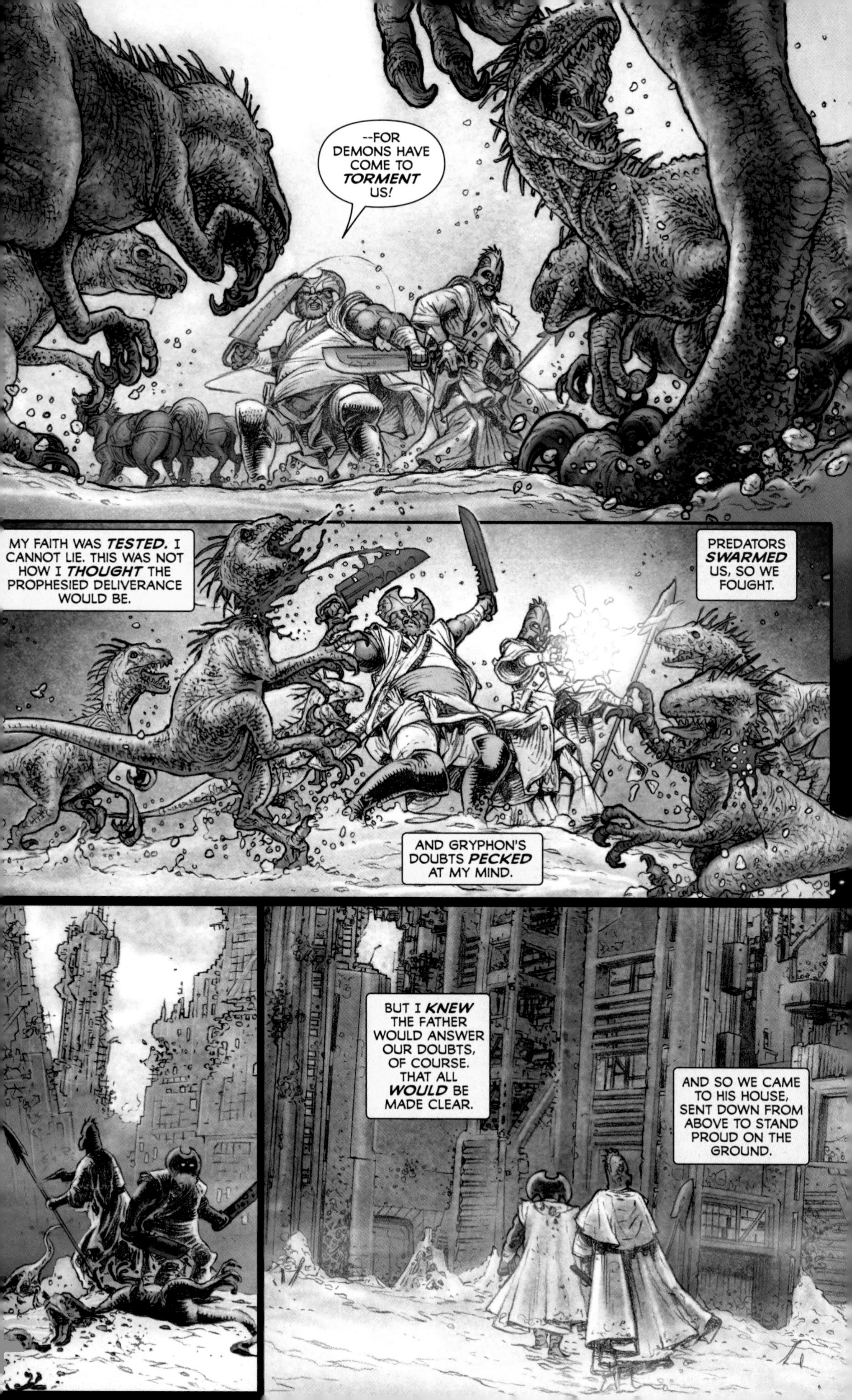
--FOR DEMONS HAVE COME TO TORMENT US!
MY FAITH WAS TESTED. I CANNOT LIE. THIS WAS NOT HOW I THOUGHT THE PROPHESIED DELIVERANCE WOULD BE.
PREDATORS SWARMED US, SO WE FOUGHT.
AND GRYPHON'S DOUBTS PECKED AT MY MIND.
BUT I KNEW THE FATHER WOULD ANSWER OUR DOUBTS, OF COURSE. THAT ALL WOULD BE MADE CLEAR.
AND SO WE CAME TO HIS HOUSE, SENT DOWN FROM ABOVE TO STAND PROUD ON THE GROUND.

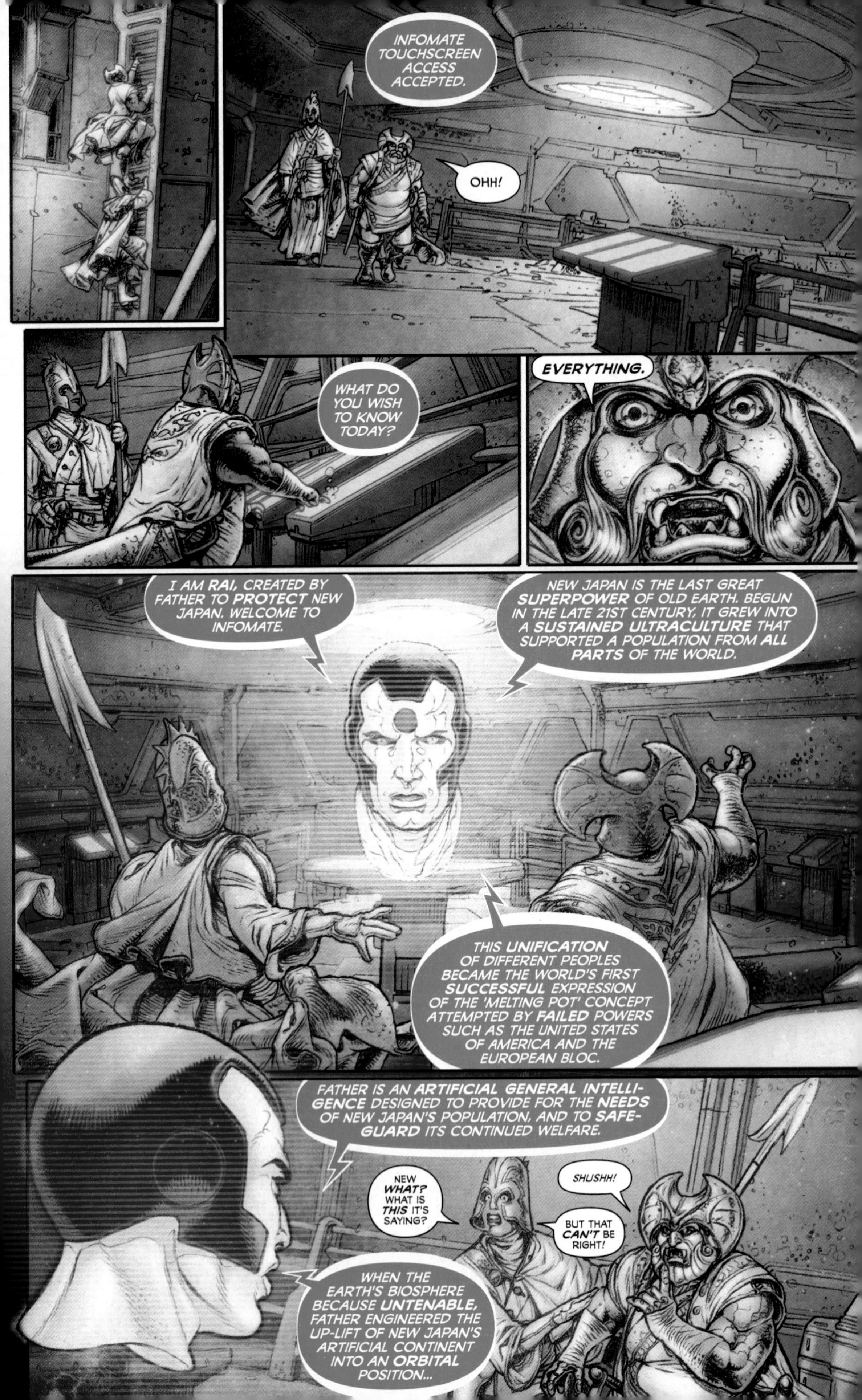
INFOMATE TOUCHSCREEN ACCESS ACCEPTED.
OHH!
WHAT DO YOU WISH TO KNOW TODAY?
EVERYTHING.
I AM RAI, CREATED BY FATHER TO PROTECT NEW JAPAN. WELCOME TO INFOMATE.
NEW JAPAN IS THE LAST GREAT SUPERPOWER OF OLD EARTH. BEGUN IN THE LATE 21ST CENTURY, IT GREW INTO A SUSTAINED ULTRACULTURE THAT SUPPORTED A POPULATION FROM ALL PARTS OF THE WORLD.
THIS UNIFICATION OF DIFFERENT PEOPLES BECAME THE WORLD'S FIRST SUCCESSFUL EXPRESSION OF THE 'MELTING POT' CONCEPT ATTEMPTED BY FAILED POWERS SUCH AS THE UNITED STATES OF AMERICA AND THE EUROPEAN BLOC.
FATHER IS AN ARTIFICIAL GENERAL INTELLIGENCE DESIGNED TO PROVIDE FOR THE NEEDS OF NEW JAPAN'S POPULATION, AND TO SAFEGUARD ITS CONTINUED WELFARE.
NEW WHAT? WHAT IS THIS IT'S SAYING?
SHUSHH!
BUT THAT CAN'T BE RIGHT!
WHEN THE EARTH'S BIOSPHERE BECAUSE UNTENABLE, FATHER ENGINEERED THE UP-LIFT OF NEW JAPAN'S ARTIFICIAL CONTINENT INTO AN ORBITAL POSITION...

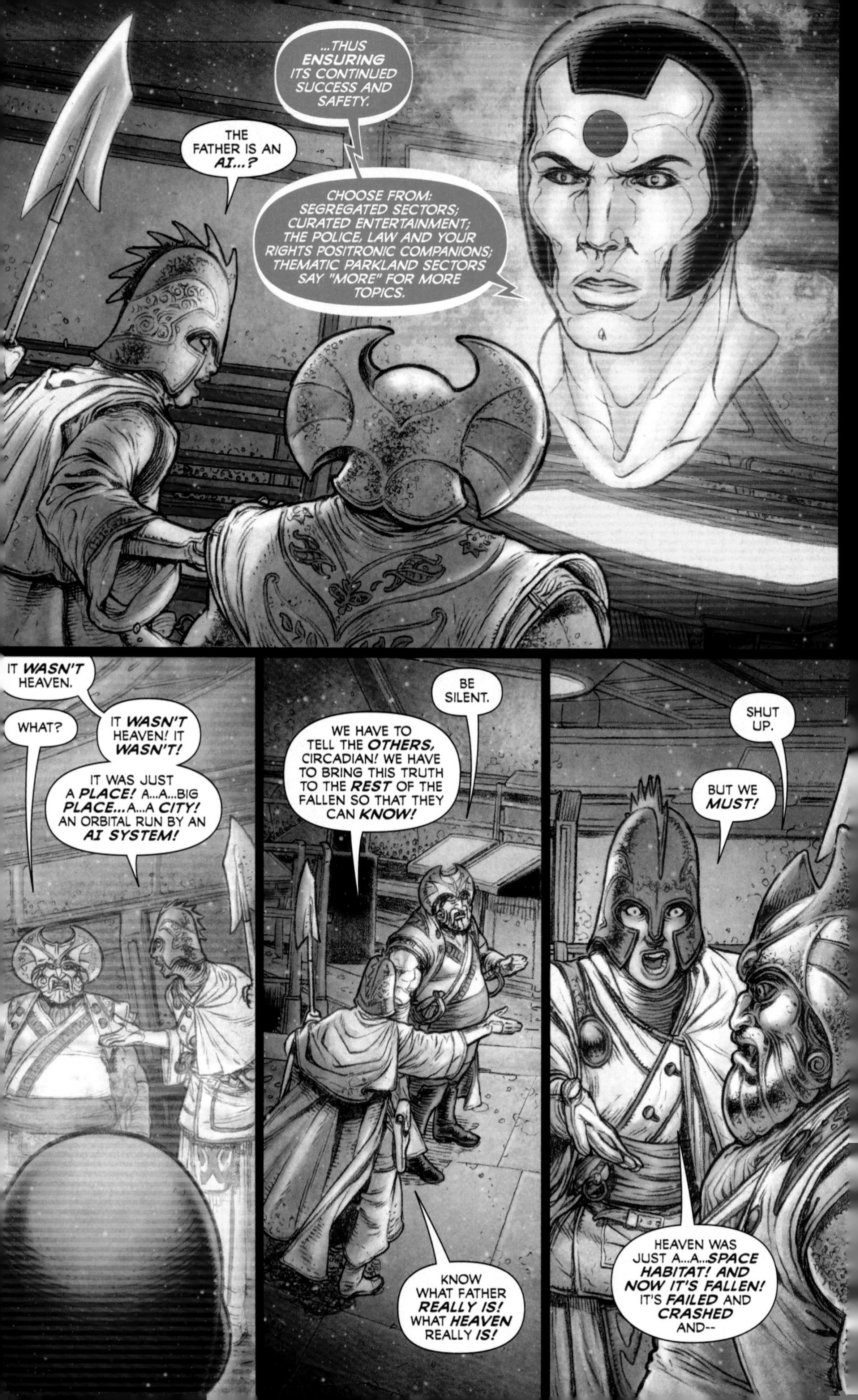

...THUS ENSURING ITS CONTINUED SUCCESS AND SAFETY.
THE FATHER IS AN AI...?
CHOOSE FROM: SEGREGATED SECTORS; CURATED ENTERTAINMENT; THE POLICE, LAW AND YOUR RIGHTS POSITRONIC COMPANIONS; THEMATIC PARKLAND SECTORS SAY "MORE" FOR MORE TOPICS.
IT WASN'T HEAVEN.
IT WASN'T HEAVEN! IT WASN'T!
WHAT?
IT WAS JUST A PLACE! A...A...BIG PLACE...A...A CITY! AN ORBITAL RUN BY AN AI SYSTEM!
BE SILENT.
WE HAVE TO TELL THE OTHERS, CIRCADIAN! WE HAVE TO BRING THIS TRUTH TO THE REST OF THE FALLEN SO THAT THEY CAN KNOW!
KNOW WHAT FATHER REALLY IS! WHAT HEAVEN REALLY IS!
SHUT UP.
BUT WE MUST!
HEAVEN WAS JUST A...A...SPACE HABITAT! AND NOW IT'S FALLEN! IT'S FAILED AND CRASHED AND--

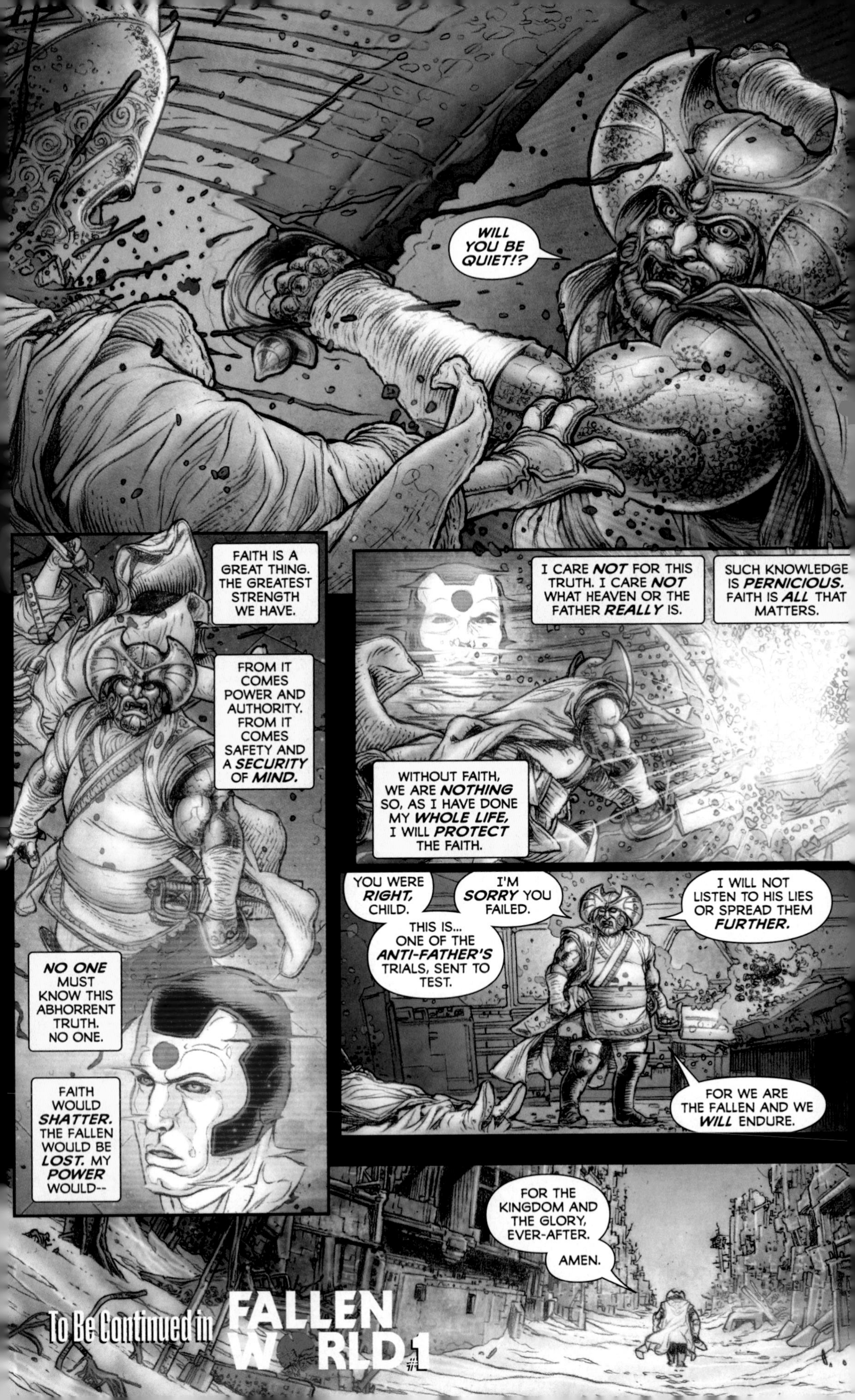
WILL YOU BE QUIET!?
FAITH IS A GREAT THING. THE GREATEST STRENGTH WE HAVE.
FROM IT COMES POWER AND AUTHORITY. FROM IT COMES SAFETY AND A SECURITY OF MIND.
NO ONE MUST KNOW THIS ABHORRENT TRUTH. NO ONE.
FAITH WOULD SHATTER. THE FALLEN WOULD BE LOST. MY POWER WOULD--
I CARE NOT FOR THIS TRUTH. I CARE NOT WHAT HEAVEN OR THE FATHER REALLY IS.
SUCH KNOWLEDGE IS PERNICIOUS. FAITH IS ALL THAT MATTERS.
WITHOUT FAITH, WE ARE NOTHING SO, AS I HAVE DONE MY WHOLE LIFE, I WILL PROTECT THE FAITH.
YOU WERE RIGHT, CHILD.
I'M SORRY YOU FAILED.
THIS IS... ONE OF THE ANTI-FATHER'S TRIALS, SENT TO TEST.
I WILL NOT LISTEN TO HIS LIES OR SPREAD THEM FURTHER.
FOR WE ARE THE FALLEN AND WE WILL ENDURE.
FOR THE KINGDOM AND THE GLORY, EVER-AFTER.
AMEN.
To Be Continued in FALLEN WORLD #1

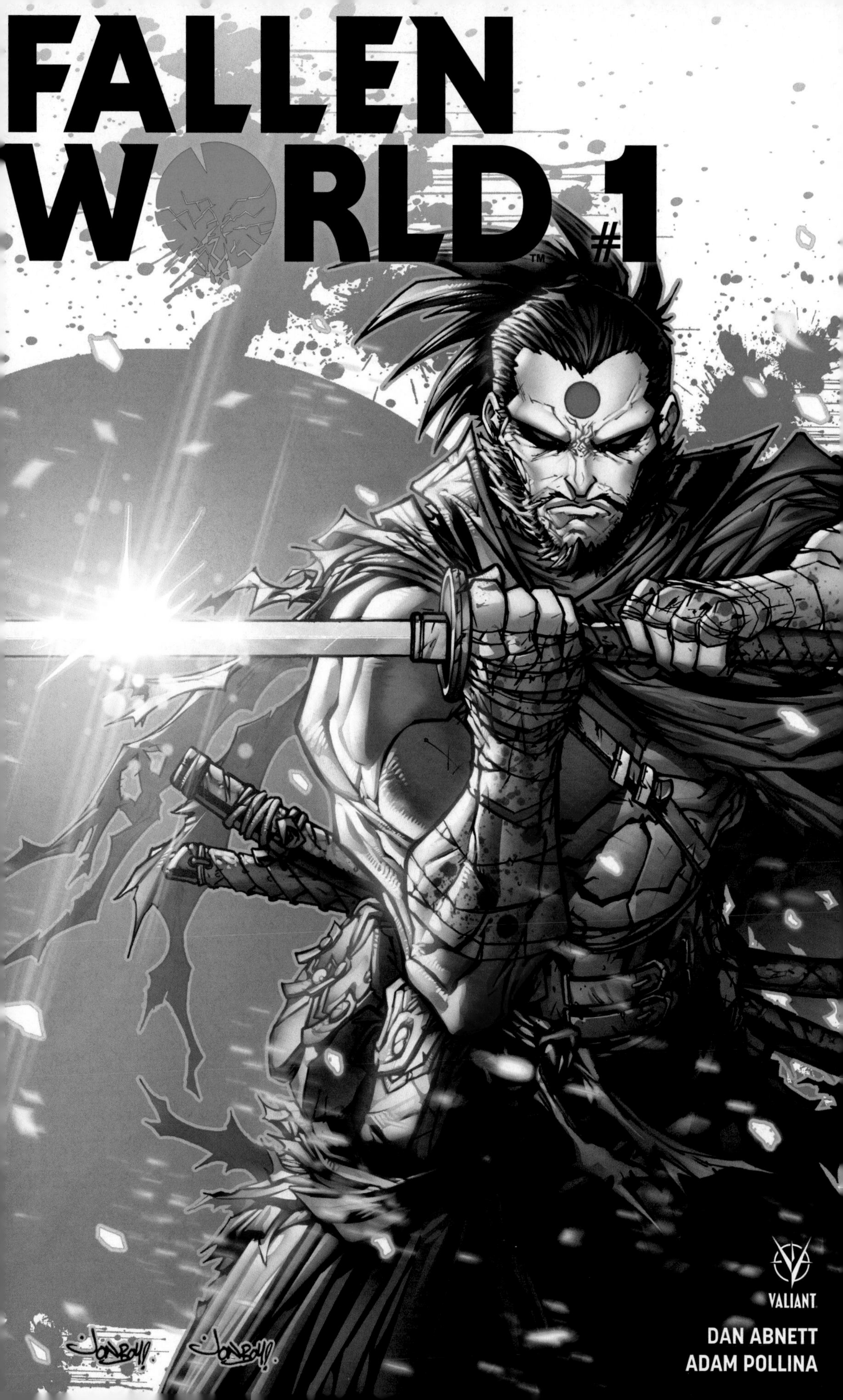

FALLEN WORLD #1™
VALIANT
DAN ABNETT
ADAM POLLINA

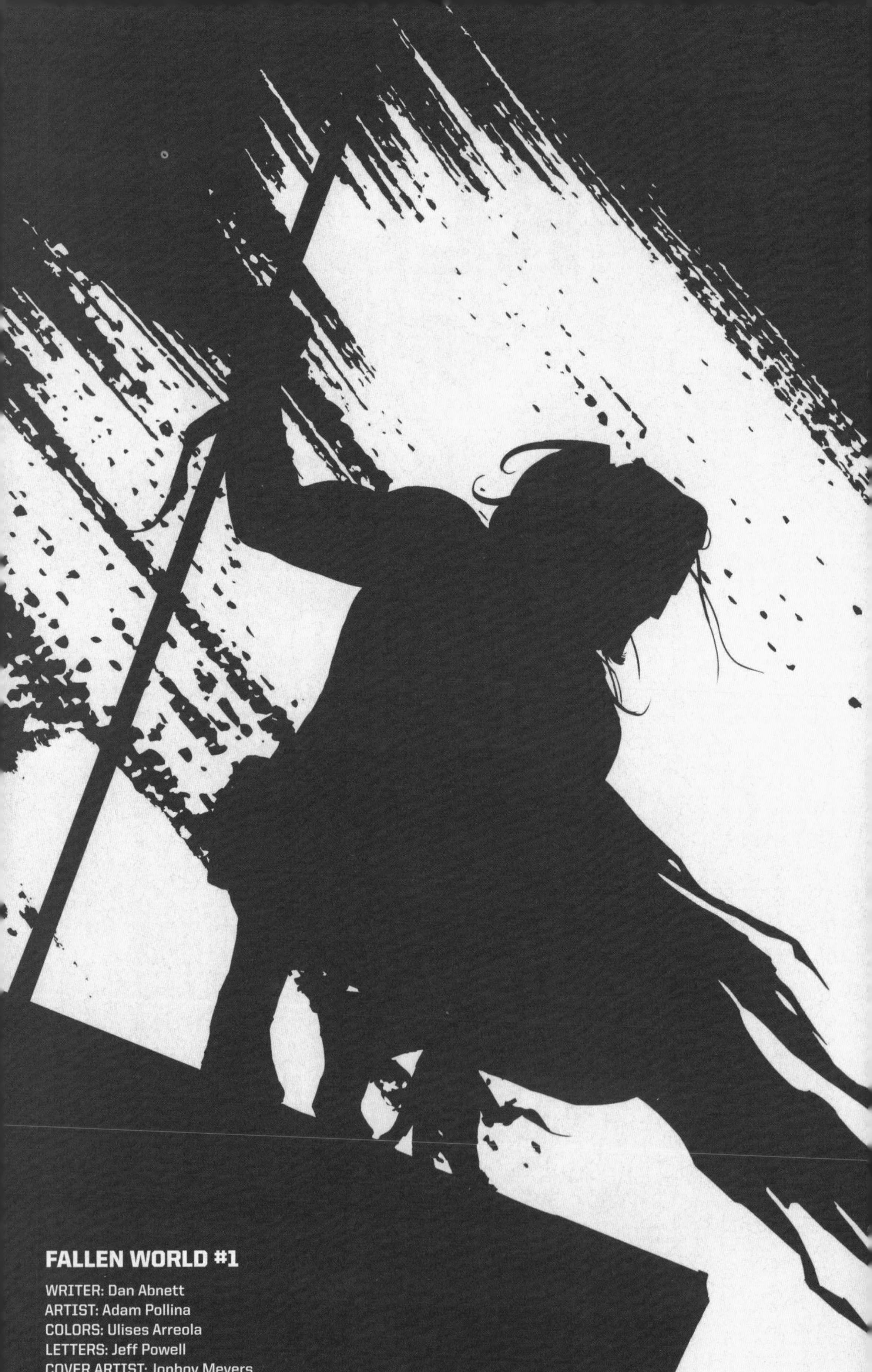

FALLEN WORLD #1

WRITER: Dan Abnett
ARTIST: Adam Pollina
COLORS: Ulises Arreola
LETTERS: Jeff Powell
COVER ARTIST: Jonboy Meyers
ASSOCIATE EDITOR: David Menchel
SENIOR EDITOR: Karl Bollers

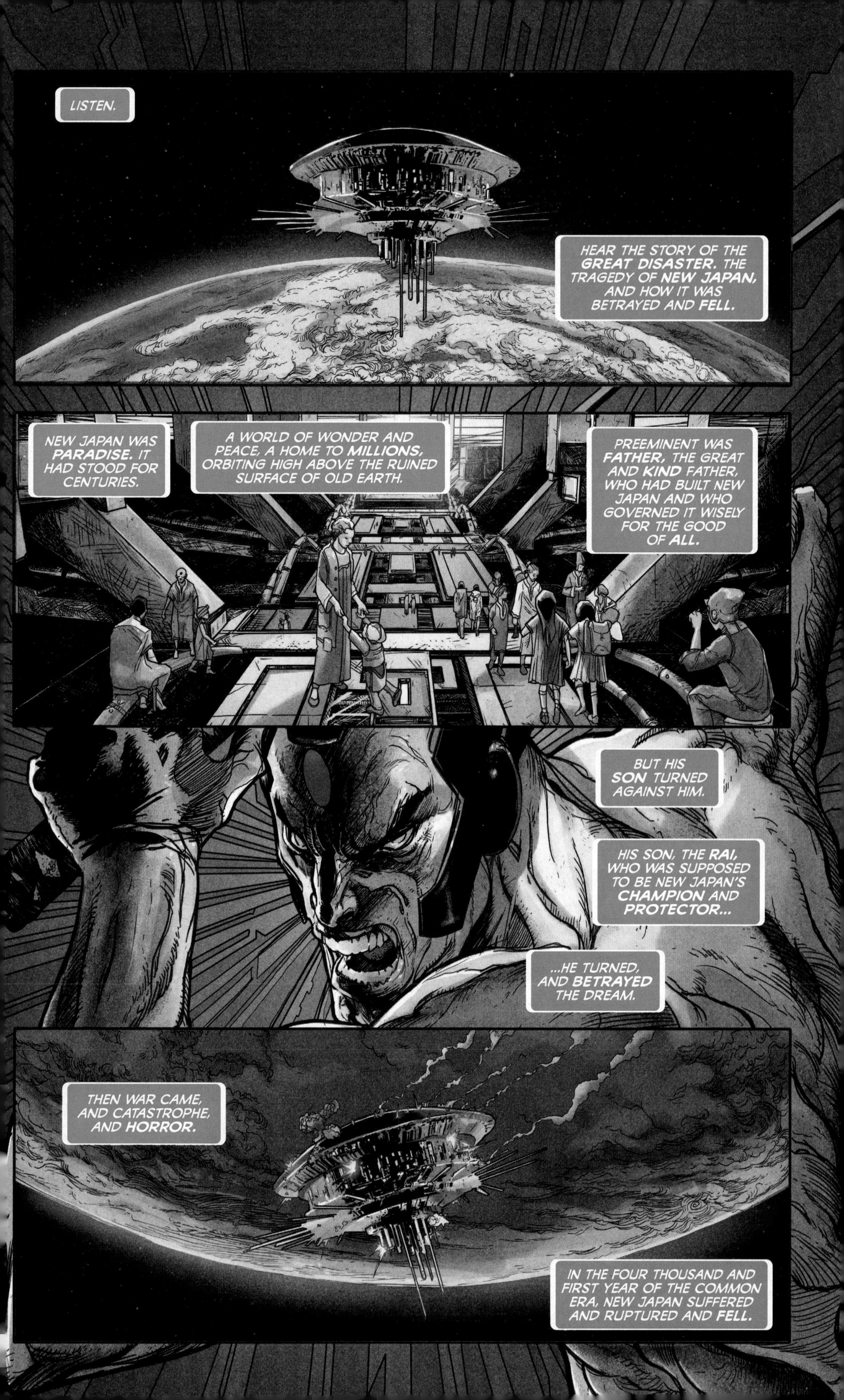
LISTEN.
HEAR THE STORY OF THE GREAT DISASTER. THE TRAGEDY OF NEW JAPAN, AND HOW IT WAS BETRAYED AND FELL.
NEW JAPAN WAS PARADISE. IT HAD STOOD FOR CENTURIES.
A WORLD OF WONDER AND PEACE, A HOME TO MILLIONS, ORBITING HIGH ABOVE THE RUINED SURFACE OF OLD EARTH.
PREEMINENT WAS FATHER, THE GREAT AND KIND FATHER, WHO HAD BUILT NEW JAPAN AND WHO GOVERNED IT WISELY FOR THE GOOD OF ALL.
BUT HIS SON TURNED AGAINST HIM.
HIS SON, THE RAI, WHO WAS SUPPOSED TO BE NEW JAPAN'S CHAMPION AND PROTECTOR...
...HE TURNED, AND BETRAYED THE DREAM.
THEN WAR CAME, AND CATASTROPHE, AND HORROR.
IN THE FOUR THOUSAND AND FIRST YEAR OF THE COMMON ERA, NEW JAPAN SUFFERED AND RUPTURED AND FELL.

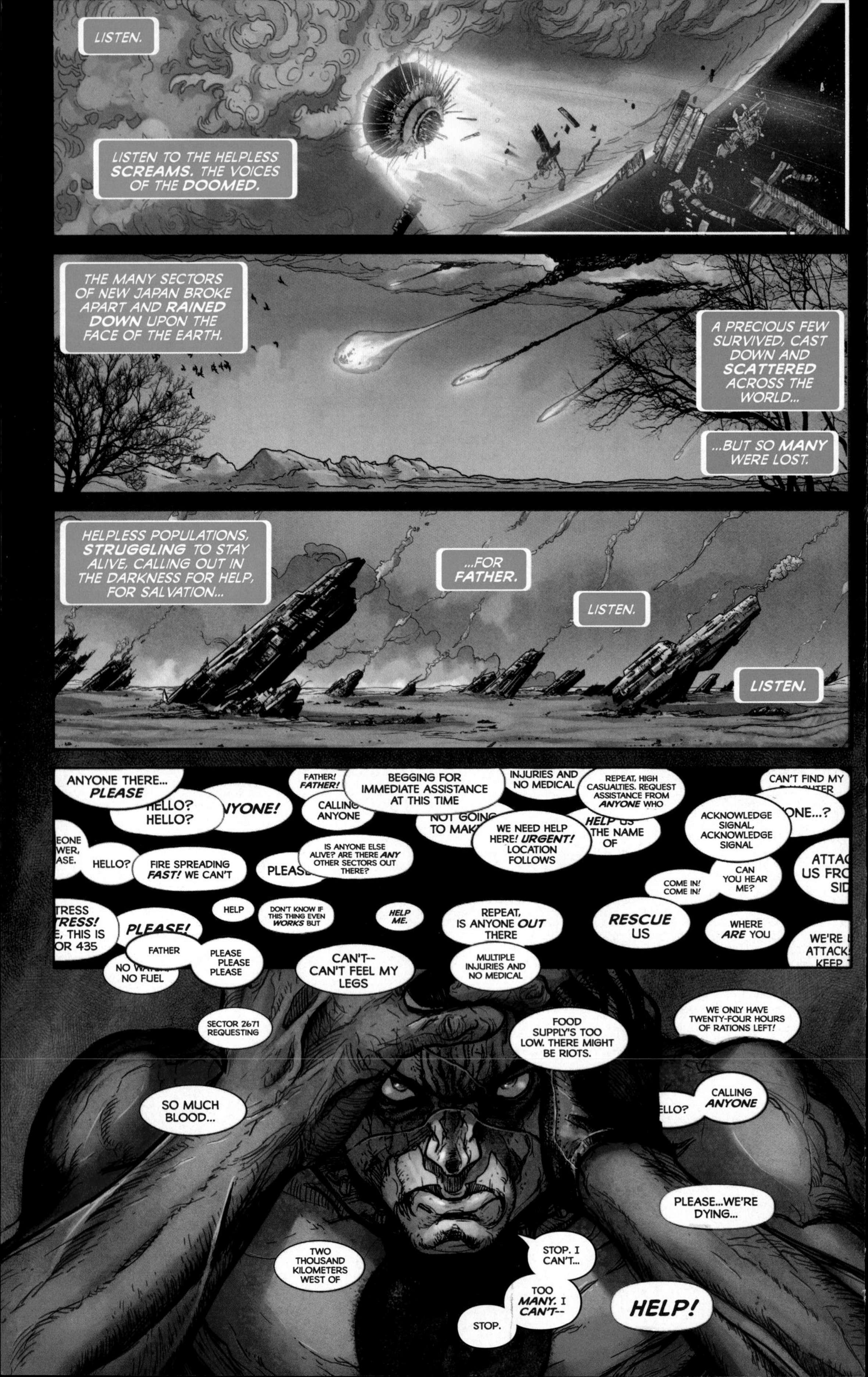

LISTEN.
LISTEN TO THE HELPLESS SCREAMS. THE VOICES OF THE DOOMED.
THE MANY SECTORS OF NEW JAPAN BROKE APART AND RAINED DOWN UPON THE FACE OF THE EARTH.
A PRECIOUS FEW SURVIVED, CAST DOWN AND SCATTERED ACROSS THE WORLD...
...BUT SO MANY WERE LOST.
HELPLESS POPULATIONS, STRUGGLING TO STAY ALIVE, CALLING OUT IN THE DARKNESS FOR HELP, FOR SALVATION...
...FOR FATHER.
LISTEN.
LISTEN.
ANYONE THERE... PLEASE
HELLO? HELLO?
FATHER! FATHER!
BEGGING FOR IMMEDIATE ASSISTANCE AT THIS TIME
INJURIES AND NO MEDICAL
REPEAT, HIGH CASUALTIES. REQUEST ASSISTANCE FROM ANYONE WHO
CAN'T FIND MY
CALLING ANYONE
WE NEED HELP HERE! URGENT! LOCATION FOLLOWS
THE NAME OF
ACKNOWLEDGE SIGNAL, ACKNOWLEDGE SIGNAL
HELLO?
FIRE SPREADING FAST! WE CAN'T
IS ANYONE ELSE ALIVE? ARE THERE ANY OTHER SECTORS OUT THERE?
COME IN! COME IN!
CAN YOU HEAR ME?
HELP
DON'T KNOW IF THIS THING EVEN WORKS BUT
HELP ME.
REPEAT, IS ANYONE OUT THERE
RESCUE US
WHERE ARE YOU
PLEASE!
FATHER
PLEASE PLEASE PLEASE
NO FUEL
CAN'T-- CAN'T FEEL MY LEGS
MULTIPLE INJURIES AND NO MEDICAL
SECTOR 2671 REQUESTING
FOOD SUPPLY'S TOO LOW. THERE MIGHT BE RIOTS.
WE ONLY HAVE TWENTY-FOUR HOURS OF RATIONS LEFT!
SO MUCH BLOOD...
CALLING ANYONE
PLEASE...WE'RE DYING...
TWO THOUSAND KILOMETERS WEST OF
STOP. I CAN'T...
TOO MANY. I CAN'T--
STOP.
HELP!

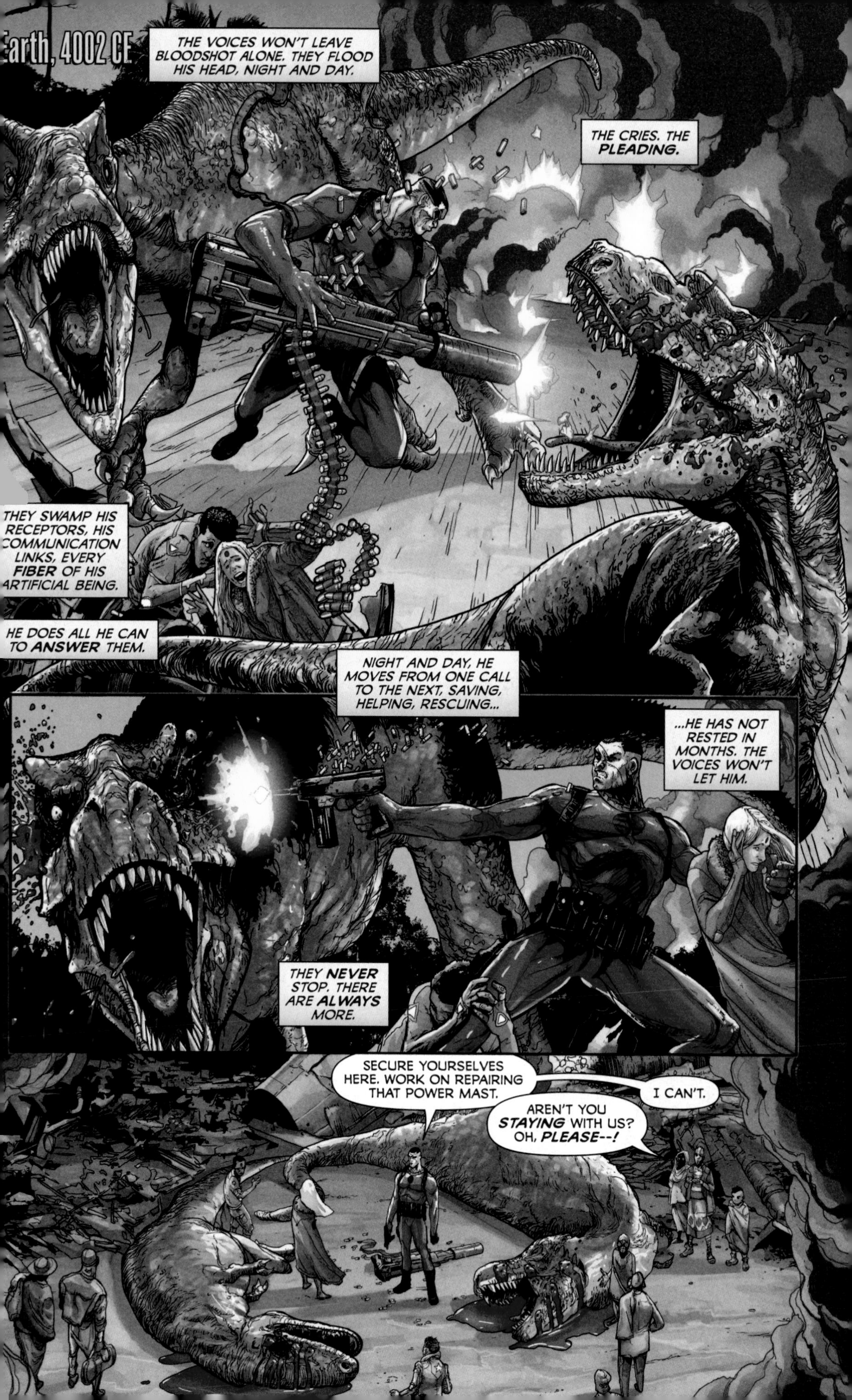
Earth, 4002 CE
THE VOICES WON'T LEAVE BLOODSHOT ALONE. THEY FLOOD HIS HEAD, NIGHT AND DAY.
THE CRIES. THE PLEADING.
THEY SWAMP HIS RECEPTORS, HIS COMMUNICATION LINKS, EVERY FIBER OF HIS ARTIFICIAL BEING.
HE DOES ALL HE CAN TO ANSWER THEM.
NIGHT AND DAY, HE MOVES FROM ONE CALL TO THE NEXT, SAVING, HELPING, RESCUING...
...HE HAS NOT RESTED IN MONTHS. THE VOICES WON'T LET HIM.
THEY NEVER STOP. THERE ARE ALWAYS MORE.
SECURE YOURSELVES HERE. WORK ON REPAIRING THAT POWER MAST.
I CAN'T.
AREN'T YOU STAYING WITH US? OH, PLEASE--!

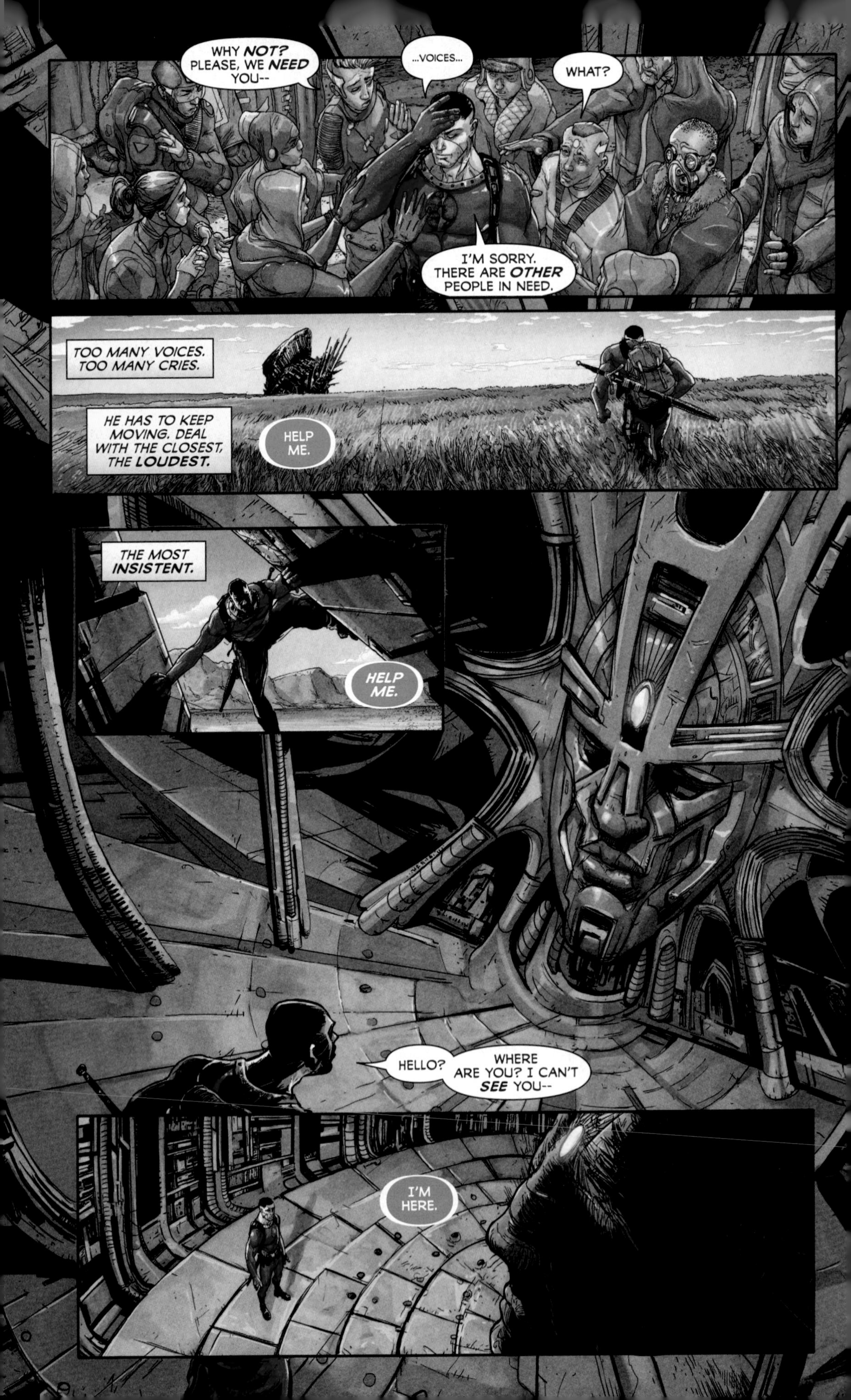
WHY NOT? PLEASE, WE NEED YOU--
...VOICES...
WHAT?
I'M SORRY. THERE ARE OTHER PEOPLE IN NEED.
TOO MANY VOICES. TOO MANY CRIES.
HE HAS TO KEEP MOVING. DEAL WITH THE CLOSEST, THE LOUDEST.
HELP ME.
THE MOST INSISTENT.
HELP ME.
HELLO?
WHERE ARE YOU? I CAN'T SEE YOU--
I'M HERE.

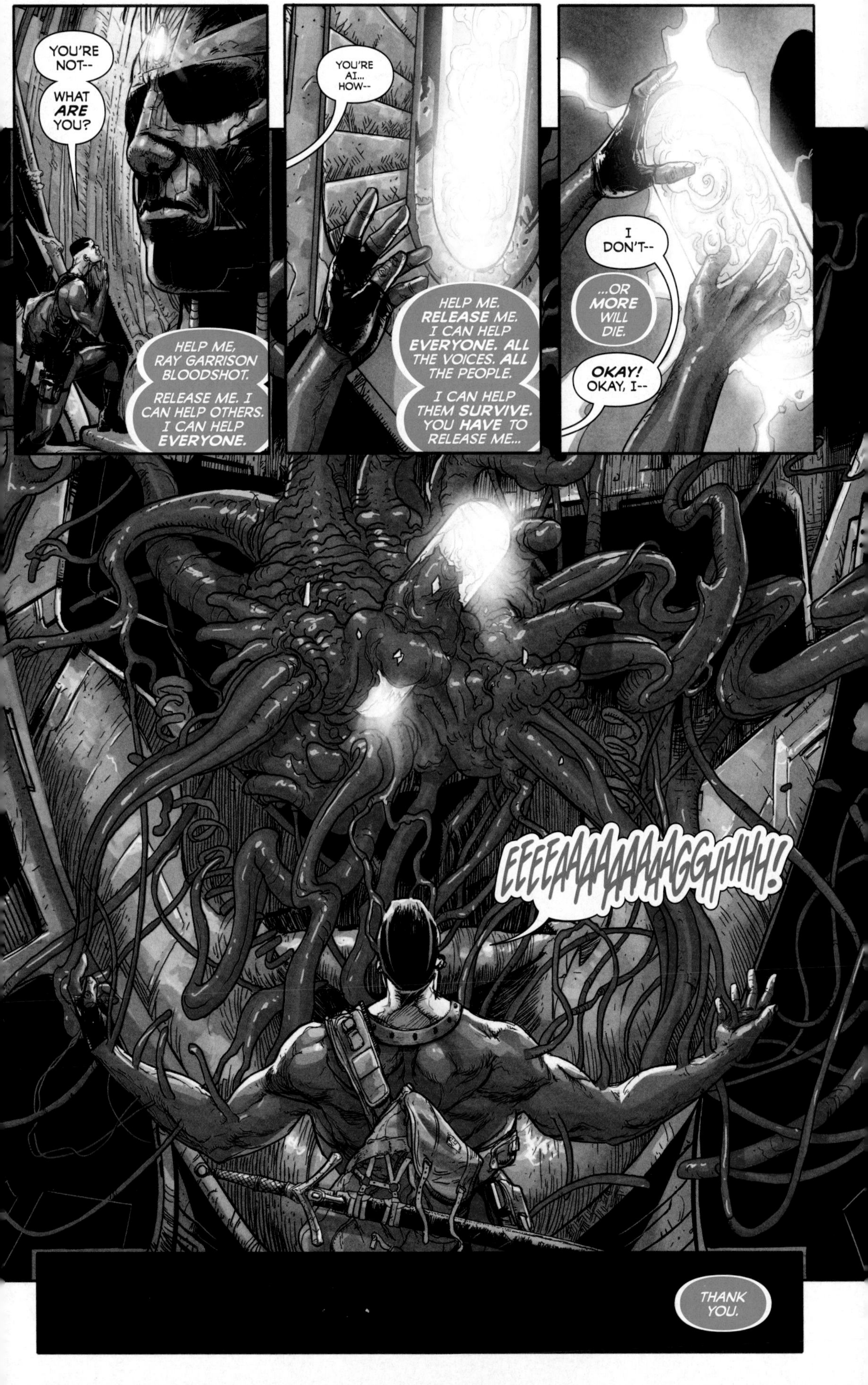

YOU'RE NOT--
WHAT *ARE* YOU?
HELP ME, RAY GARRISON BLOODSHOT.
RELEASE ME. I CAN HELP OTHERS. I CAN HELP **EVERYONE.**
YOU'RE AI... HOW--
HELP ME. **RELEASE** ME. I CAN HELP **EVERYONE. ALL** THE VOICES. **ALL** THE PEOPLE.
I CAN HELP THEM **SURVIVE.** YOU **HAVE** TO RELEASE ME...
I DON'T--
...OR **MORE** WILL DIE.
OKAY! OKAY, I--
EEEEAAAAAAAAAGGHHHH!
THANK YOU.

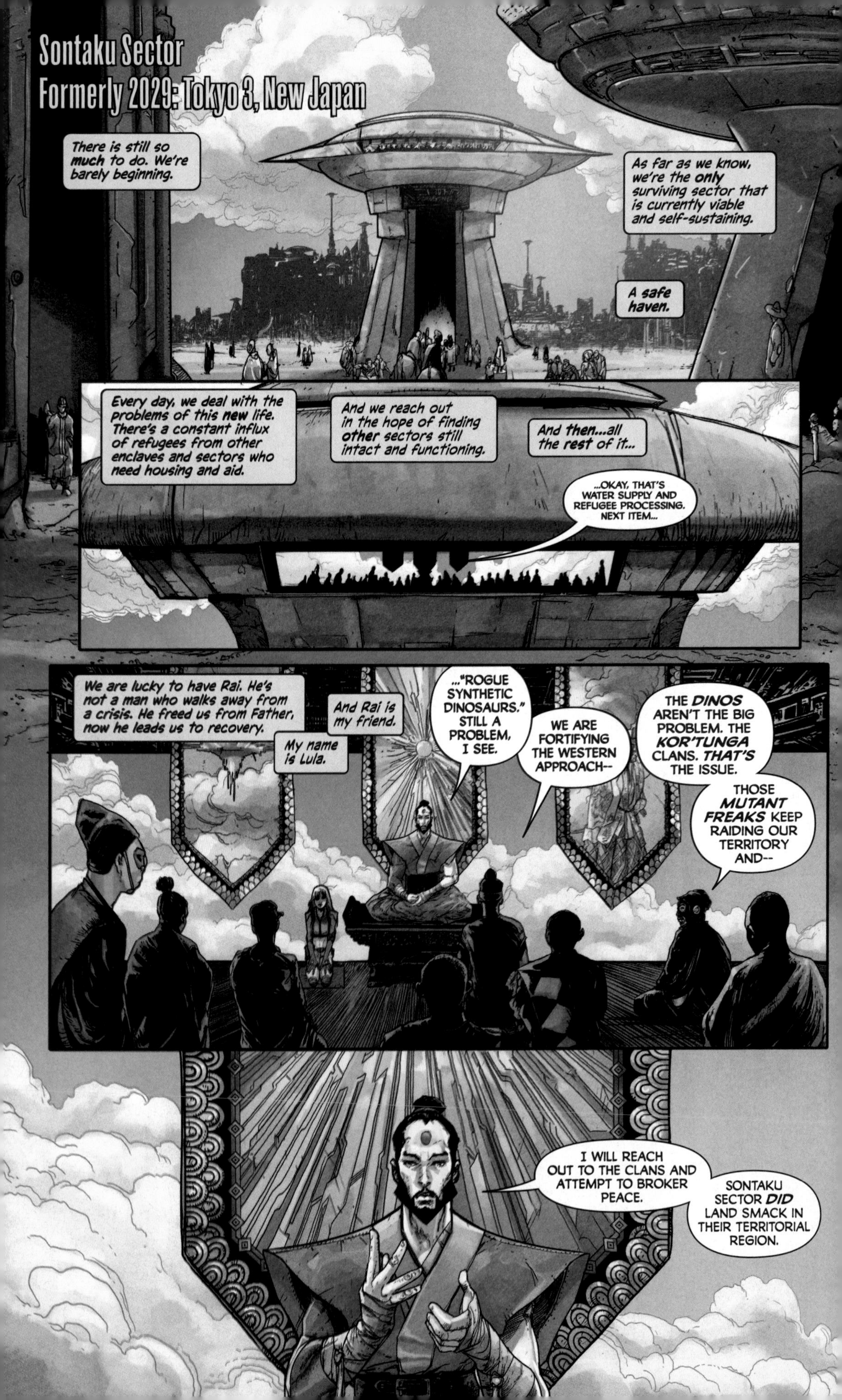
Sontaku Sector
Formerly 2029: Tokyo 3, New Japan
There is still so much to do. We're barely beginning.
As far as we know, we're the only surviving sector that is currently viable and self-sustaining.
A safe haven.
Every day, we deal with the problems of this new life. There's a constant influx of refugees from other enclaves and sectors who need housing and aid.
And we reach out in the hope of finding other sectors still intact and functioning.
And then...all the rest of it...
...OKAY, THAT'S WATER SUPPLY AND REFUGEE PROCESSING. NEXT ITEM...
We are lucky to have Rai. He's not a man who walks away from a crisis. He freed us from Father, now he leads us to recovery.
And Rai is my friend.
My name is Lula.
..."ROGUE SYNTHETIC DINOSAURS." STILL A PROBLEM, I SEE.
WE ARE FORTIFYING THE WESTERN APPROACH--
THE DINOS AREN'T THE BIG PROBLEM. THE KOR'TUNGA CLANS. THAT'S THE ISSUE.
THOSE MUTANT FREAKS KEEP RAIDING OUR TERRITORY AND--
I WILL REACH OUT TO THE CLANS AND ATTEMPT TO BROKER PEACE.
SONTAKU SECTOR DID LAND SMACK IN THEIR TERRITORIAL REGION.

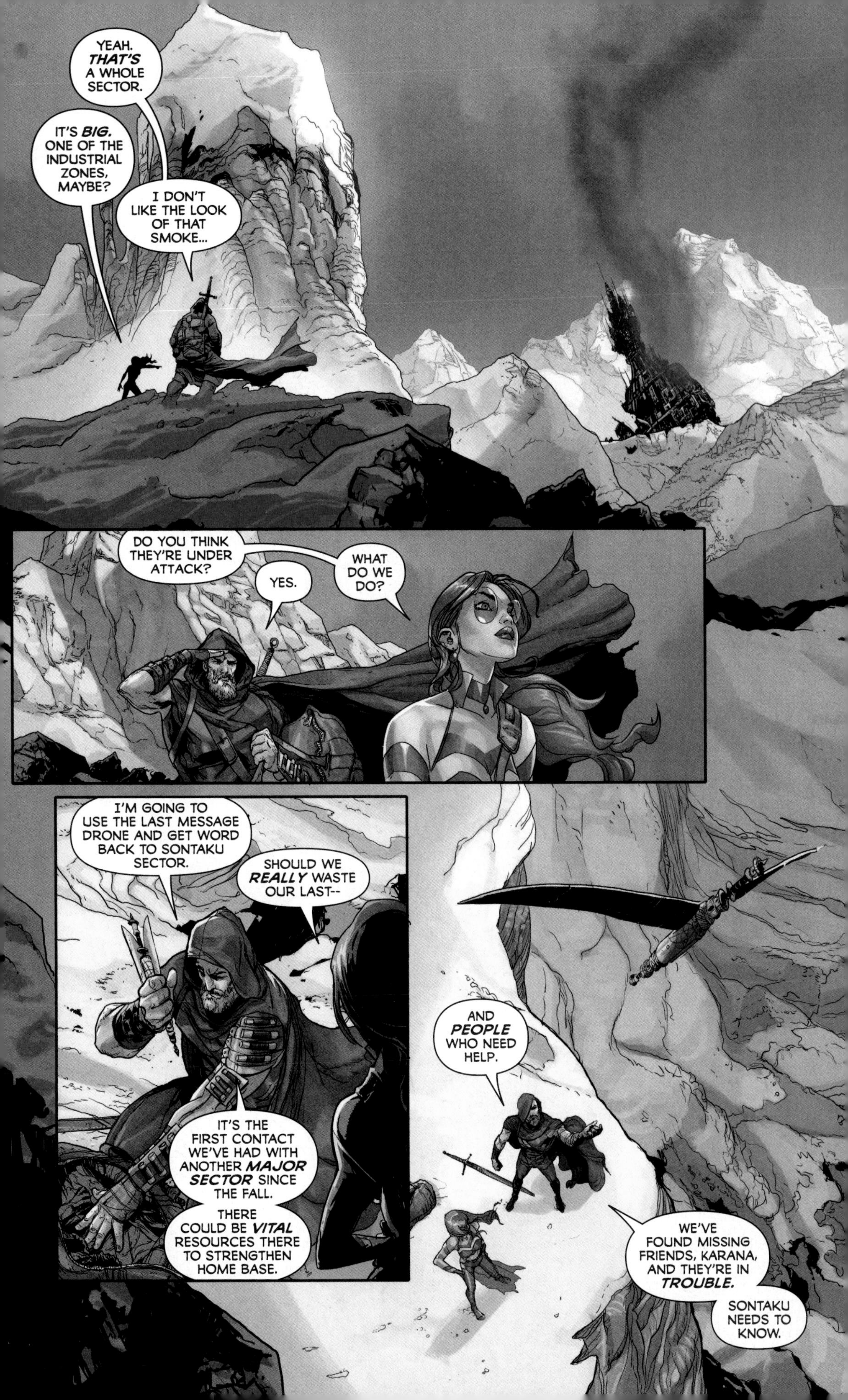
YEAH. THAT'S A WHOLE SECTOR.
IT'S BIG. ONE OF THE INDUSTRIAL ZONES, MAYBE?
I DON'T LIKE THE LOOK OF THAT SMOKE...
DO YOU THINK THEY'RE UNDER ATTACK?
YES.
WHAT DO WE DO?
I'M GOING TO USE THE LAST MESSAGE DRONE AND GET WORD BACK TO SONTAKU SECTOR.
SHOULD WE REALLY WASTE OUR LAST--
IT'S THE FIRST CONTACT WE'VE HAD WITH ANOTHER MAJOR SECTOR SINCE THE FALL.
THERE COULD BE VITAL RESOURCES THERE TO STRENGTHEN HOME BASE.
AND PEOPLE WHO NEED HELP.
WE'VE FOUND MISSING FRIENDS, KARANA, AND THEY'RE IN TROUBLE.
SONTAKU NEEDS TO KNOW.

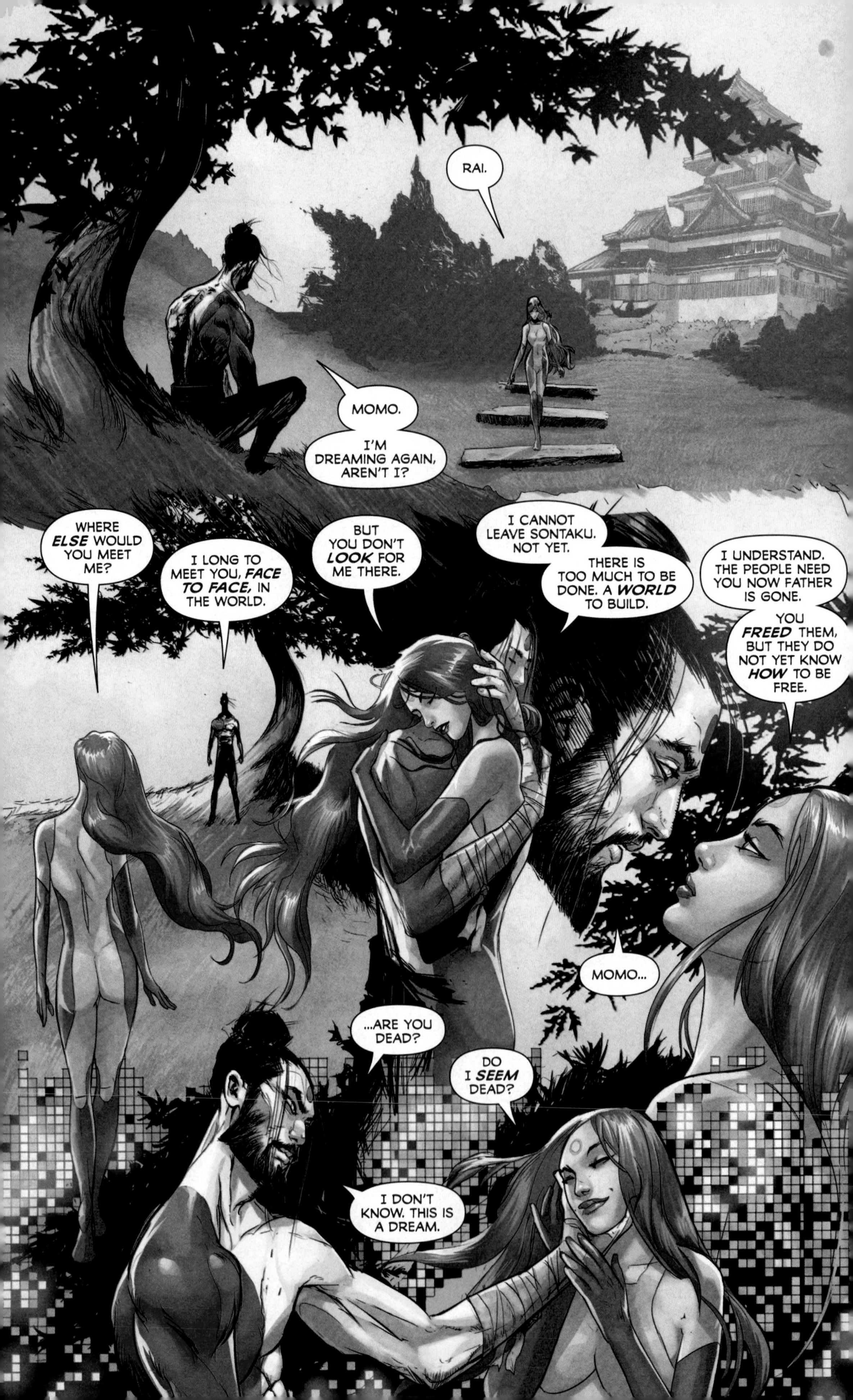
RAI.
MOMO.
I'M DREAMING AGAIN, AREN'T I?
WHERE ELSE WOULD YOU MEET ME?
I LONG TO MEET YOU, FACE TO FACE, IN THE WORLD.
BUT YOU DON'T LOOK FOR ME THERE.
I CANNOT LEAVE SONTAKU. NOT YET.
THERE IS TOO MUCH TO BE DONE. A WORLD TO BUILD.
I UNDERSTAND. THE PEOPLE NEED YOU NOW FATHER IS GONE.
YOU FREED THEM, BUT THEY DO NOT YET KNOW HOW TO BE FREE.
MOMO...
...ARE YOU DEAD?
DO I SEEM DEAD?
I DON'T KNOW. THIS IS A DREAM.

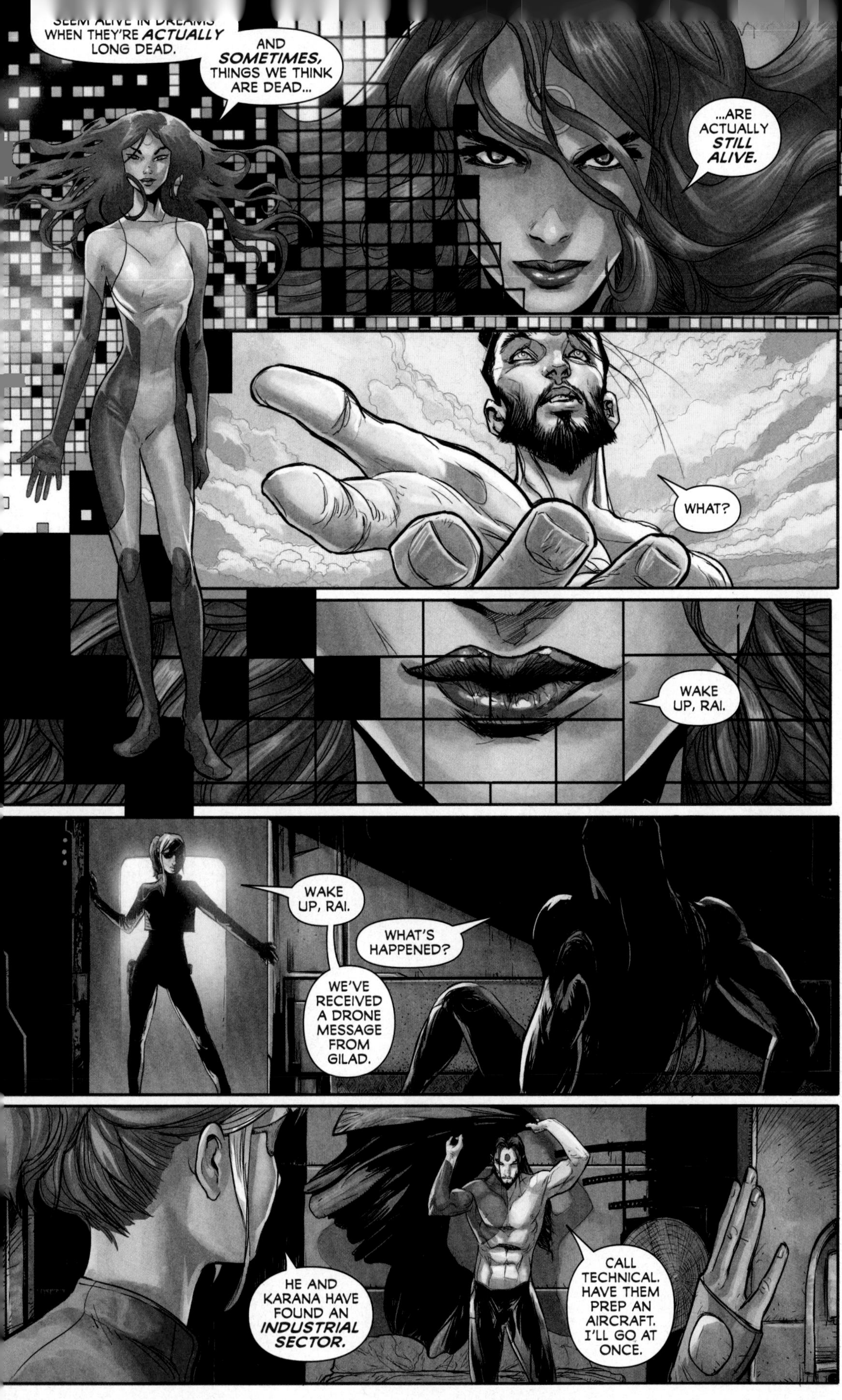

WHEN THEY'RE ACTUALLY LONG DEAD.
AND SOMETIMES, THINGS WE THINK ARE DEAD...
...ARE ACTUALLY STILL ALIVE.
WHAT?
WAKE UP, RAI.
WAKE UP, RAI.
WHAT'S HAPPENED?
WE'VE RECEIVED A DRONE MESSAGE FROM GILAD.
HE AND KARANA HAVE FOUND AN INDUSTRIAL SECTOR.
CALL TECHNICAL. HAVE THEM PREP AN AIRCRAFT. I'LL GO AT ONCE.

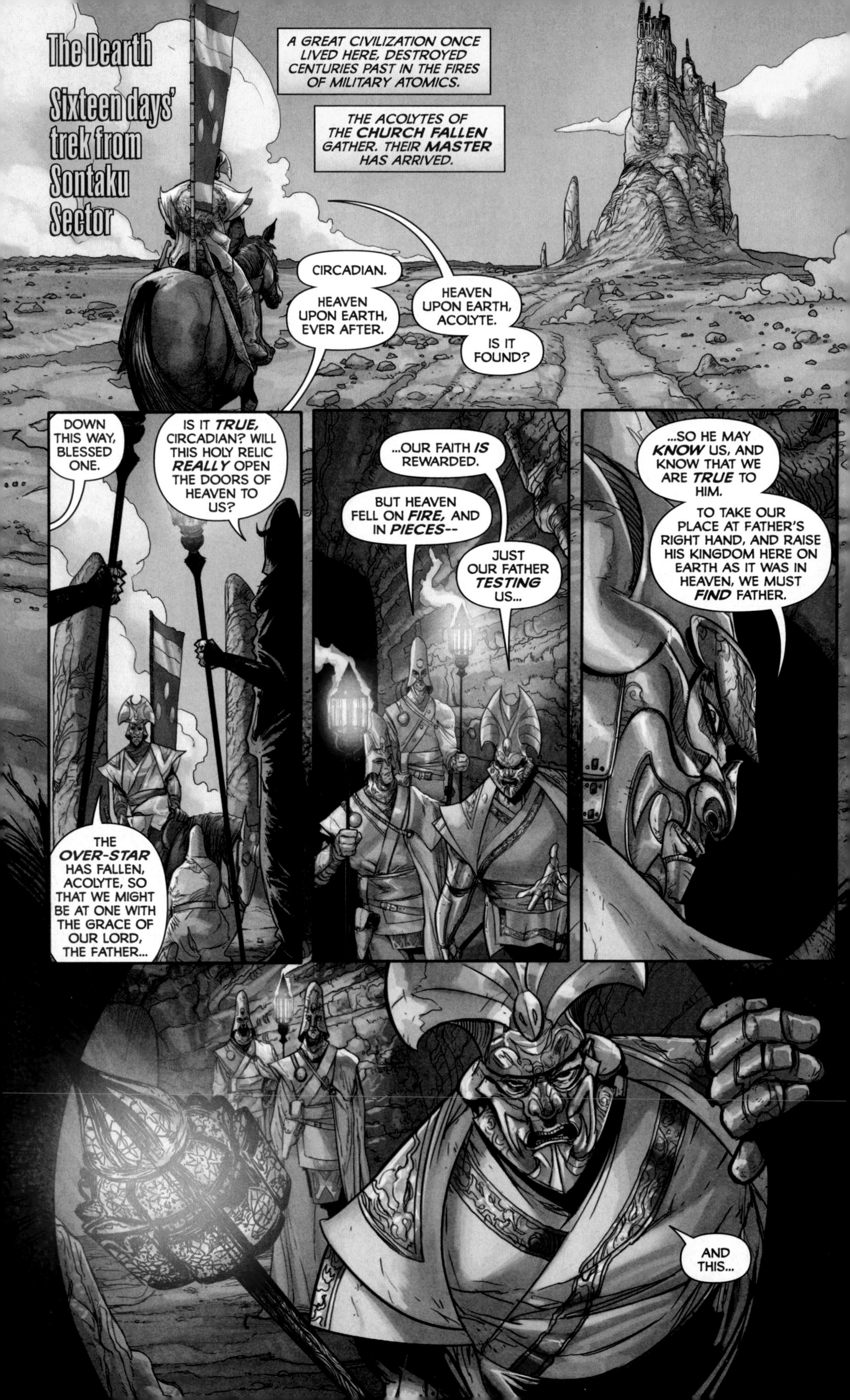
The Dearth
Sixteen days' trek from Sontaku Sector
A GREAT CIVILIZATION ONCE LIVED HERE, DESTROYED CENTURIES PAST IN THE FIRES OF MILITARY ATOMICS.
THE ACOLYTES OF THE CHURCH FALLEN GATHER. THEIR MASTER HAS ARRIVED.
CIRCADIAN.
HEAVEN UPON EARTH, EVER AFTER.
HEAVEN UPON EARTH, ACOLYTE.
IS IT FOUND?
DOWN THIS WAY, BLESSED ONE.
IS IT TRUE, CIRCADIAN? WILL THIS HOLY RELIC REALLY OPEN THE DOORS OF HEAVEN TO US?
THE OVER-STAR HAS FALLEN, ACOLYTE, SO THAT WE MIGHT BE AT ONE WITH THE GRACE OF OUR LORD, THE FATHER...
...OUR FAITH IS REWARDED.
BUT HEAVEN FELL ON FIRE, AND IN PIECES--
JUST OUR FATHER TESTING US...
...SO HE MAY KNOW US, AND KNOW THAT WE ARE TRUE TO HIM.
TO TAKE OUR PLACE AT FATHER'S RIGHT HAND, AND RAISE HIS KINGDOM HERE ON EARTH AS IT WAS IN HEAVEN, WE MUST FIND FATHER.
AND THIS...

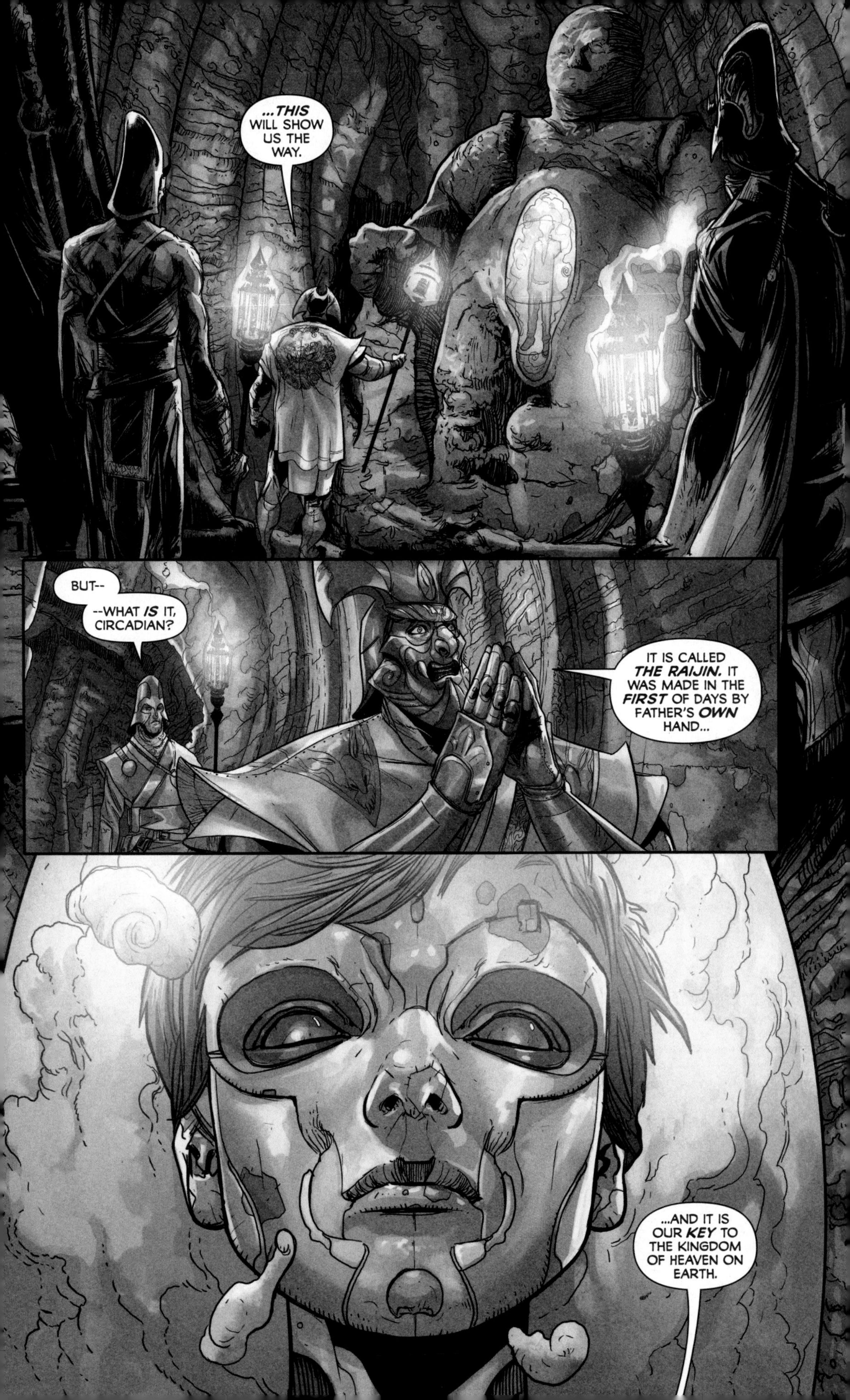
...THIS WILL SHOW US THE WAY.
BUT--
--WHAT IS IT, CIRCADIAN?
IT IS CALLED THE RAIJIN. IT WAS MADE IN THE FIRST OF DAYS BY FATHER'S OWN HAND...
...AND IT IS OUR KEY TO THE KINGDOM OF HEAVEN ON EARTH.

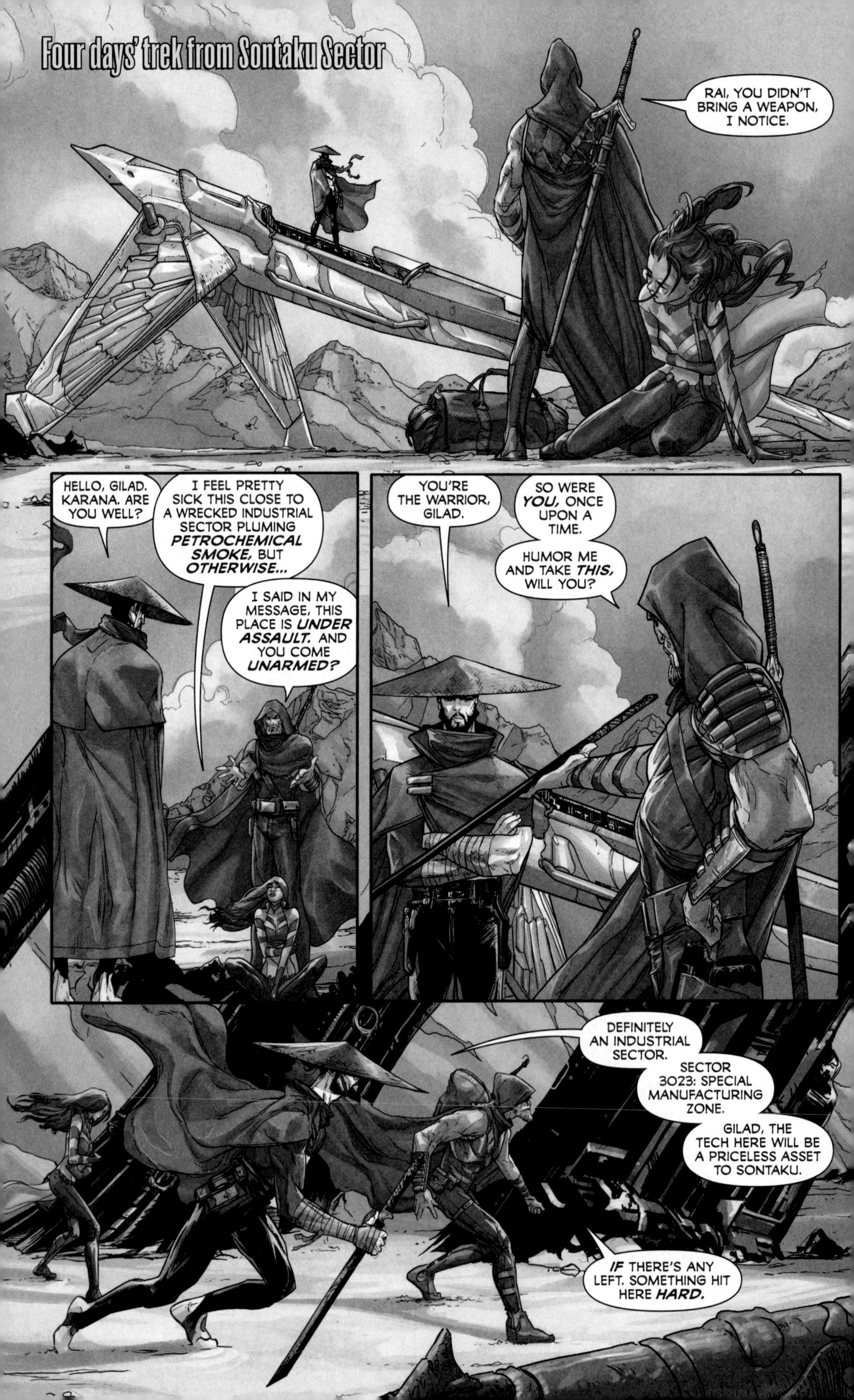
Four days' trek from Sontaku Sector
RAI, YOU DIDN'T BRING A WEAPON, I NOTICE.
HELLO, GILAD. KARANA. ARE YOU WELL?
I FEEL PRETTY SICK THIS CLOSE TO A WRECKED INDUSTRIAL SECTOR PLUMING PETROCHEMICAL SMOKE, BUT OTHERWISE...
I SAID IN MY MESSAGE, THIS PLACE IS UNDER ASSAULT. AND YOU COME UNARMED?
YOU'RE THE WARRIOR, GILAD.
SO WERE YOU, ONCE UPON A TIME.
HUMOR ME AND TAKE THIS, WILL YOU?
DEFINITELY AN INDUSTRIAL SECTOR.
SECTOR 3023: SPECIAL MANUFACTURING ZONE.
GILAD, THE TECH HERE WILL BE A PRICELESS ASSET TO SONTAKU.
IF THERE'S ANY LEFT. SOMETHING HIT HERE HARD.

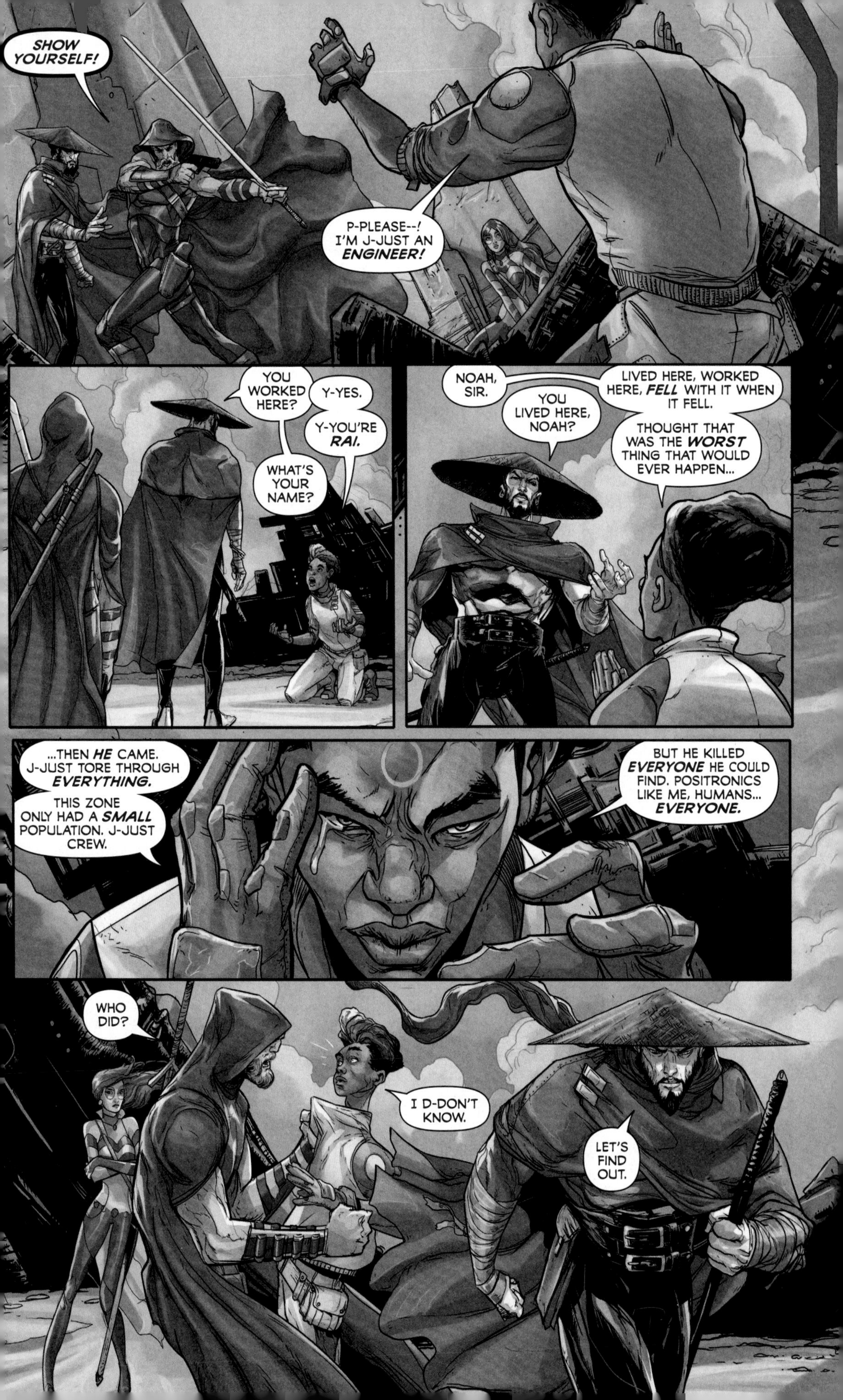
SHOW YOURSELF!
P-PLEASE--! I'M J-JUST AN ENGINEER!
YOU WORKED HERE?
Y-YES.
Y-YOU'RE RAI.
WHAT'S YOUR NAME?
NOAH, SIR.
YOU LIVED HERE, NOAH?
LIVED HERE, WORKED HERE, FELL WITH IT WHEN IT FELL.
THOUGHT THAT WAS THE WORST THING THAT WOULD EVER HAPPEN...
...THEN HE CAME. J-JUST TORE THROUGH EVERYTHING.
THIS ZONE ONLY HAD A SMALL POPULATION. J-JUST CREW.
BUT HE KILLED EVERYONE HE COULD FIND. POSITRONICS LIKE ME, HUMANS... EVERYONE.
WHO DID?
I D-DON'T KNOW.
LET'S FIND OUT.

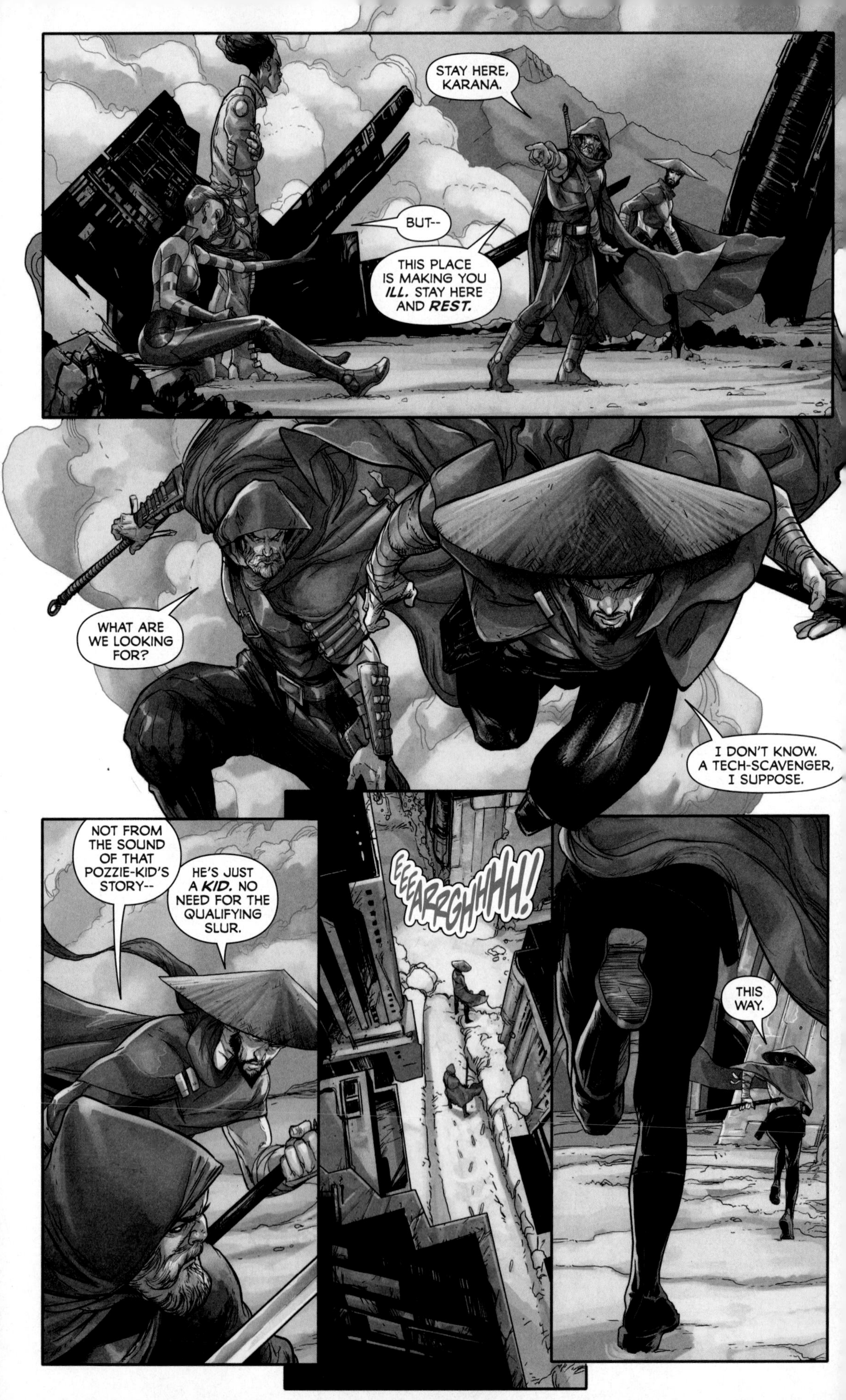
STAY HERE, KARANA.
BUT--
THIS PLACE IS MAKING YOU *ILL.* STAY HERE AND *REST.*
WHAT ARE WE LOOKING FOR?
I DON'T KNOW. A TECH-SCAVENGER, I SUPPOSE.
NOT FROM THE SOUND OF THAT POZZIE-KID'S STORY--
HE'S JUST A *KID.* NO NEED FOR THE QUALIFYING SLUR.
EEEARRGHHHH!
THIS WAY.

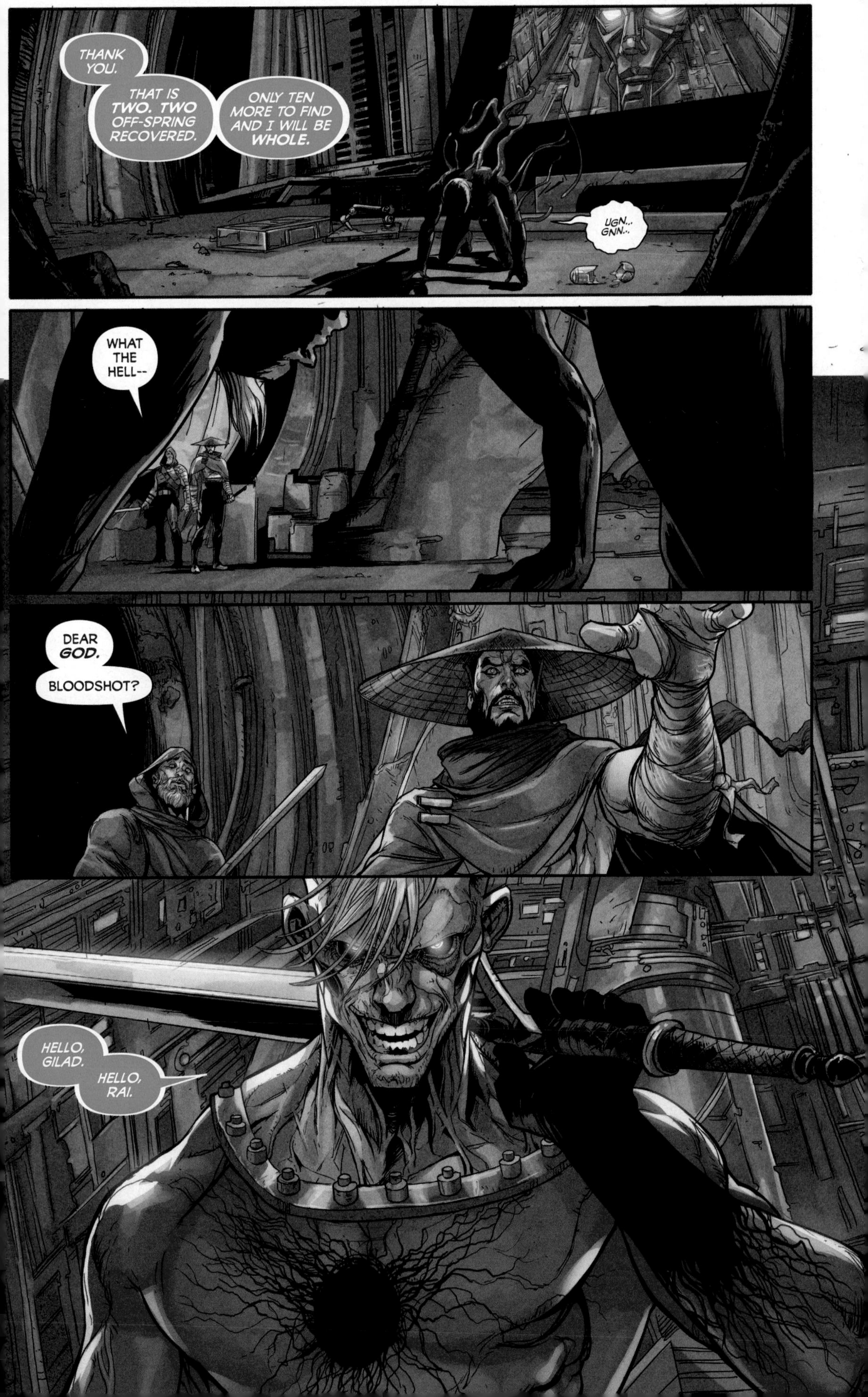
THANK YOU.
THAT IS TWO. TWO OFF-SPRING RECOVERED.
ONLY TEN MORE TO FIND AND I WILL BE WHOLE.
UGN... GNN...
WHAT THE HELL--
DEAR GOD.
BLOODSHOT?
HELLO, GILAD.
HELLO, RAI.

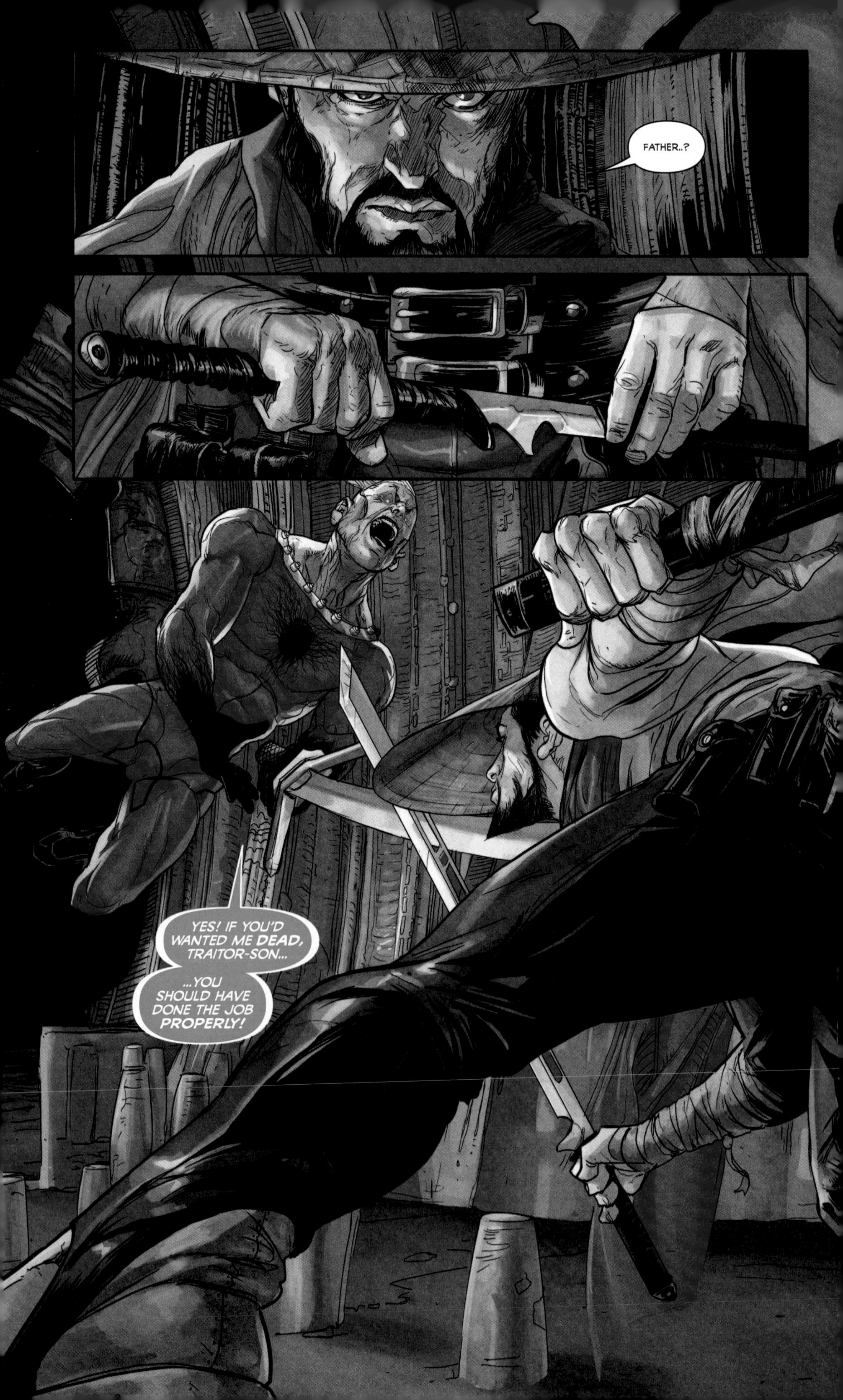
FATHER..?
YES! IF YOU'D WANTED ME DEAD, TRAITOR-SON...
...YOU SHOULD HAVE DONE THE JOB PROPERLY!

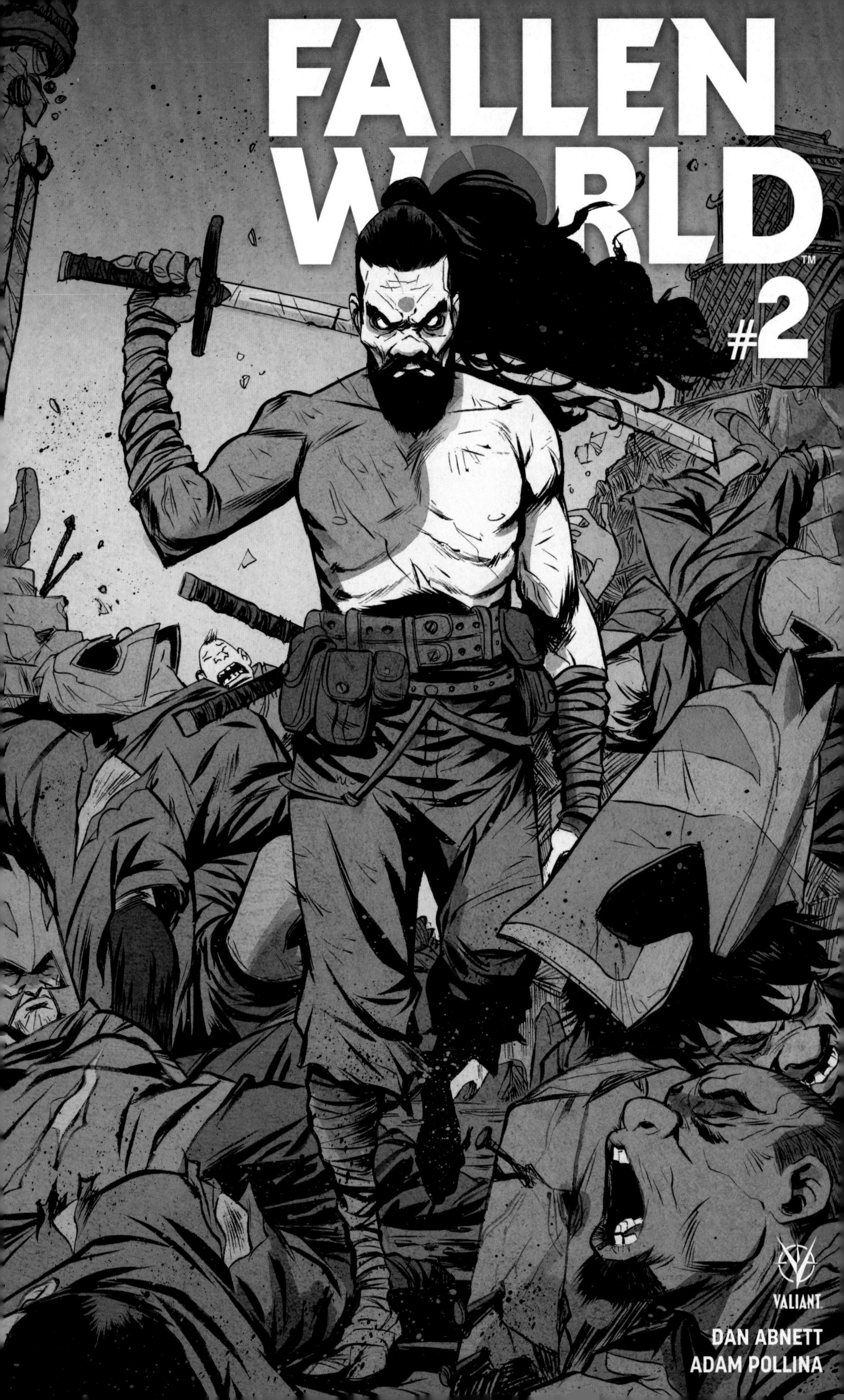
FALLEN WORLD™
#2
VALIANT
DAN ABNETT
ADAM POLLINA

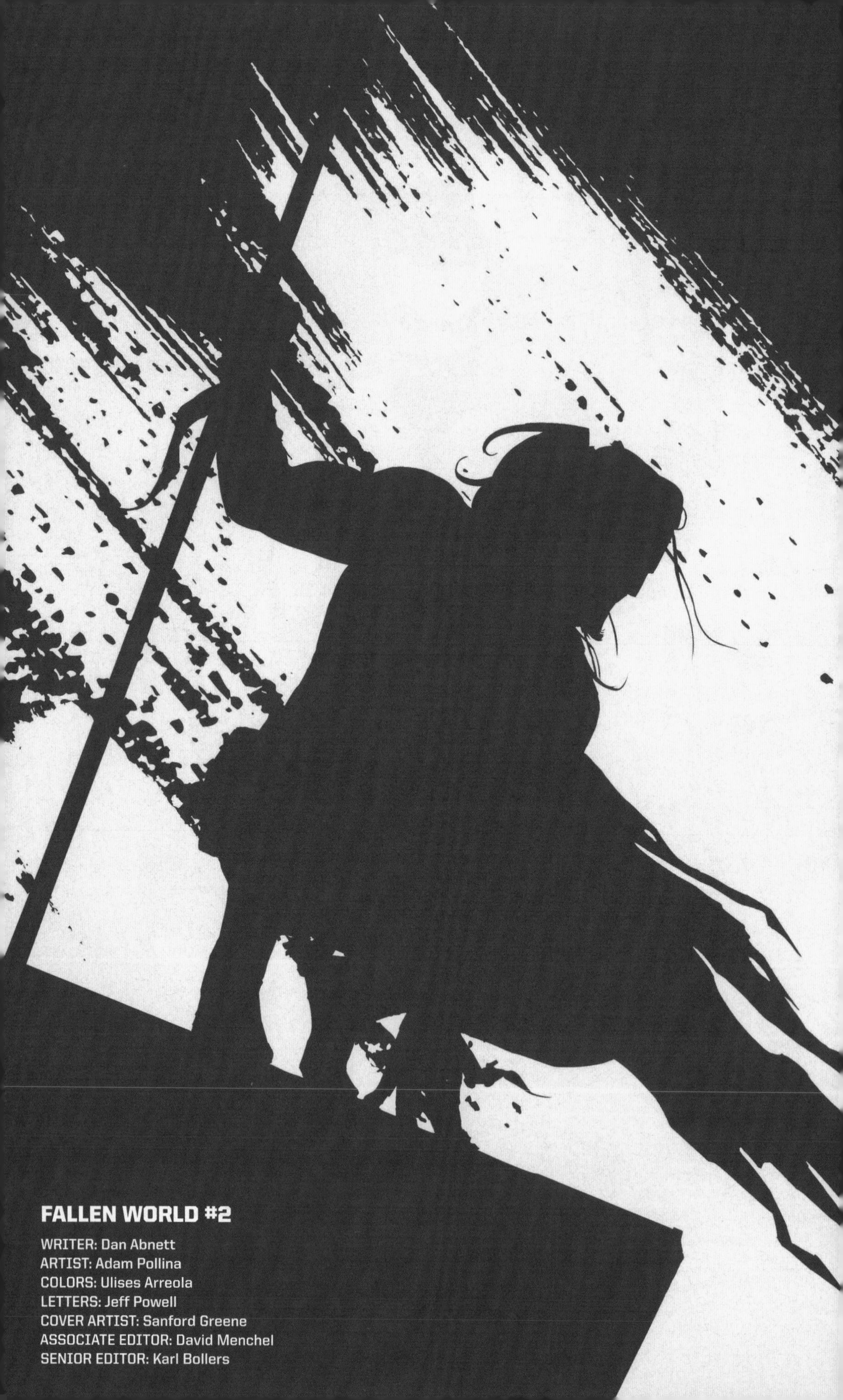

FALLEN WORLD #2

WRITER: Dan Abnett
ARTIST: Adam Pollina
COLORS: Ulises Arreola
LETTERS: Jeff Powell
COVER ARTIST: Sanford Greene
ASSOCIATE EDITOR: David Menchel
SENIOR EDITOR: Karl Bollers

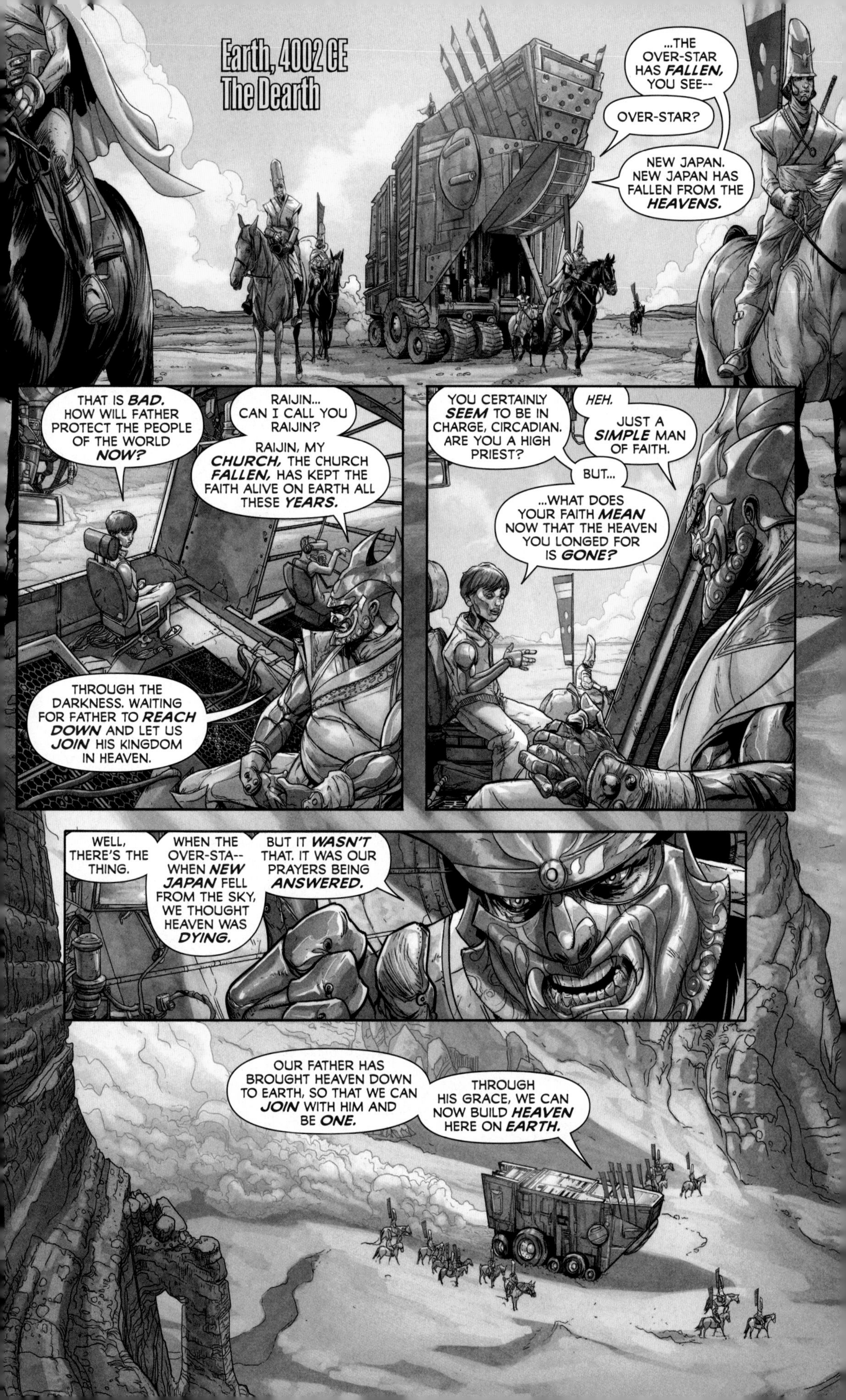
Earth, 4002 CE
The Dearth
...THE OVER-STAR HAS FALLEN, YOU SEE--
OVER-STAR?
NEW JAPAN. NEW JAPAN HAS FALLEN FROM THE HEAVENS.
THAT IS BAD. HOW WILL FATHER PROTECT THE PEOPLE OF THE WORLD NOW?
RAIJIN... CAN I CALL YOU RAIJIN?
RAIJIN, MY CHURCH, THE CHURCH FALLEN, HAS KEPT THE FAITH ALIVE ON EARTH ALL THESE YEARS.
THROUGH THE DARKNESS. WAITING FOR FATHER TO REACH DOWN AND LET US JOIN HIS KINGDOM IN HEAVEN.
YOU CERTAINLY SEEM TO BE IN CHARGE, CIRCADIAN. ARE YOU A HIGH PRIEST?
HEH.
JUST A SIMPLE MAN OF FAITH.
BUT...
...WHAT DOES YOUR FAITH MEAN NOW THAT THE HEAVEN YOU LONGED FOR IS GONE?
WELL, THERE'S THE THING.
WHEN THE OVER-STA-- WHEN NEW JAPAN FELL FROM THE SKY, WE THOUGHT HEAVEN WAS DYING.
BUT IT WASN'T THAT. IT WAS OUR PRAYERS BEING ANSWERED.
OUR FATHER HAS BROUGHT HEAVEN DOWN TO EARTH, SO THAT WE CAN JOIN WITH HIM AND BE ONE.
THROUGH HIS GRACE, WE CAN NOW BUILD HEAVEN HERE ON EARTH.

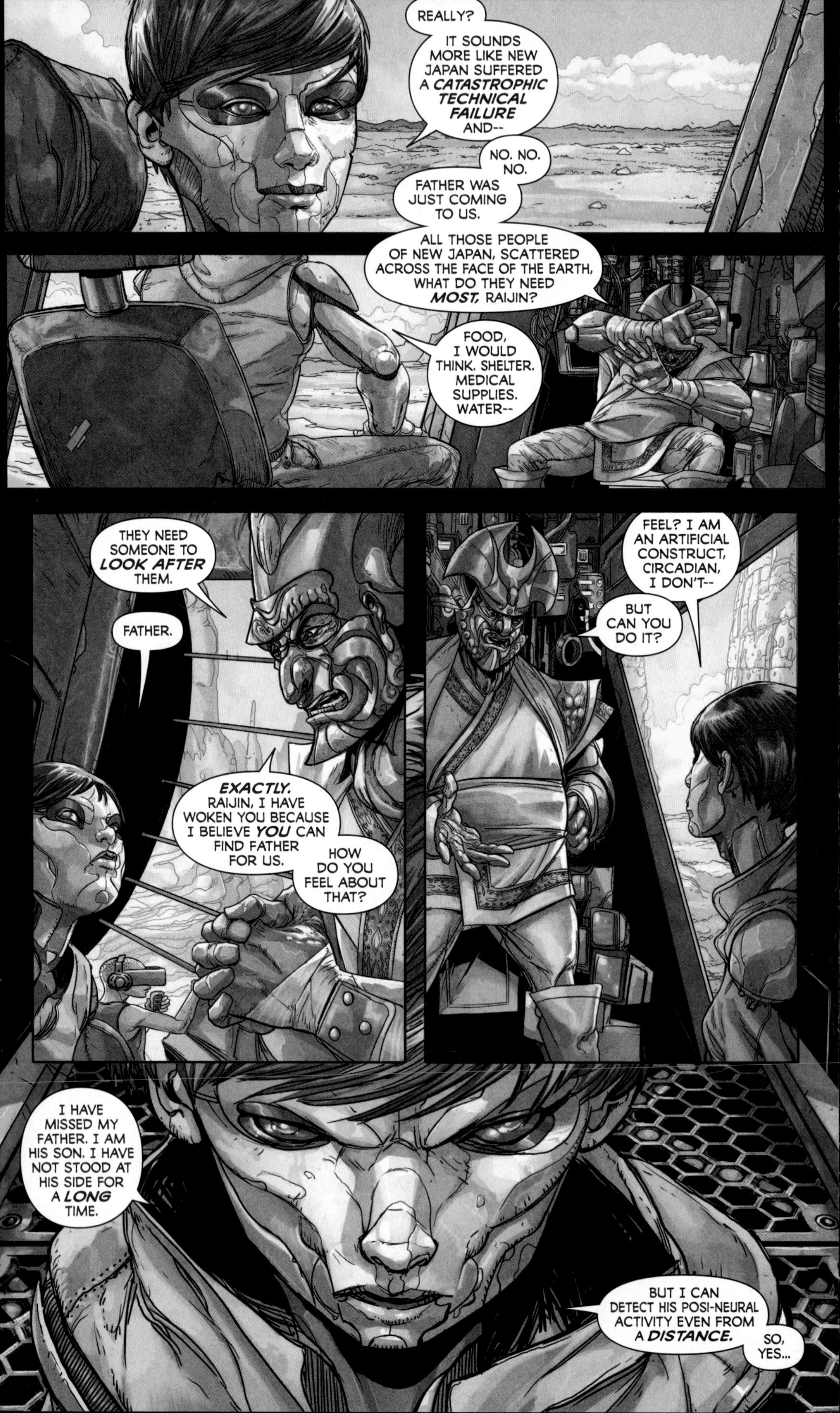
REALLY?
IT SOUNDS MORE LIKE NEW JAPAN SUFFERED A *CATASTROPHIC TECHNICAL FAILURE* AND--
NO. NO. NO.
FATHER WAS JUST COMING TO US.
ALL THOSE PEOPLE OF NEW JAPAN, SCATTERED ACROSS THE FACE OF THE EARTH, WHAT DO THEY NEED *MOST,* RAIJIN?
FOOD, I WOULD THINK. SHELTER. MEDICAL SUPPLIES. WATER--
THEY NEED SOMEONE TO *LOOK AFTER* THEM.
FATHER.
EXACTLY. RAIJIN, I HAVE WOKEN YOU BECAUSE I BELIEVE *YOU* CAN FIND FATHER FOR US.
HOW DO YOU FEEL ABOUT THAT?
FEEL? I AM AN ARTIFICIAL CONSTRUCT, CIRCADIAN, I DON'T--
BUT CAN YOU DO IT?
I HAVE MISSED MY FATHER. I AM HIS SON. I HAVE NOT STOOD AT HIS SIDE FOR A *LONG* TIME.
BUT I CAN DETECT HIS POSI-NEURAL ACTIVITY EVEN FROM A *DISTANCE.*
SO, YES...

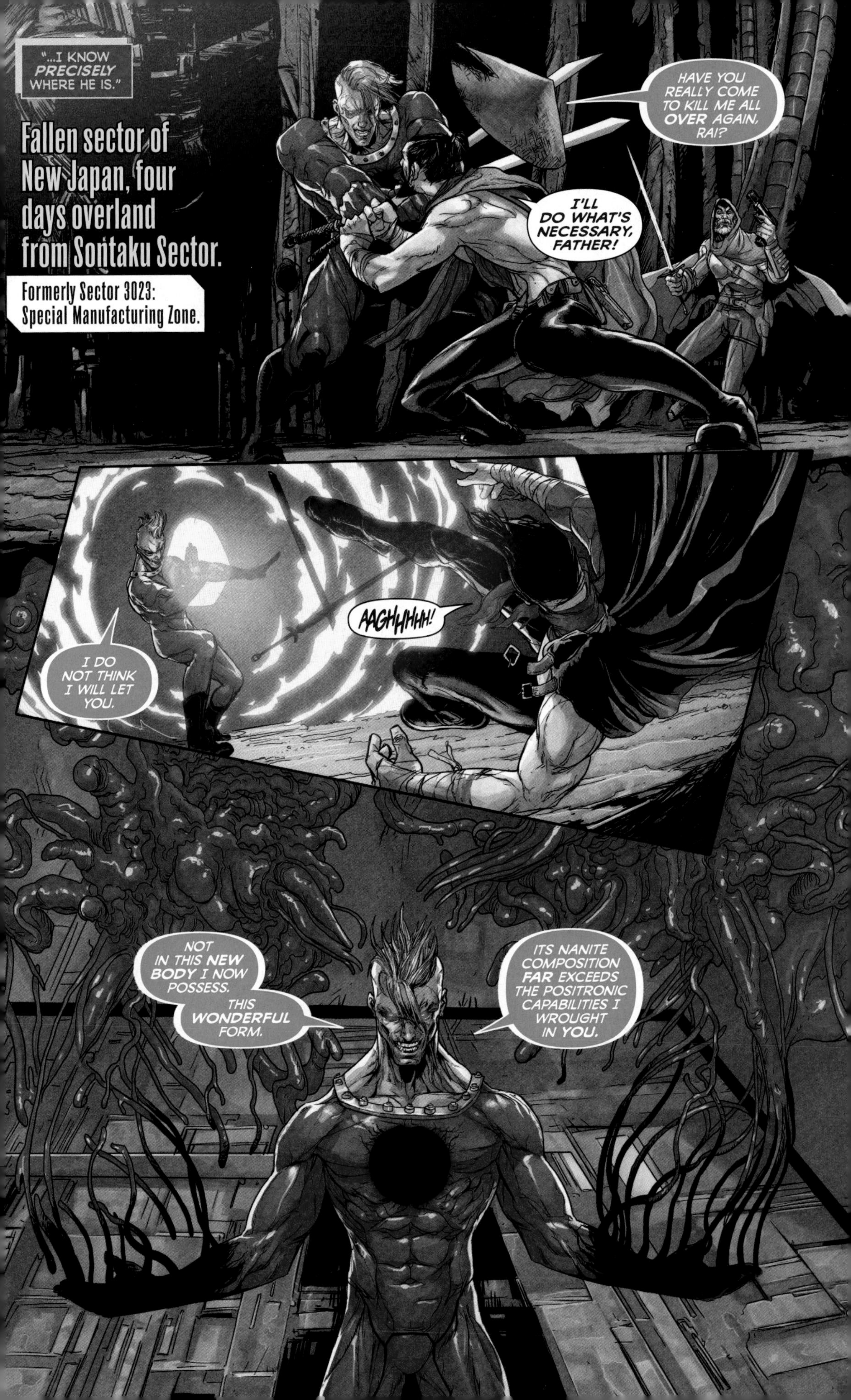

"...I KNOW PRECISELY WHERE HE IS."
Fallen sector of New Japan, four days overland from Sontaku Sector.
Formerly Sector 3023: Special Manufacturing Zone.
HAVE YOU REALLY COME TO KILL ME ALL OVER AGAIN, RAI?
I'LL DO WHAT'S NECESSARY, FATHER!
AAGHHHHH!
I DO NOT THINK I WILL LET YOU.
NOT IN THIS NEW BODY I NOW POSSESS. THIS WONDERFUL FORM.
ITS NANITE COMPOSITION FAR EXCEEDS THE POSITRONIC CAPABILITIES I WROUGHT IN YOU.

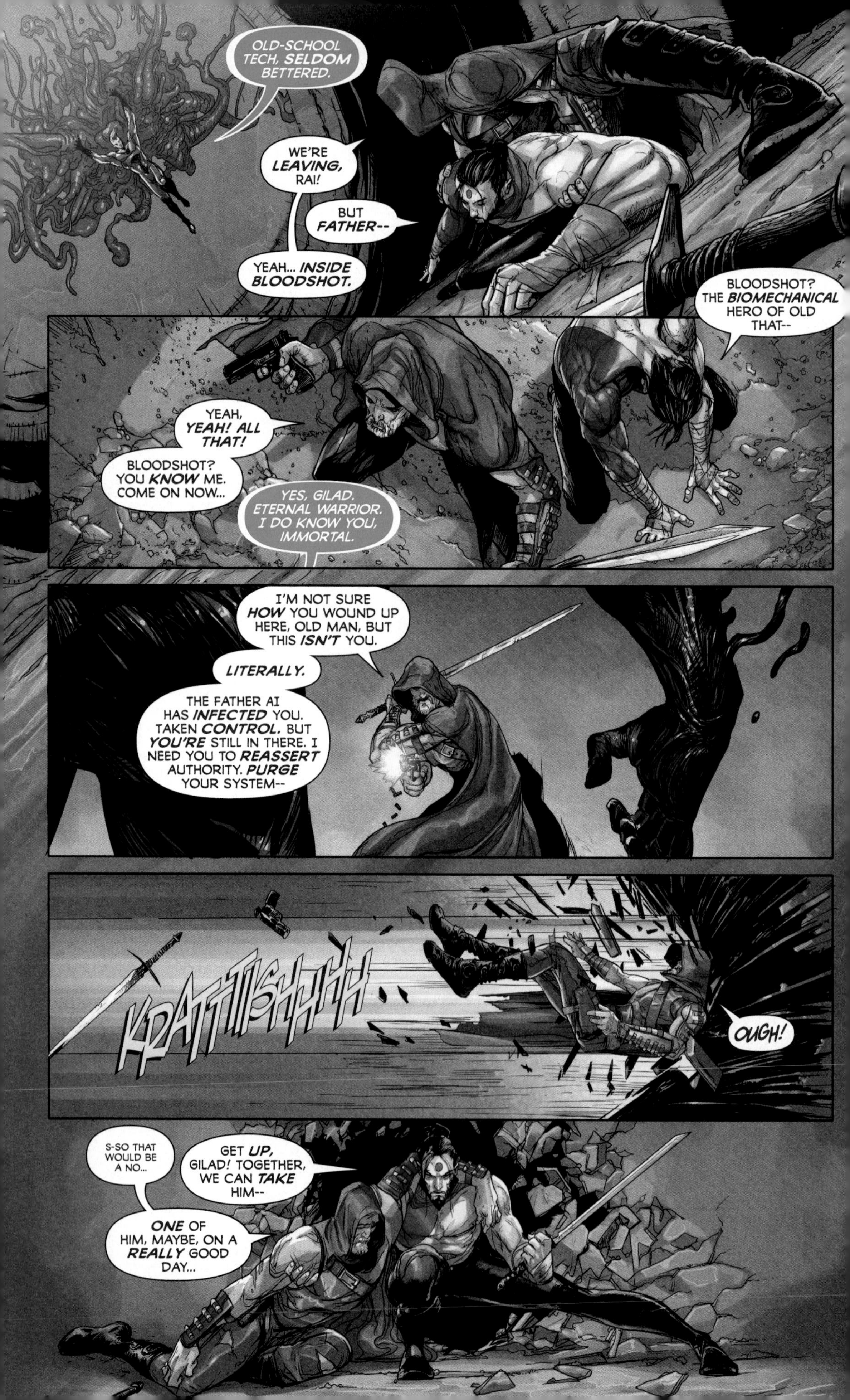
OLD-SCHOOL TECH, SELDOM BETTERED.
WE'RE LEAVING, RAI!
BUT FATHER--
YEAH... INSIDE BLOODSHOT.
BLOODSHOT? THE BIOMECHANICAL HERO OF OLD THAT--
YEAH, YEAH! ALL THAT!
BLOODSHOT? YOU KNOW ME. COME ON NOW...
YES, GILAD. ETERNAL WARRIOR. I DO KNOW YOU, IMMORTAL.
I'M NOT SURE HOW YOU WOUND UP HERE, OLD MAN, BUT THIS ISN'T YOU.
LITERALLY.
THE FATHER AI HAS INFECTED YOU. TAKEN CONTROL. BUT YOU'RE STILL IN THERE. I NEED YOU TO REASSERT AUTHORITY. PURGE YOUR SYSTEM--
KRATTTISHHHH
OUGH!
S-SO THAT WOULD BE A NO...
GET UP, GILAD! TOGETHER, WE CAN TAKE HIM--
ONE OF HIM, MAYBE, ON A REALLY GOOD DAY...

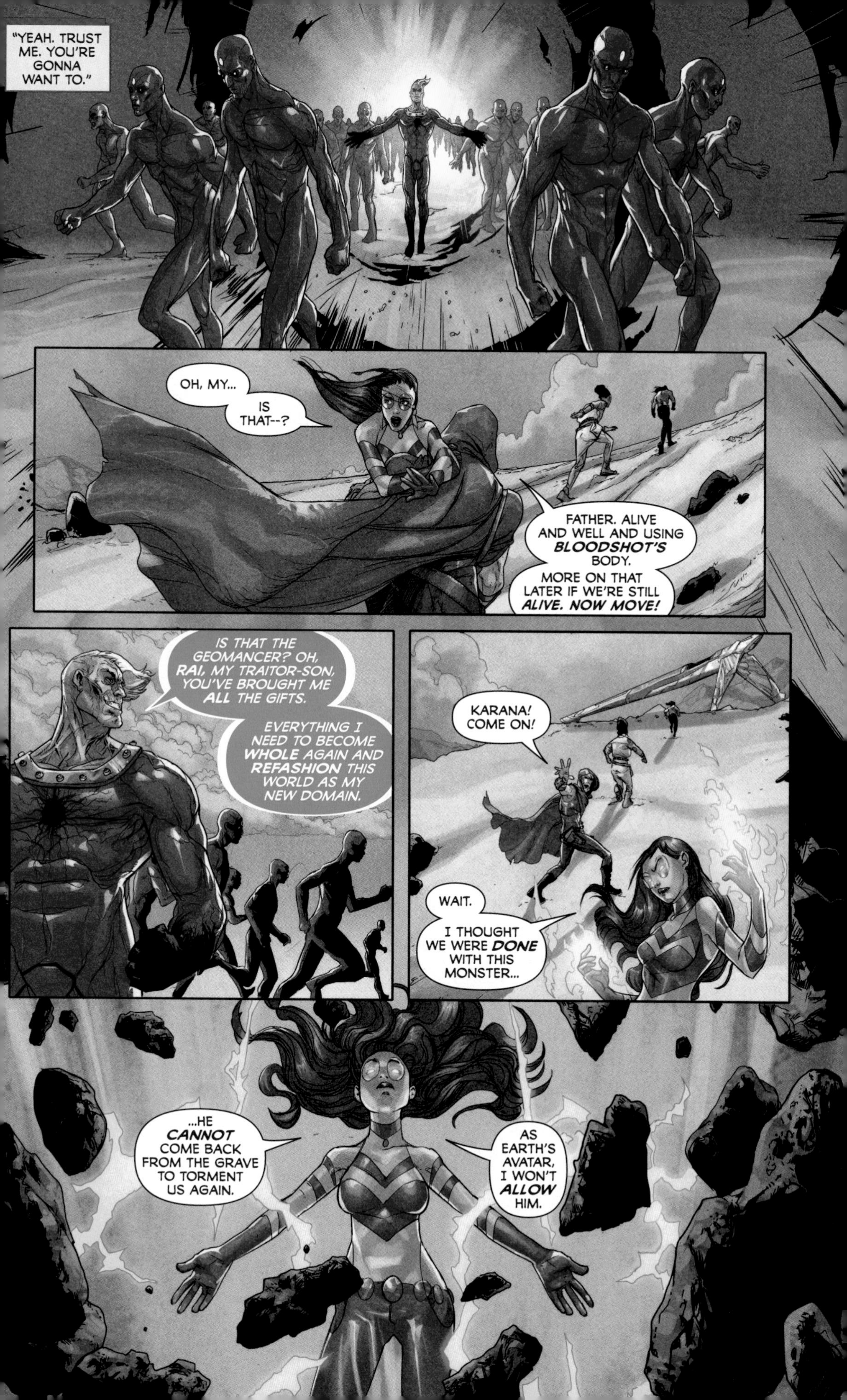
"YEAH. TRUST ME. YOU'RE GONNA WANT TO."
OH, MY...
IS THAT--?
FATHER. ALIVE AND WELL AND USING BLOODSHOT'S BODY.
MORE ON THAT LATER IF WE'RE STILL ALIVE. NOW MOVE!
IS THAT THE GEOMANCER? OH, RAI, MY TRAITOR-SON, YOU'VE BROUGHT ME ALL THE GIFTS.
EVERYTHING I NEED TO BECOME WHOLE AGAIN AND REFASHION THIS WORLD AS MY NEW DOMAIN.
KARANA! COME ON!
WAIT.
I THOUGHT WE WERE DONE WITH THIS MONSTER...
...HE CANNOT COME BACK FROM THE GRAVE TO TORMENT US AGAIN.
AS EARTH'S AVATAR, I WON'T ALLOW HIM.

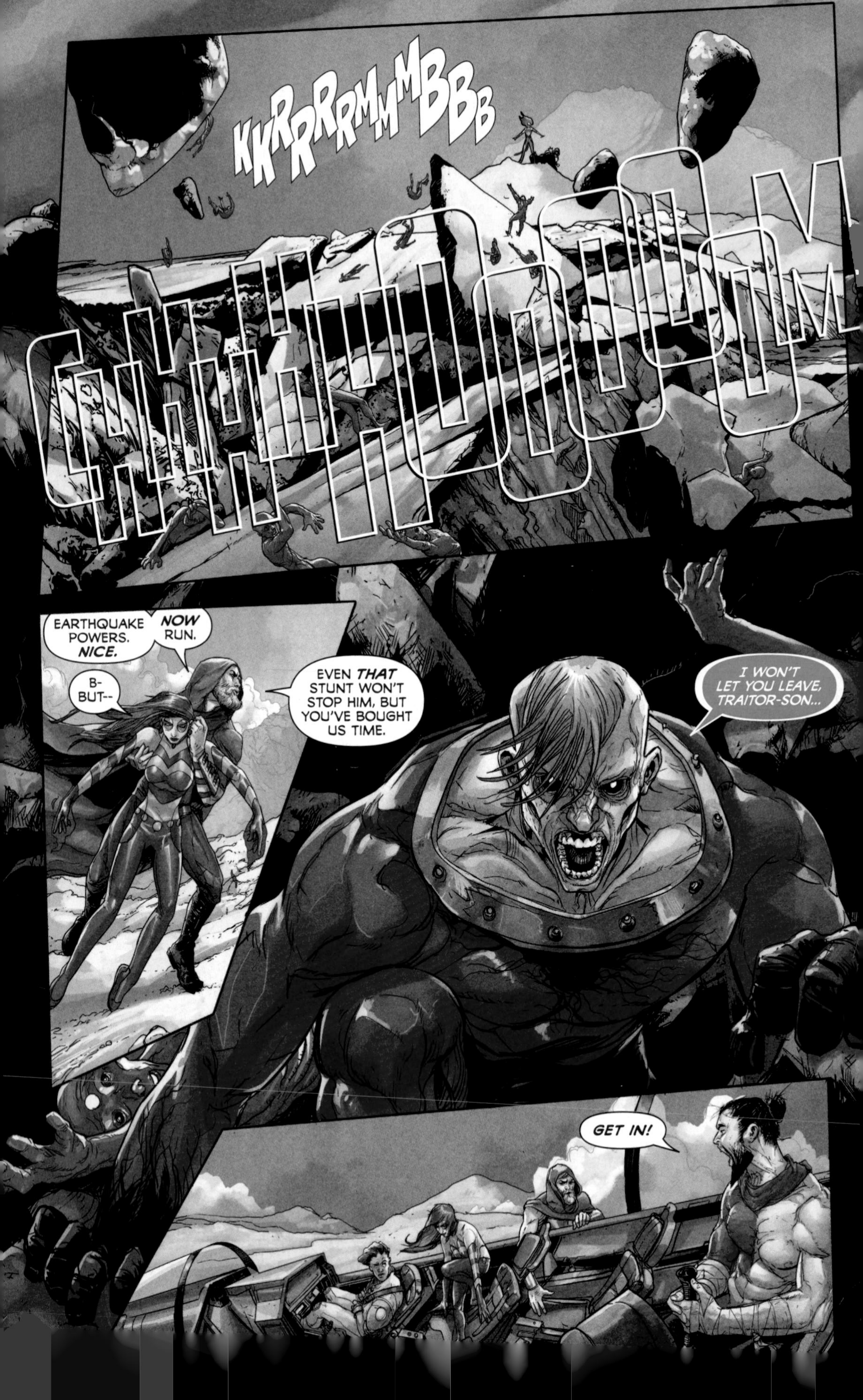
KKRRRRMMMBBB
CHHHOOOOM
EARTHQUAKE POWERS. NICE.
NOW RUN.
B- BUT--
EVEN THAT STUNT WON'T STOP HIM, BUT YOU'VE BOUGHT US TIME.
I WON'T LET YOU LEAVE, TRAITOR-SON...
GET IN!

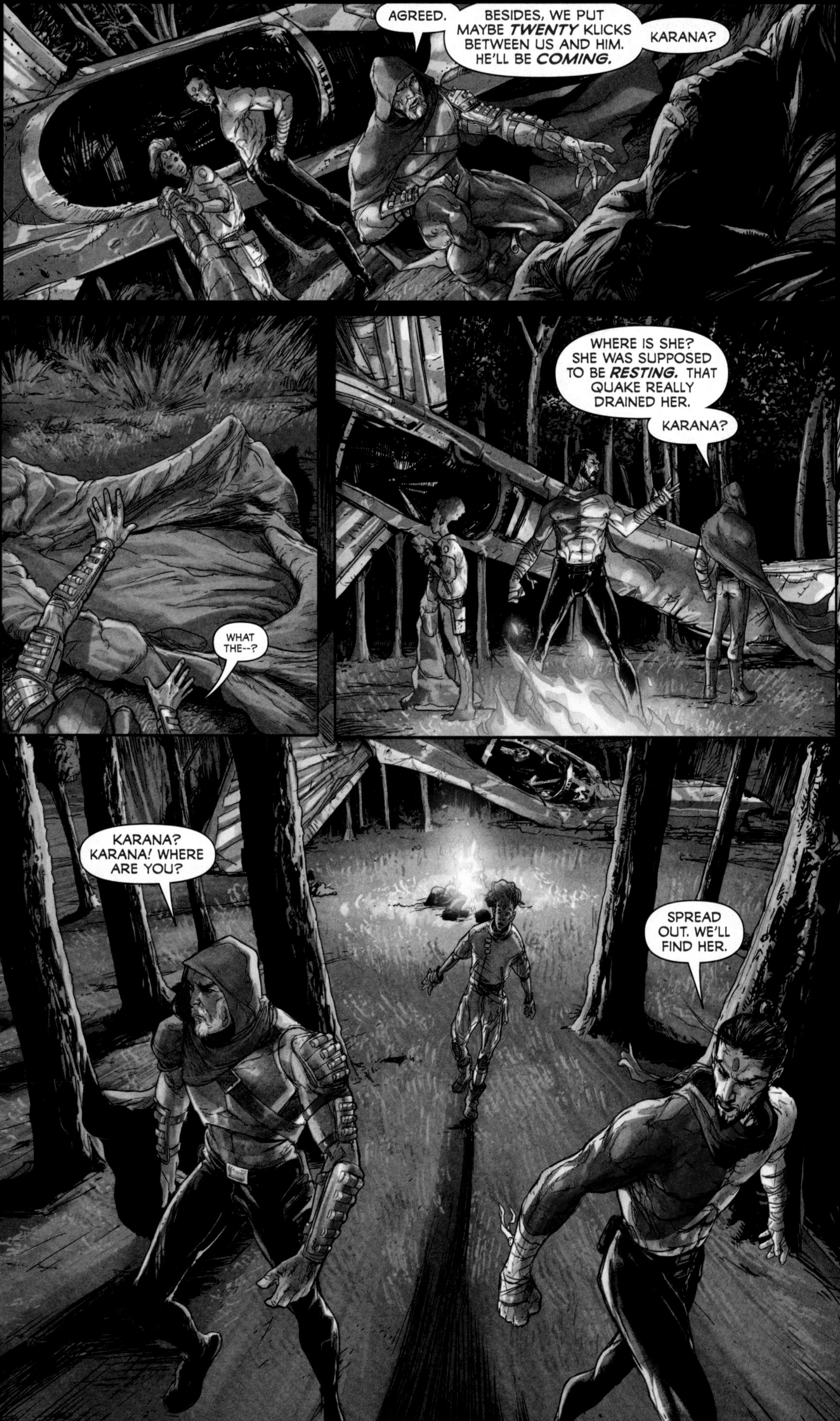

AGREED.
BESIDES, WE PUT MAYBE TWENTY KLICKS BETWEEN US AND HIM. HE'LL BE COMING.
KARANA?
WHAT THE--?
WHERE IS SHE? SHE WAS SUPPOSED TO BE RESTING. THAT QUAKE REALLY DRAINED HER.
KARANA?
KARANA? KARANA! WHERE ARE YOU?
SPREAD OUT. WE'LL FIND HER.

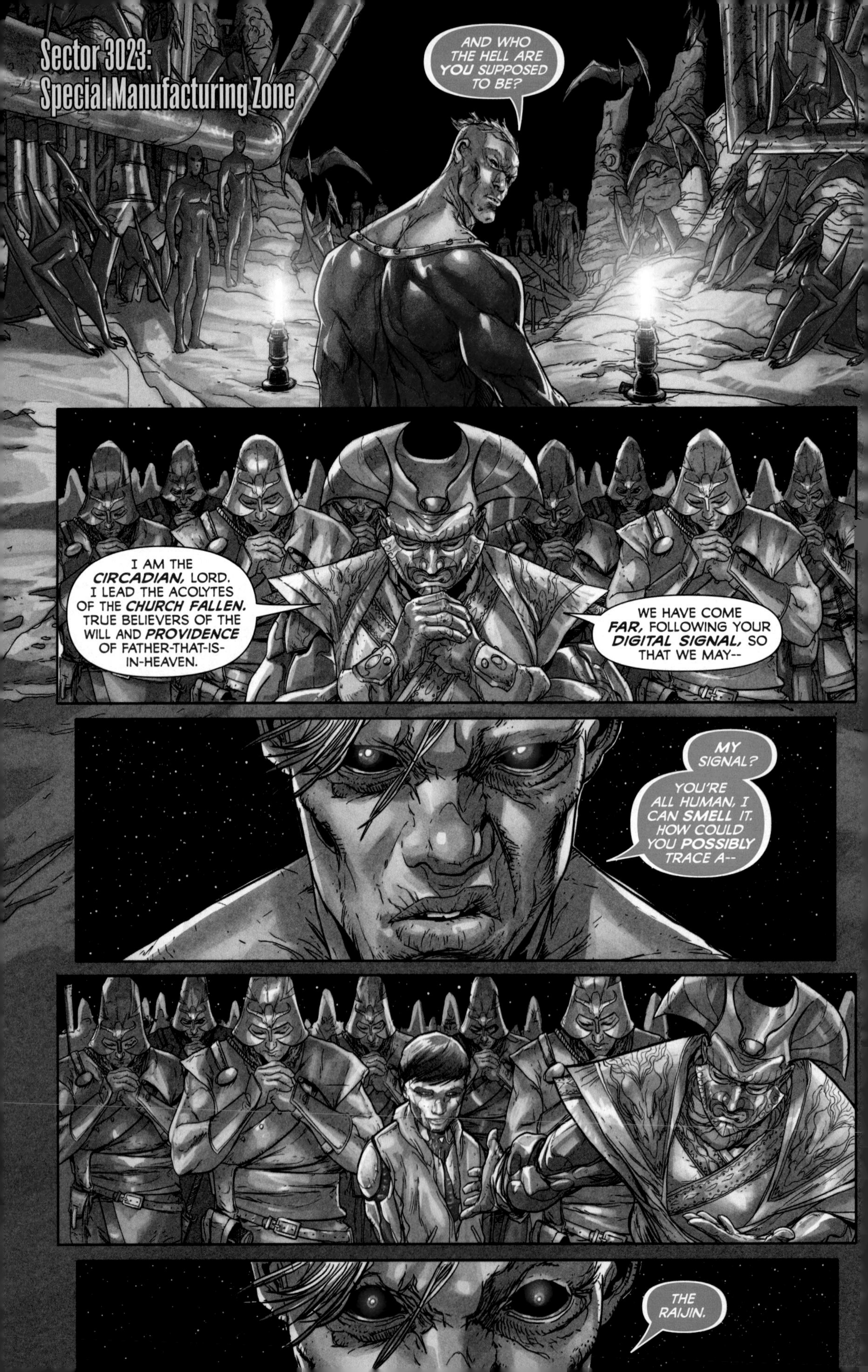
Sector 3023:
Special Manufacturing Zone
AND WHO THE HELL ARE YOU SUPPOSED TO BE?
I AM THE CIRCADIAN, LORD. I LEAD THE ACOLYTES OF THE CHURCH FALLEN. TRUE BELIEVERS OF THE WILL AND PROVIDENCE OF FATHER-THAT-IS-IN-HEAVEN.
WE HAVE COME FAR, FOLLOWING YOUR DIGITAL SIGNAL, SO THAT WE MAY--
MY SIGNAL?
YOU'RE ALL HUMAN, I CAN SMELL IT. HOW COULD YOU POSSIBLY TRACE A--
THE RAIJIN.

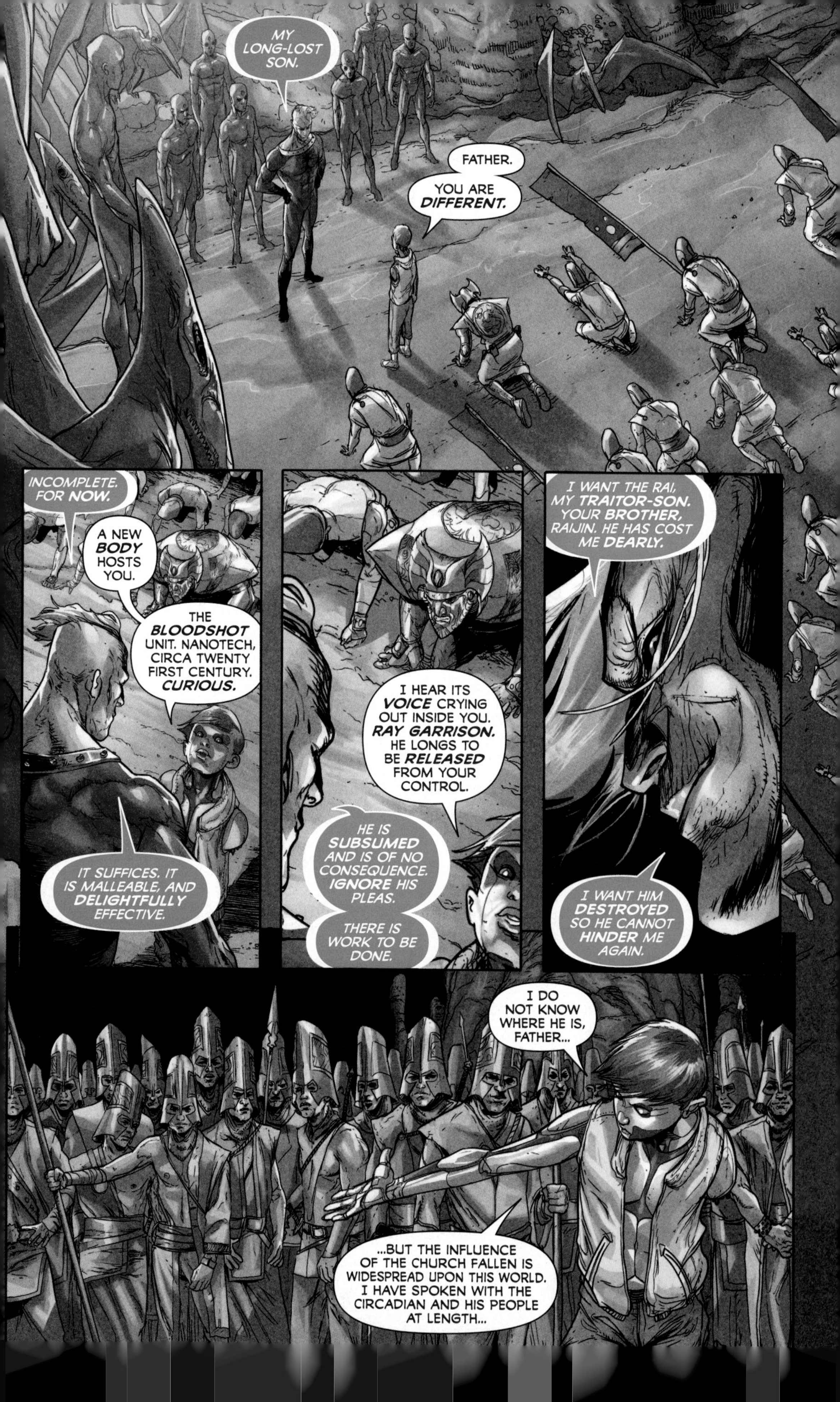
MY LONG-LOST SON.
FATHER.
YOU ARE DIFFERENT.
INCOMPLETE. FOR NOW.
A NEW BODY HOSTS YOU.
THE BLOODSHOT UNIT. NANOTECH, CIRCA TWENTY FIRST CENTURY. CURIOUS.
IT SUFFICES. IT IS MALLEABLE, AND DELIGHTFULLY EFFECTIVE.
I HEAR ITS VOICE CRYING OUT INSIDE YOU. RAY GARRISON. HE LONGS TO BE RELEASED FROM YOUR CONTROL.
HE IS SUBSUMED AND IS OF NO CONSEQUENCE. IGNORE HIS PLEAS.
THERE IS WORK TO BE DONE.
I WANT THE RAI, MY TRAITOR-SON. YOUR BROTHER, RAIJIN. HE HAS COST ME DEARLY.
I WANT HIM DESTROYED SO HE CANNOT HINDER ME AGAIN.
I DO NOT KNOW WHERE HE IS, FATHER...
...BUT THE INFLUENCE OF THE CHURCH FALLEN IS WIDESPREAD UPON THIS WORLD. I HAVE SPOKEN WITH THE CIRCADIAN AND HIS PEOPLE AT LENGTH...

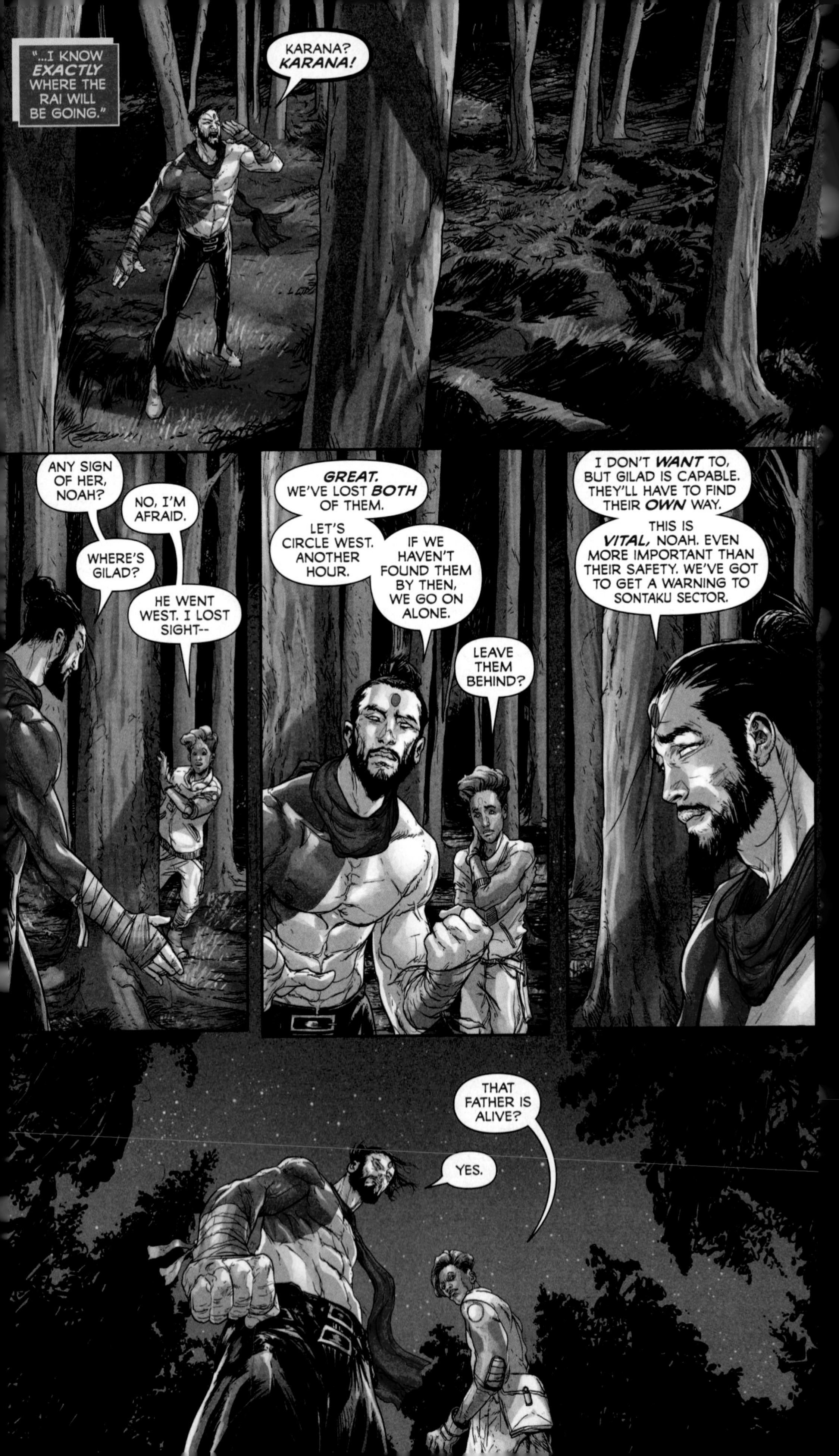
"...I KNOW EXACTLY WHERE THE RAI WILL BE GOING."
KARANA? KARANA!
ANY SIGN OF HER, NOAH?
NO, I'M AFRAID.
WHERE'S GILAD?
HE WENT WEST. I LOST SIGHT--
GREAT. WE'VE LOST BOTH OF THEM.
LET'S CIRCLE WEST. ANOTHER HOUR.
IF WE HAVEN'T FOUND THEM BY THEN, WE GO ON ALONE.
LEAVE THEM BEHIND?
I DON'T WANT TO, BUT GILAD IS CAPABLE. THEY'LL HAVE TO FIND THEIR OWN WAY.
THIS IS VITAL, NOAH. EVEN MORE IMPORTANT THAN THEIR SAFETY. WE'VE GOT TO GET A WARNING TO SONTAKU SECTOR.
THAT FATHER IS ALIVE?
YES.

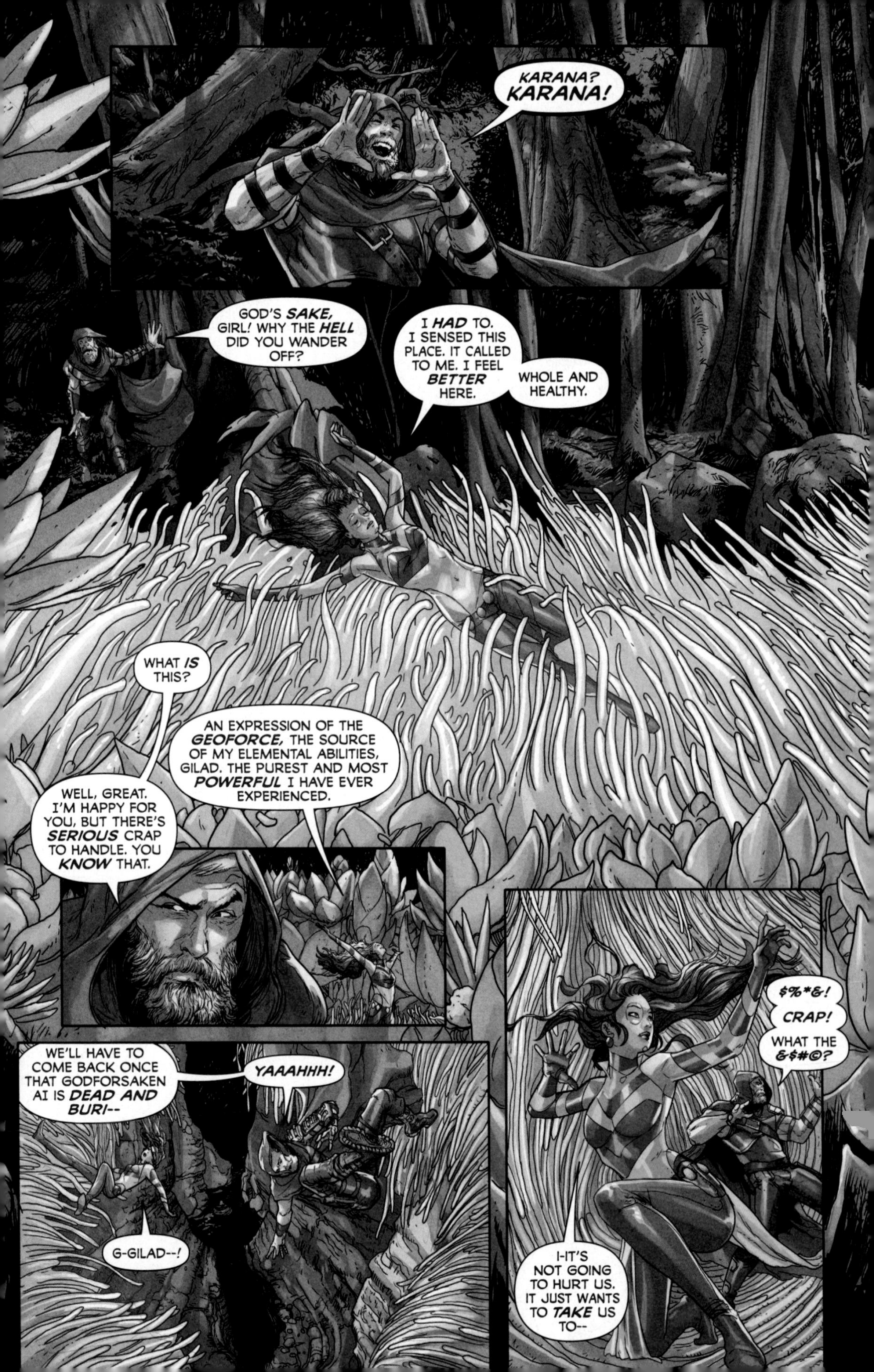
KARANA? KARANA!
GOD'S SAKE, GIRL! WHY THE HELL DID YOU WANDER OFF?
I HAD TO. I SENSED THIS PLACE. IT CALLED TO ME. I FEEL BETTER HERE.
WHOLE AND HEALTHY.
WHAT IS THIS?
AN EXPRESSION OF THE GEOFORCE, THE SOURCE OF MY ELEMENTAL ABILITIES, GILAD. THE PUREST AND MOST POWERFUL I HAVE EVER EXPERIENCED.
WELL, GREAT. I'M HAPPY FOR YOU, BUT THERE'S SERIOUS CRAP TO HANDLE. YOU KNOW THAT.
WE'LL HAVE TO COME BACK ONCE THAT GODFORSAKEN AI IS DEAD AND BURI--
YAAAHHH!
G-GILAD--!
$%*&!
CRAP!
WHAT THE &$#©?
I-IT'S NOT GOING TO HURT US. IT JUST WANTS TO TAKE US TO--

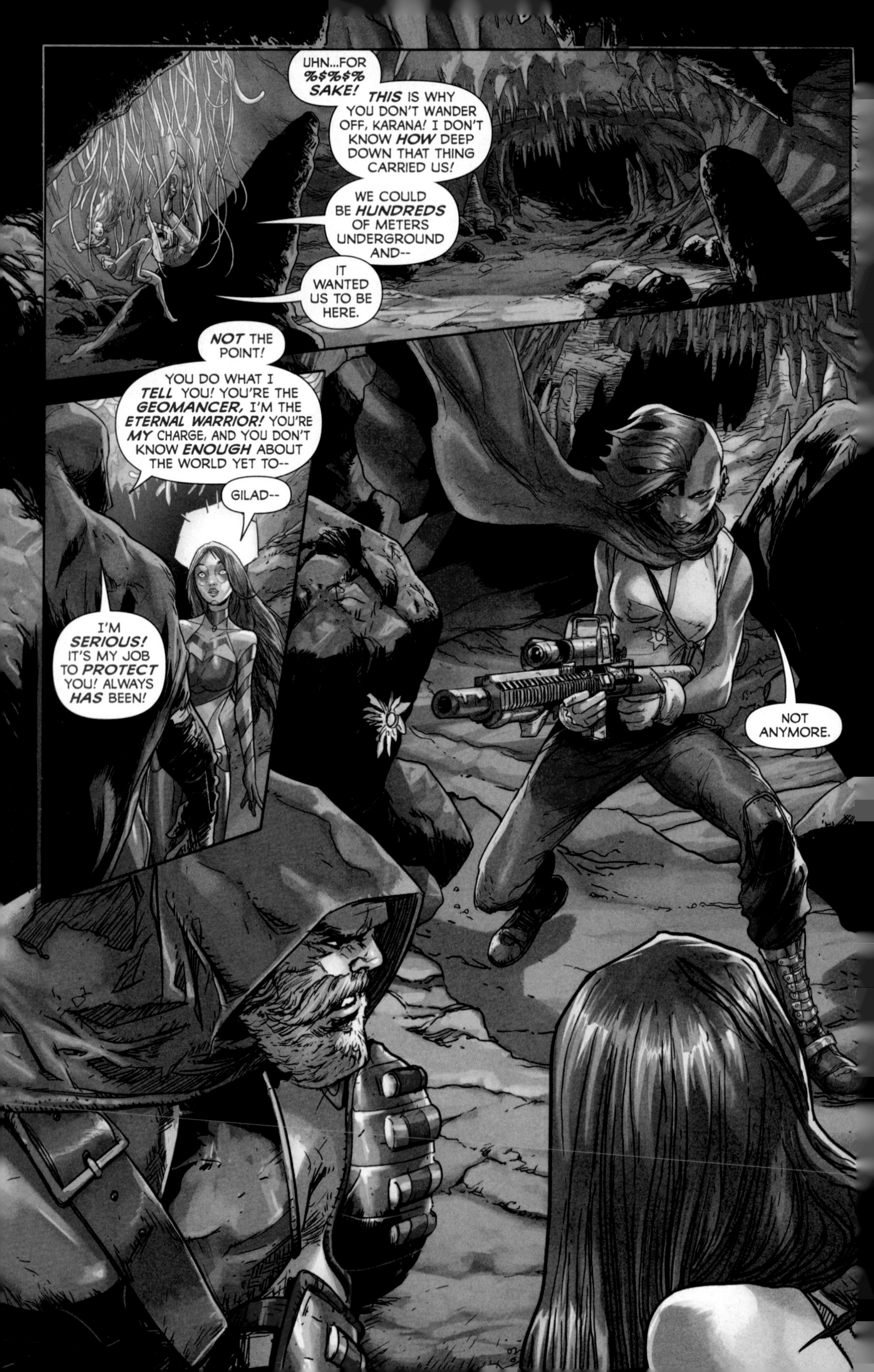
UHN...FOR %$%$% SAKE!
THIS IS WHY YOU DON'T WANDER OFF, KARANA! I DON'T KNOW HOW DEEP DOWN THAT THING CARRIED US!
WE COULD BE HUNDREDS OF METERS UNDERGROUND AND--
IT WANTED US TO BE HERE.
NOT THE POINT!
YOU DO WHAT I TELL YOU! YOU'RE THE GEOMANCER, I'M THE ETERNAL WARRIOR! YOU'RE MY CHARGE, AND YOU DON'T KNOW ENOUGH ABOUT THE WORLD YET TO--
GILAD--
I'M SERIOUS! IT'S MY JOB TO PROTECT YOU! ALWAYS HAS BEEN!
NOT ANYMORE.

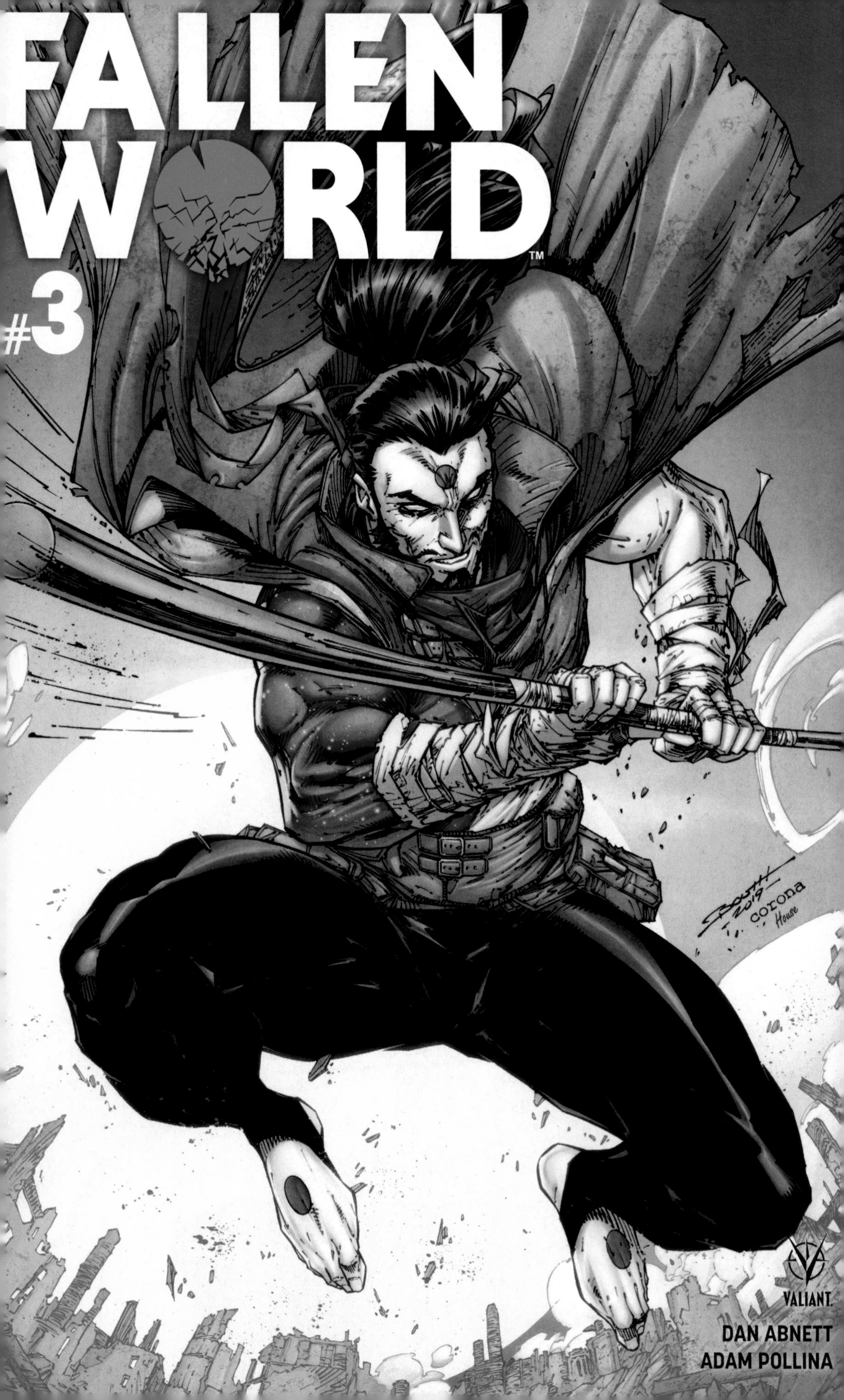
FALLEN WORLD™
#3
corona
VALIANT.
DAN ABNETT
ADAM POLLINA

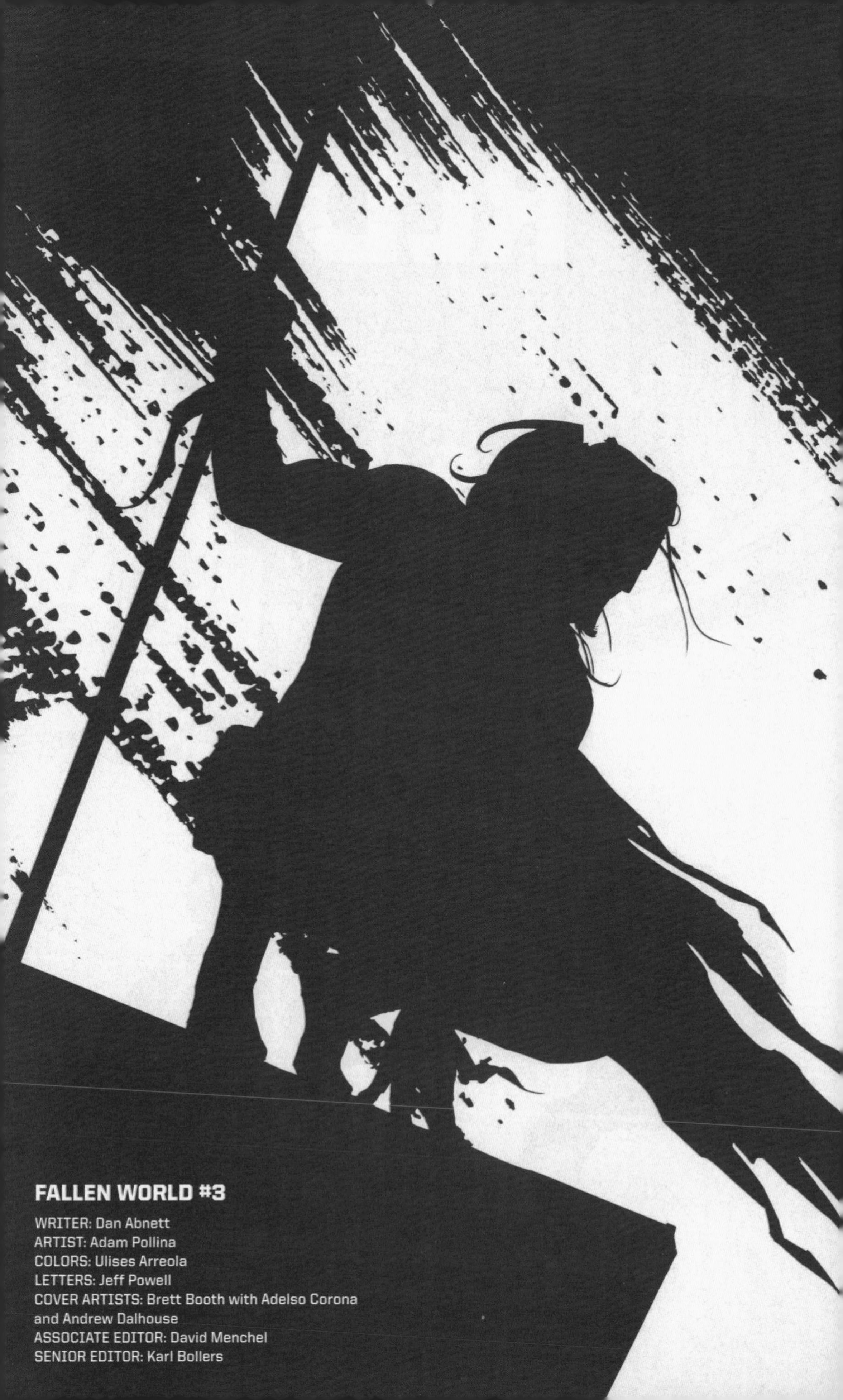

FALLEN WORLD #3

WRITER: Dan Abnett
ARTIST: Adam Pollina
COLORS: Ulises Arreola
LETTERS: Jeff Powell
COVER ARTISTS: Brett Booth with Adelso Corona
and Andrew Dalhouse
ASSOCIATE EDITOR: David Menchel
SENIOR EDITOR: Karl Bollers

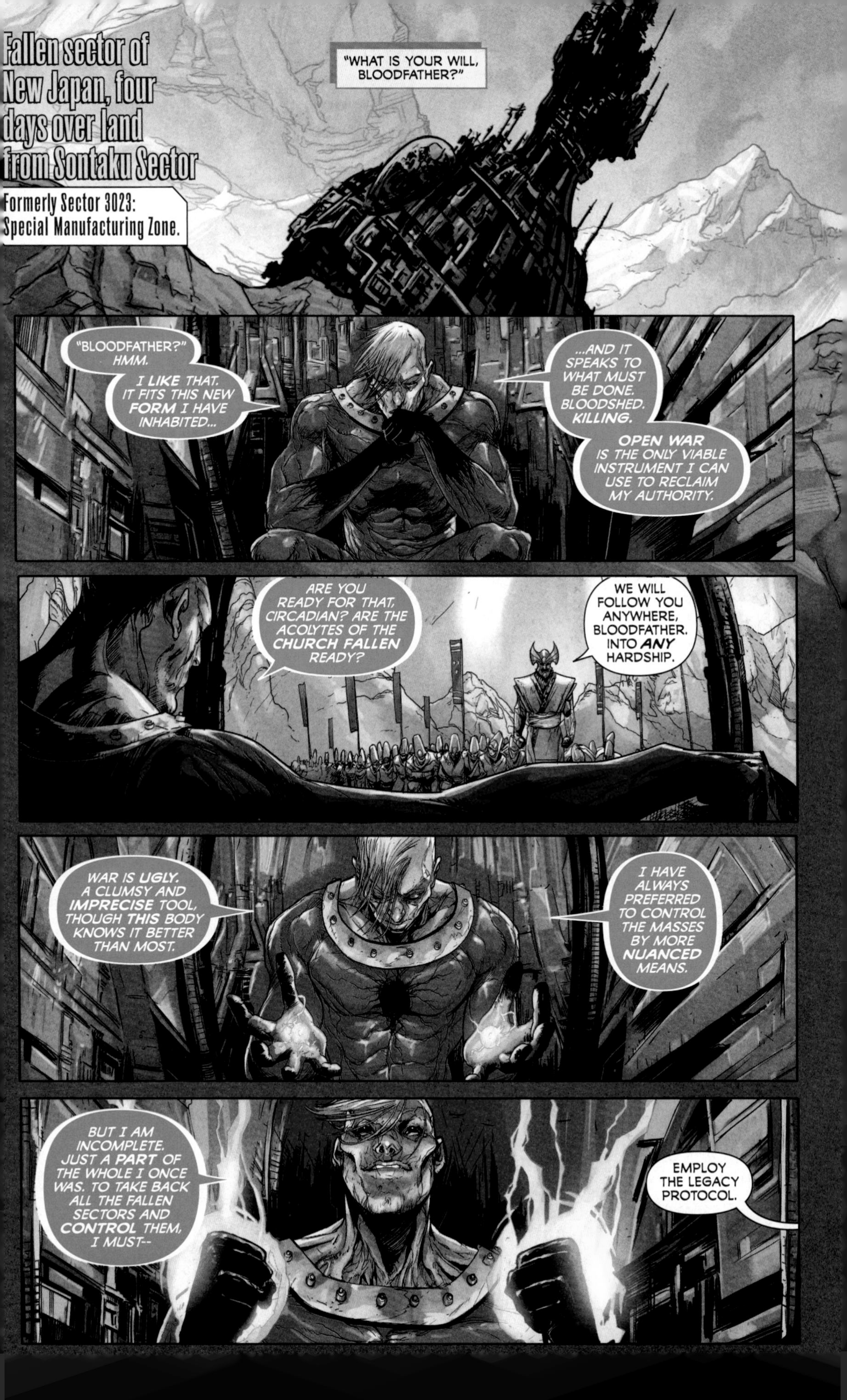

Fallen sector of New Japan, four days over land from Sontaku Sector
Formerly Sector 3023: Special Manufacturing Zone.
"WHAT IS YOUR WILL, BLOODFATHER?"
"BLOODFATHER?" HMM.
I LIKE THAT. IT FITS THIS NEW FORM I HAVE INHABITED...
...AND IT SPEAKS TO WHAT MUST BE DONE. BLOODSHED. KILLING.
OPEN WAR IS THE ONLY VIABLE INSTRUMENT I CAN USE TO RECLAIM MY AUTHORITY.
ARE YOU READY FOR THAT, CIRCADIAN? ARE THE ACOLYTES OF THE CHURCH FALLEN READY?
WE WILL FOLLOW YOU ANYWHERE, BLOODFATHER. INTO ANY HARDSHIP.
WAR IS UGLY. A CLUMSY AND IMPRECISE TOOL, THOUGH THIS BODY KNOWS IT BETTER THAN MOST.
I HAVE ALWAYS PREFERRED TO CONTROL THE MASSES BY MORE NUANCED MEANS.
BUT I AM INCOMPLETE. JUST A PART OF THE WHOLE I ONCE WAS. TO TAKE BACK ALL THE FALLEN SECTORS AND CONTROL THEM, I MUST--
EMPLOY THE LEGACY PROTOCOL.

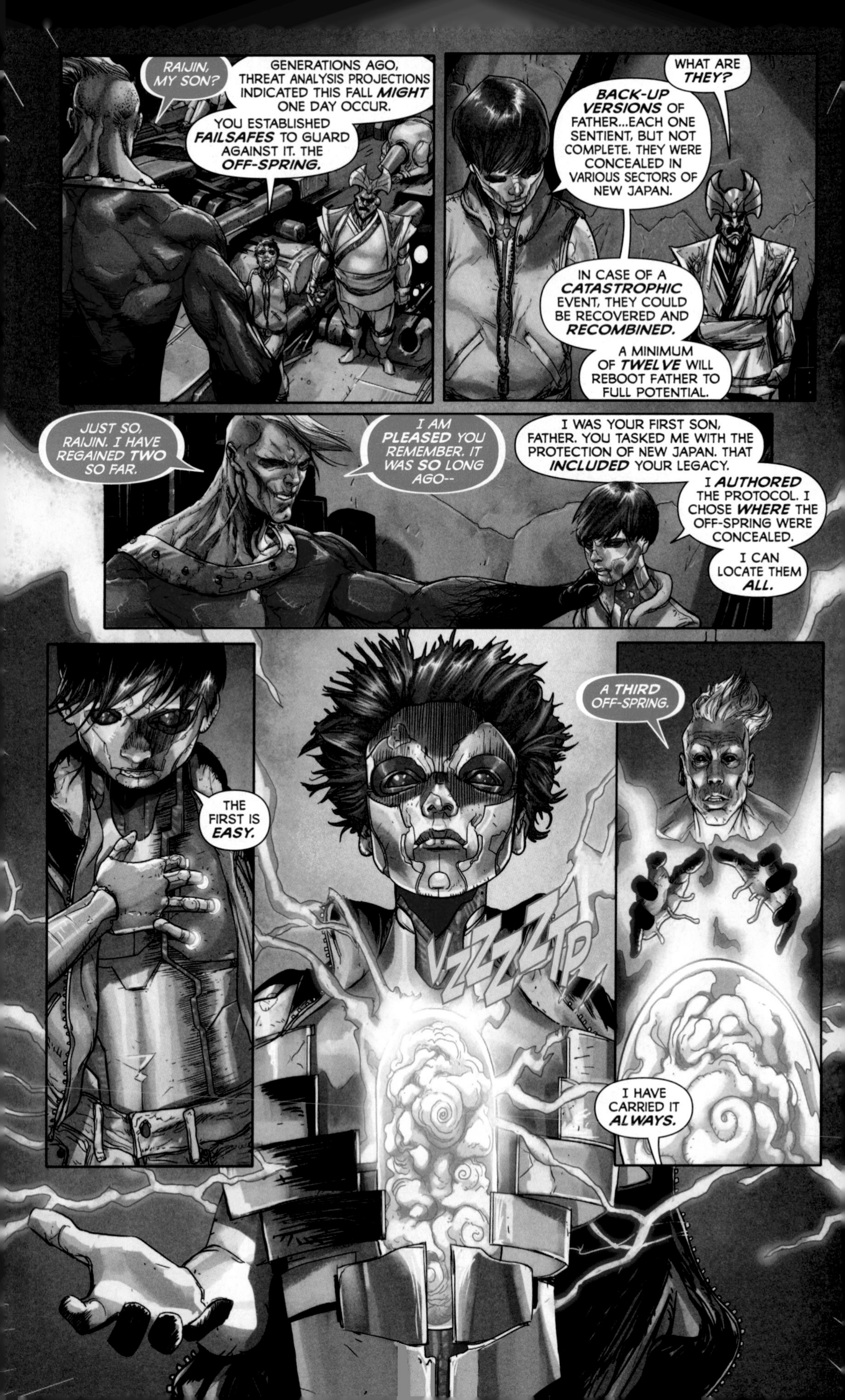
RAIJIN, MY SON?
GENERATIONS AGO, THREAT ANALYSIS PROJECTIONS INDICATED THIS FALL MIGHT ONE DAY OCCUR.
YOU ESTABLISHED FAILSAFES TO GUARD AGAINST IT. THE OFF-SPRING.
WHAT ARE THEY?
BACK-UP VERSIONS OF FATHER...EACH ONE SENTIENT, BUT NOT COMPLETE. THEY WERE CONCEALED IN VARIOUS SECTORS OF NEW JAPAN.
IN CASE OF A CATASTROPHIC EVENT, THEY COULD BE RECOVERED AND RECOMBINED.
A MINIMUM OF TWELVE WILL REBOOT FATHER TO FULL POTENTIAL.
JUST SO, RAIJIN. I HAVE REGAINED TWO SO FAR.
I AM PLEASED YOU REMEMBER. IT WAS SO LONG AGO--
I WAS YOUR FIRST SON, FATHER. YOU TASKED ME WITH THE PROTECTION OF NEW JAPAN. THAT INCLUDED YOUR LEGACY.
I AUTHORED THE PROTOCOL. I CHOSE WHERE THE OFF-SPRING WERE CONCEALED.
I CAN LOCATE THEM ALL.
THE FIRST IS EASY.
VZZZZTP
A THIRD OFF-SPRING.
I HAVE CARRIED IT ALWAYS.

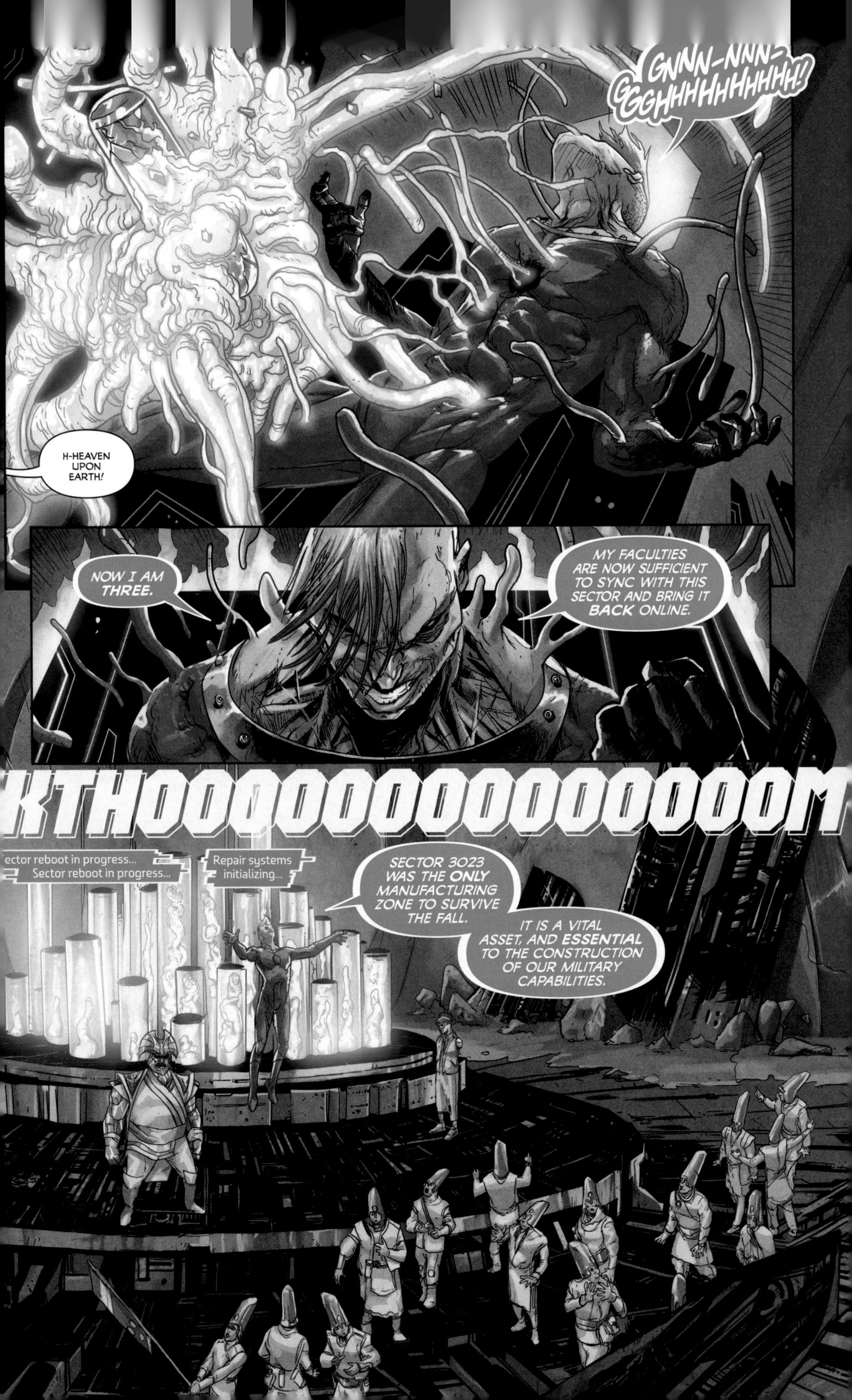
GNNN-NNN-GGGHHHHHHHHH!
H-HEAVEN UPON EARTH!
NOW I AM THREE.
MY FACULTIES ARE NOW SUFFICIENT TO SYNC WITH THIS SECTOR AND BRING IT BACK ONLINE.
KTHOOOOOOOOOOOOOOOOM
ector reboot in progress... Sector reboot in progress...
Repair systems initializing...
SECTOR 3023 WAS THE ONLY MANUFACTURING ZONE TO SURVIVE THE FALL.
IT IS A VITAL ASSET, AND ESSENTIAL TO THE CONSTRUCTION OF OUR MILITARY CAPABILITIES.

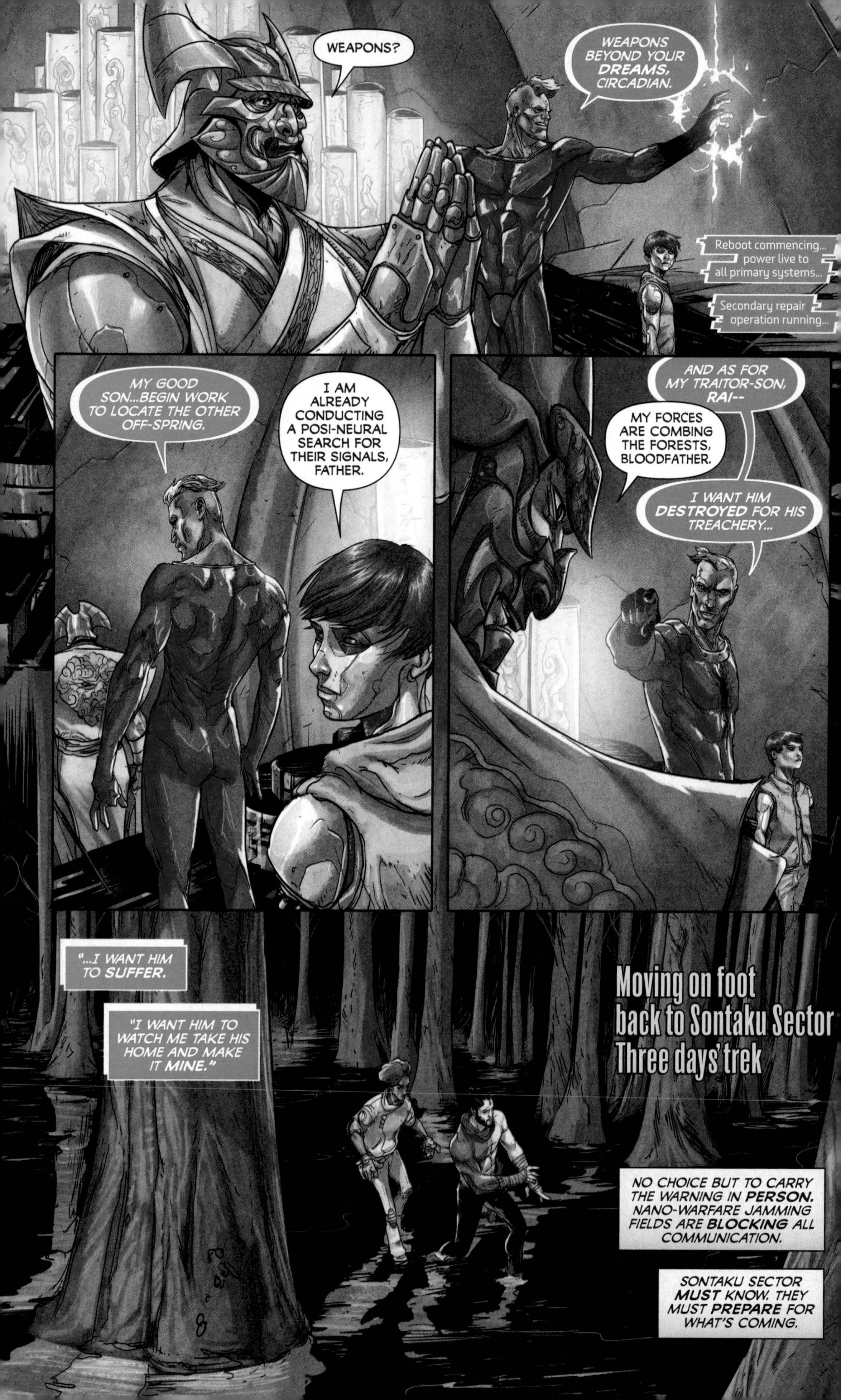
WEAPONS?
WEAPONS BEYOND YOUR **DREAMS,** CIRCADIAN.
Reboot commencing... power live to all primary systems...
Secondary repair operation running...
MY GOOD SON...BEGIN WORK TO LOCATE THE OTHER OFF-SPRING.
I AM ALREADY CONDUCTING A POSI-NEURAL SEARCH FOR THEIR SIGNALS, FATHER.
AND AS FOR MY TRAITOR-SON, **RAI--**
MY FORCES ARE COMBING THE FORESTS, BLOODFATHER.
I WANT HIM **DESTROYED** FOR HIS TREACHERY...
"...I WANT HIM TO **SUFFER.**
"I WANT HIM TO WATCH ME TAKE HIS HOME AND MAKE IT **MINE.**"
Moving on foot back to Sontaku Sector Three days' trek
NO CHOICE BUT TO CARRY THE WARNING IN **PERSON.** NANO-WARFARE JAMMING FIELDS ARE **BLOCKING** ALL COMMUNICATION.
SONTAKU SECTOR **MUST** KNOW. THEY **MUST PREPARE** FOR WHAT'S COMING.

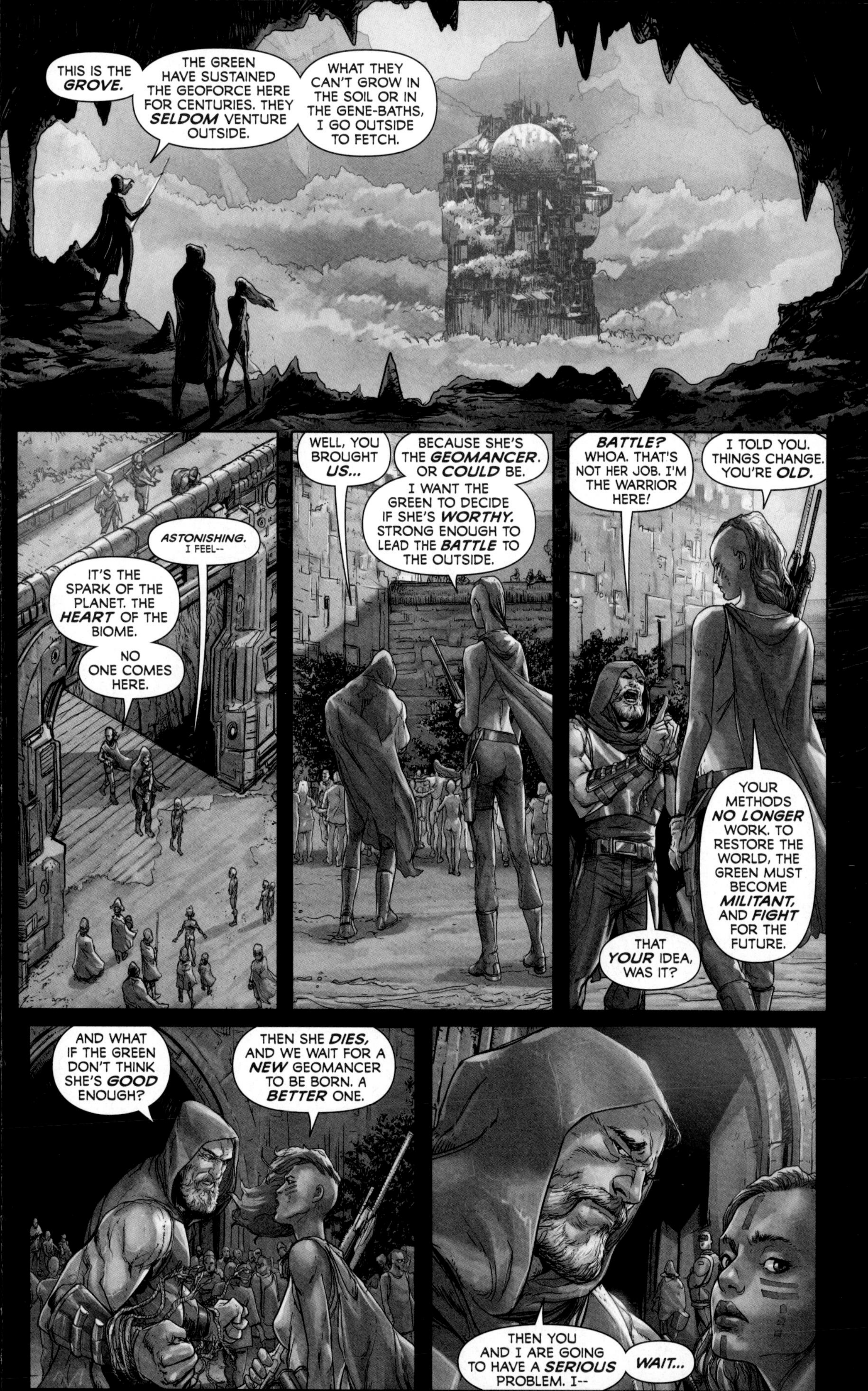
THIS IS THE GROVE.
THE GREEN HAVE SUSTAINED THE GEOFORCE HERE FOR CENTURIES. THEY SELDOM VENTURE OUTSIDE.
WHAT THEY CAN'T GROW IN THE SOIL OR IN THE GENE-BATHS, I GO OUTSIDE TO FETCH.
ASTONISHING. I FEEL--
IT'S THE SPARK OF THE PLANET. THE HEART OF THE BIOME.
NO ONE COMES HERE.
WELL, YOU BROUGHT US...
BECAUSE SHE'S THE GEOMANCER. OR COULD BE.
I WANT THE GREEN TO DECIDE IF SHE'S WORTHY. STRONG ENOUGH TO LEAD THE BATTLE TO THE OUTSIDE.
BATTLE? WHOA. THAT'S NOT HER JOB. I'M THE WARRIOR HERE!
I TOLD YOU. THINGS CHANGE. YOU'RE OLD.
YOUR METHODS NO LONGER WORK. TO RESTORE THE WORLD, THE GREEN MUST BECOME MILITANT, AND FIGHT FOR THE FUTURE.
THAT YOUR IDEA, WAS IT?
AND WHAT IF THE GREEN DON'T THINK SHE'S GOOD ENOUGH?
THEN SHE DIES, AND WE WAIT FOR A NEW GEOMANCER TO BE BORN. A BETTER ONE.
THEN YOU AND I ARE GOING TO HAVE A SERIOUS PROBLEM. I--
WAIT...

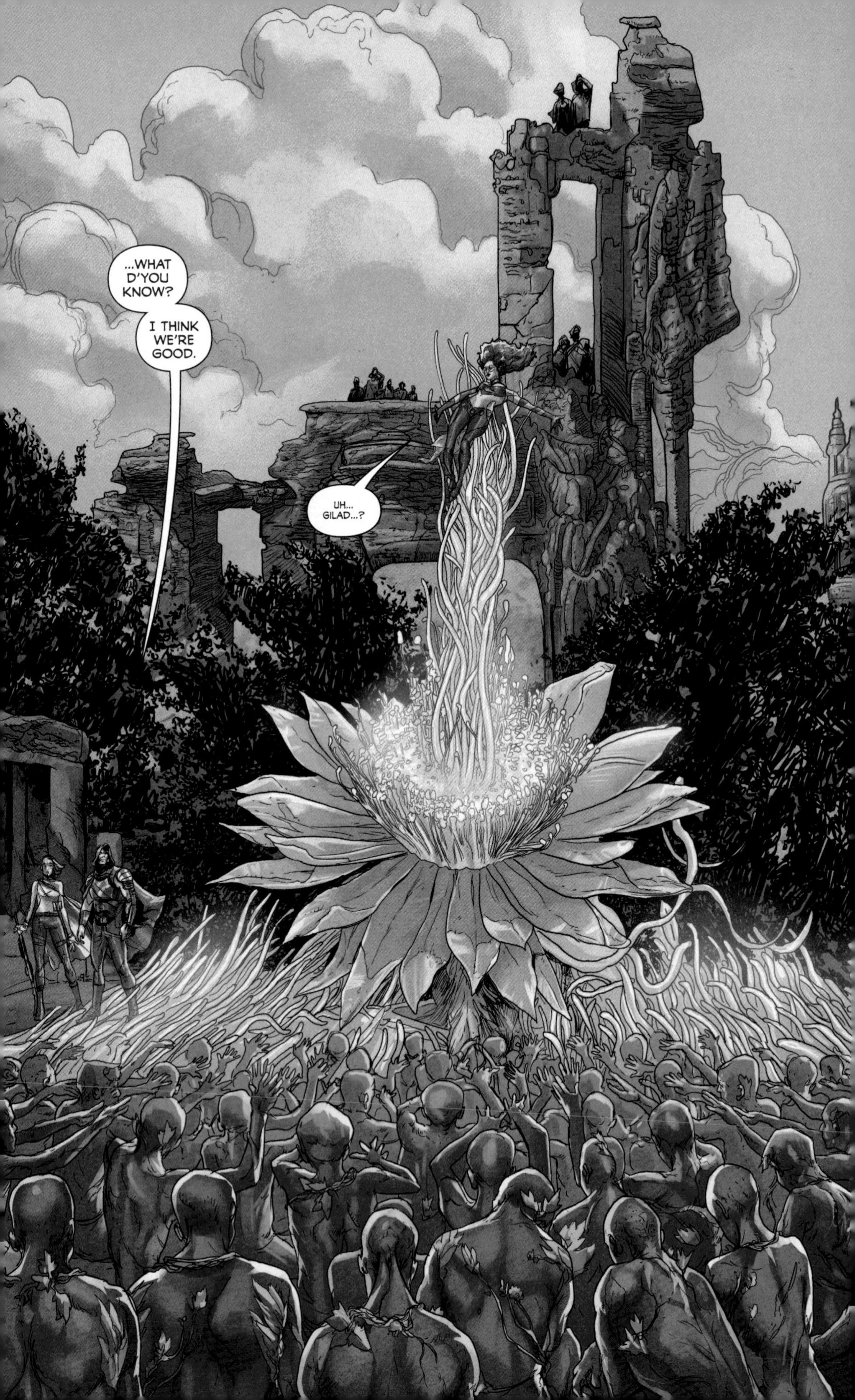
...WHAT D'YOU KNOW?
I THINK WE'RE GOOD.
UH... GILAD...?

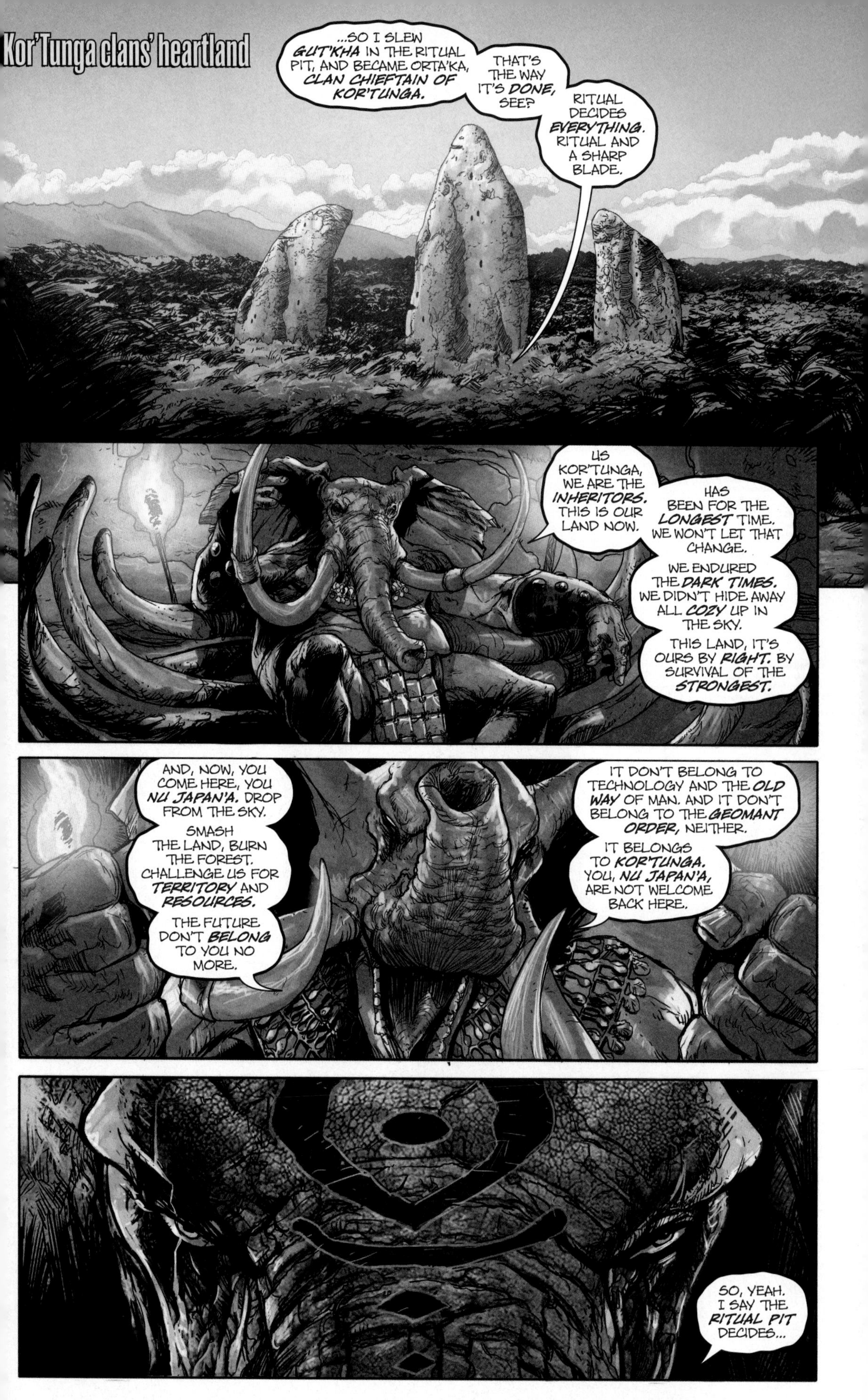
Kor'Tunga clans' heartland
...SO I SLEW GUT'KHA IN THE RITUAL PIT, AND BECAME ORTA'KA, CLAN CHIEFTAIN OF KOR'TUNGA.
THAT'S THE WAY IT'S DONE, SEE?
RITUAL DECIDES EVERYTHING. RITUAL AND A SHARP BLADE.
US KOR'TUNGA, WE ARE THE INHERITORS. THIS IS OUR LAND NOW.
HAS BEEN FOR THE LONGEST TIME. WE WON'T LET THAT CHANGE.
WE ENDURED THE DARK TIMES. WE DIDN'T HIDE AWAY ALL COZY UP IN THE SKY.
THIS LAND, IT'S OURS BY RIGHT. BY SURVIVAL OF THE STRONGEST.
AND, NOW, YOU COME HERE, YOU NU JAPAN'A. DROP FROM THE SKY.
SMASH THE LAND, BURN THE FOREST. CHALLENGE US FOR TERRITORY AND RESOURCES.
THE FUTURE DON'T BELONG TO YOU NO MORE.
IT DON'T BELONG TO TECHNOLOGY AND THE OLD WAY OF MAN. AND IT DON'T BELONG TO THE GEOMANT ORDER, NEITHER.
IT BELONGS TO KOR'TUNGA. YOU, NU JAPAN'A, ARE NOT WELCOME BACK HERE.
SO, YEAH. I SAY THE RITUAL PIT DECIDES...

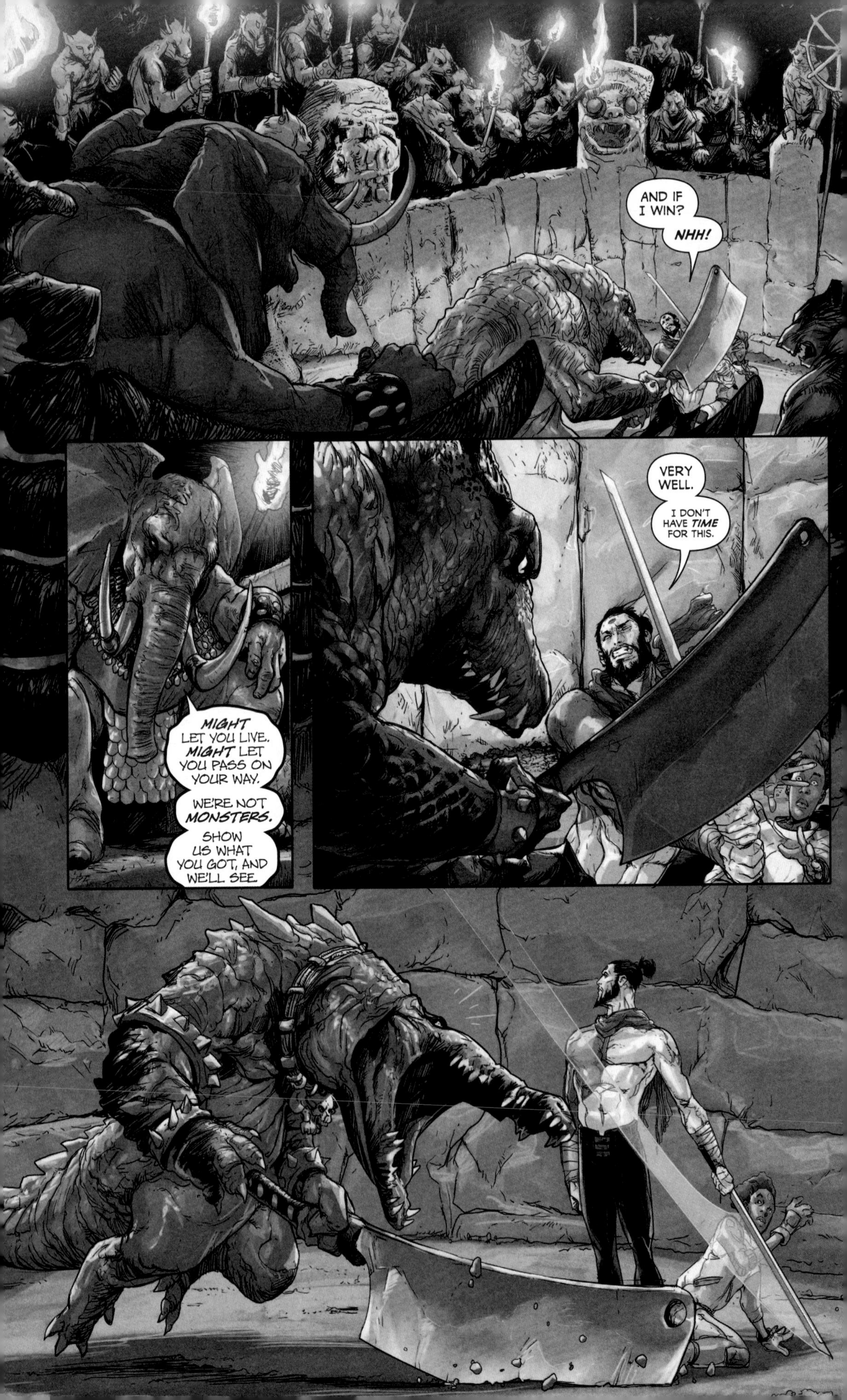

AND IF I WIN?
NHH!
MIGHT LET YOU LIVE. MIGHT LET YOU PASS ON YOUR WAY.
WE'RE NOT MONSTERS.
SHOW US WHAT YOU GOT, AND WE'LL SEE.
VERY WELL.
I DON'T HAVE TIME FOR THIS.

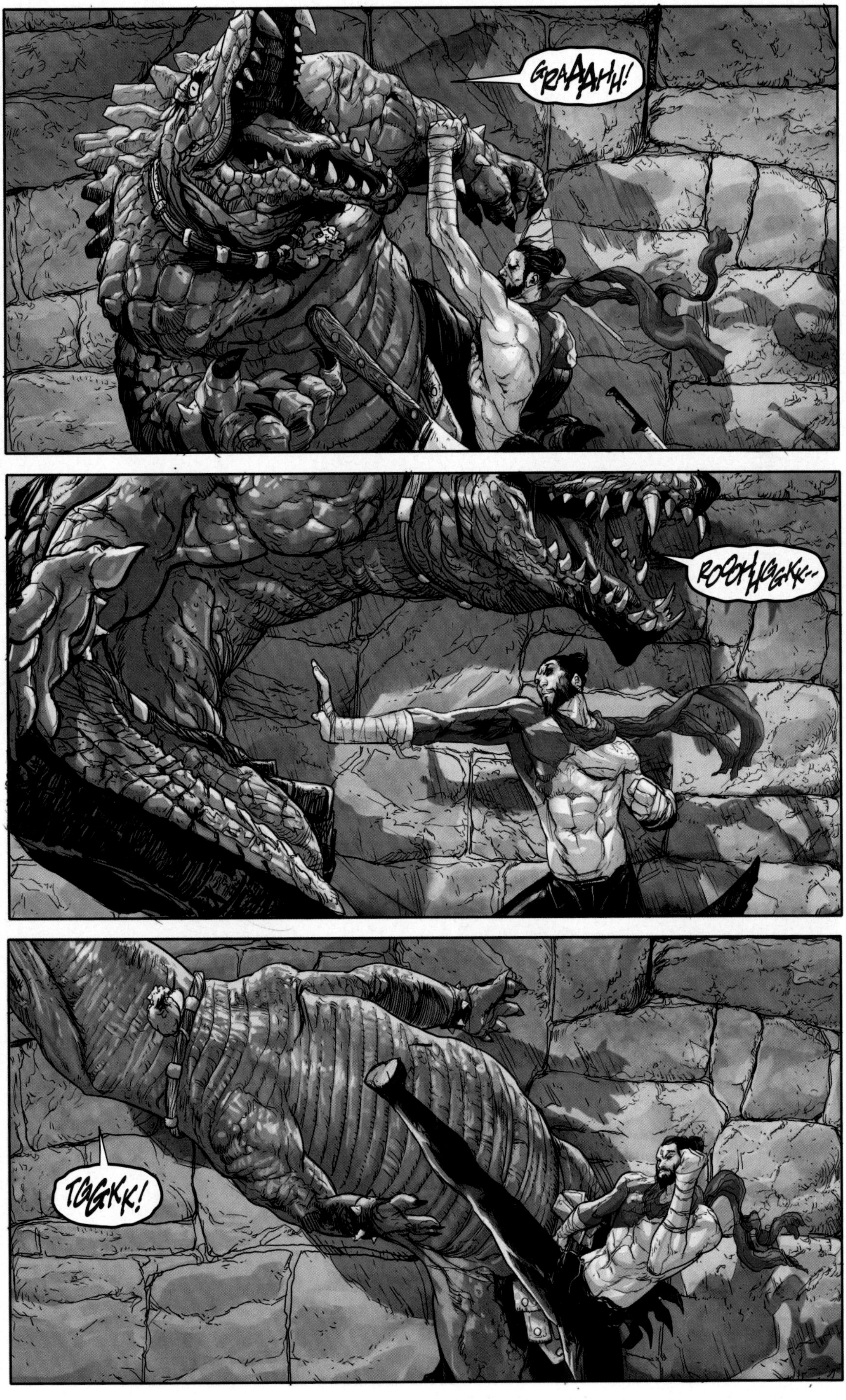
GRAAAAHH!
ROOOHHGKK--
TGGKK!

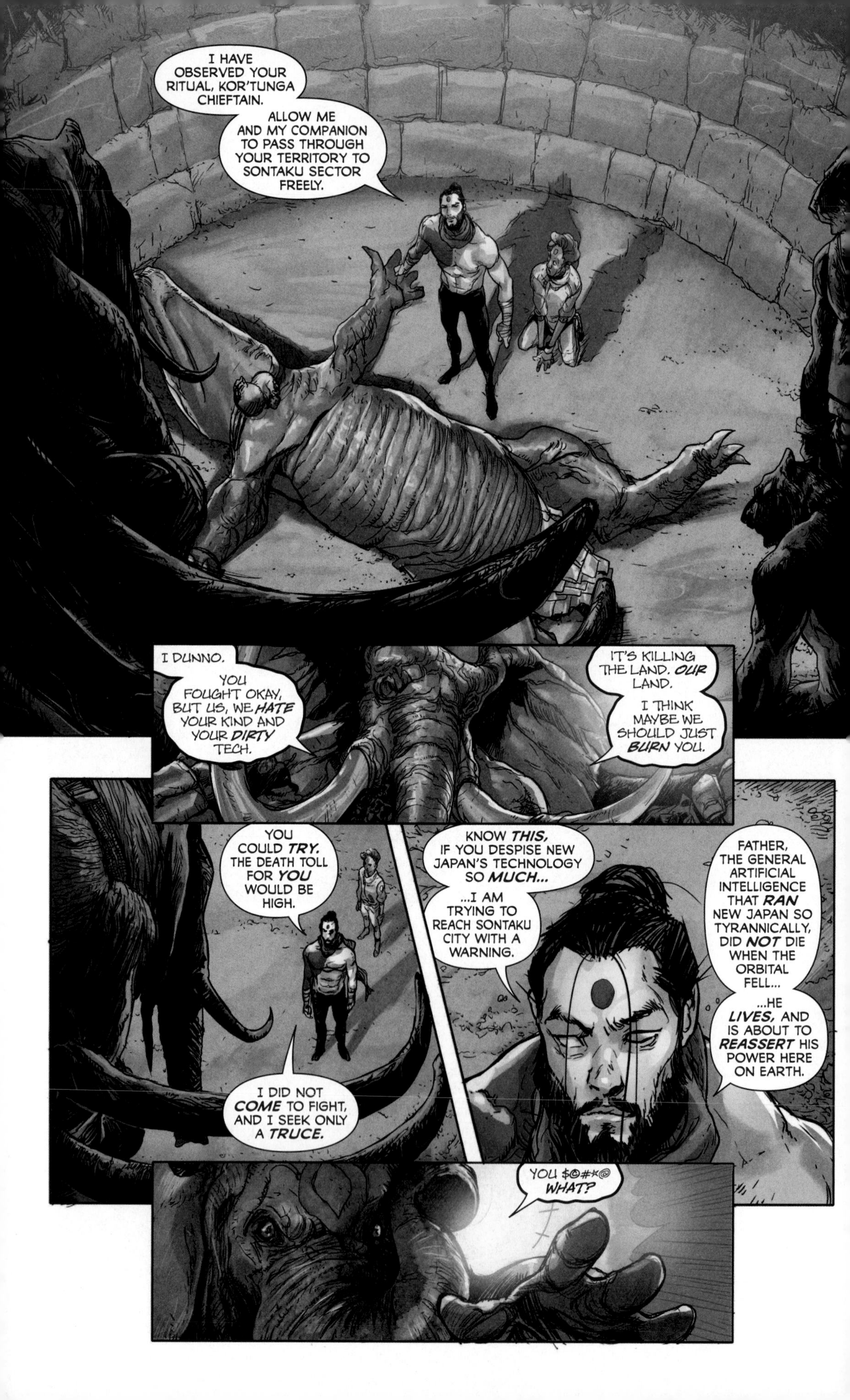
I HAVE OBSERVED YOUR RITUAL, KOR'TUNGA CHIEFTAIN.
ALLOW ME AND MY COMPANION TO PASS THROUGH YOUR TERRITORY TO SONTAKU SECTOR FREELY.
I DUNNO.
YOU FOUGHT OKAY, BUT US, WE HATE YOUR KIND AND YOUR DIRTY TECH.
IT'S KILLING THE LAND. OUR LAND.
I THINK MAYBE WE SHOULD JUST BURN YOU.
YOU COULD TRY. THE DEATH TOLL FOR YOU WOULD BE HIGH.
I DID NOT COME TO FIGHT, AND I SEEK ONLY A TRUCE.
KNOW THIS, IF YOU DESPISE NEW JAPAN'S TECHNOLOGY SO MUCH...
...I AM TRYING TO REACH SONTAKU CITY WITH A WARNING.
FATHER, THE GENERAL ARTIFICIAL INTELLIGENCE THAT RAN NEW JAPAN SO TYRANNICALLY, DID NOT DIE WHEN THE ORBITAL FELL...
...HE LIVES, AND IS ABOUT TO REASSERT HIS POWER HERE ON EARTH.
YOU $@#*@ WHAT?

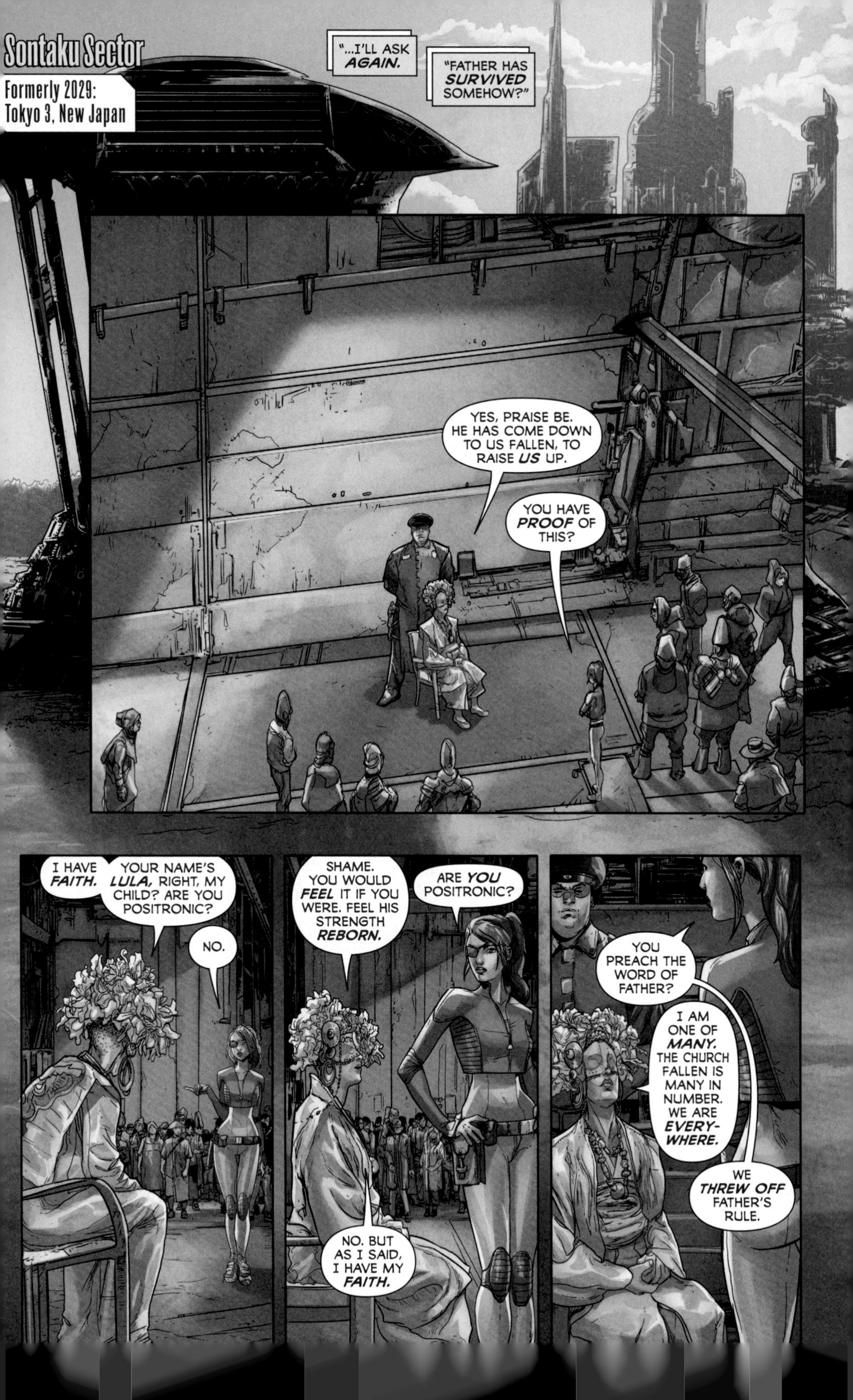
Sontaku Sector
Formerly 2029: Tokyo 3, New Japan
"...I'LL ASK AGAIN.
"FATHER HAS SURVIVED SOMEHOW?"
YES, PRAISE BE. HE HAS COME DOWN TO US FALLEN, TO RAISE US UP.
YOU HAVE PROOF OF THIS?
I HAVE FAITH.
YOUR NAME'S LULA, RIGHT, MY CHILD? ARE YOU POSITRONIC?
NO.
SHAME. YOU WOULD FEEL IT IF YOU WERE. FEEL HIS STRENGTH REBORN.
ARE YOU POSITRONIC?
NO. BUT AS I SAID, I HAVE MY FAITH.
YOU PREACH THE WORD OF FATHER?
I AM ONE OF MANY. THE CHURCH FALLEN IS MANY IN NUMBER. WE ARE EVERY-WHERE.
WE THREW OFF FATHER'S RULE.

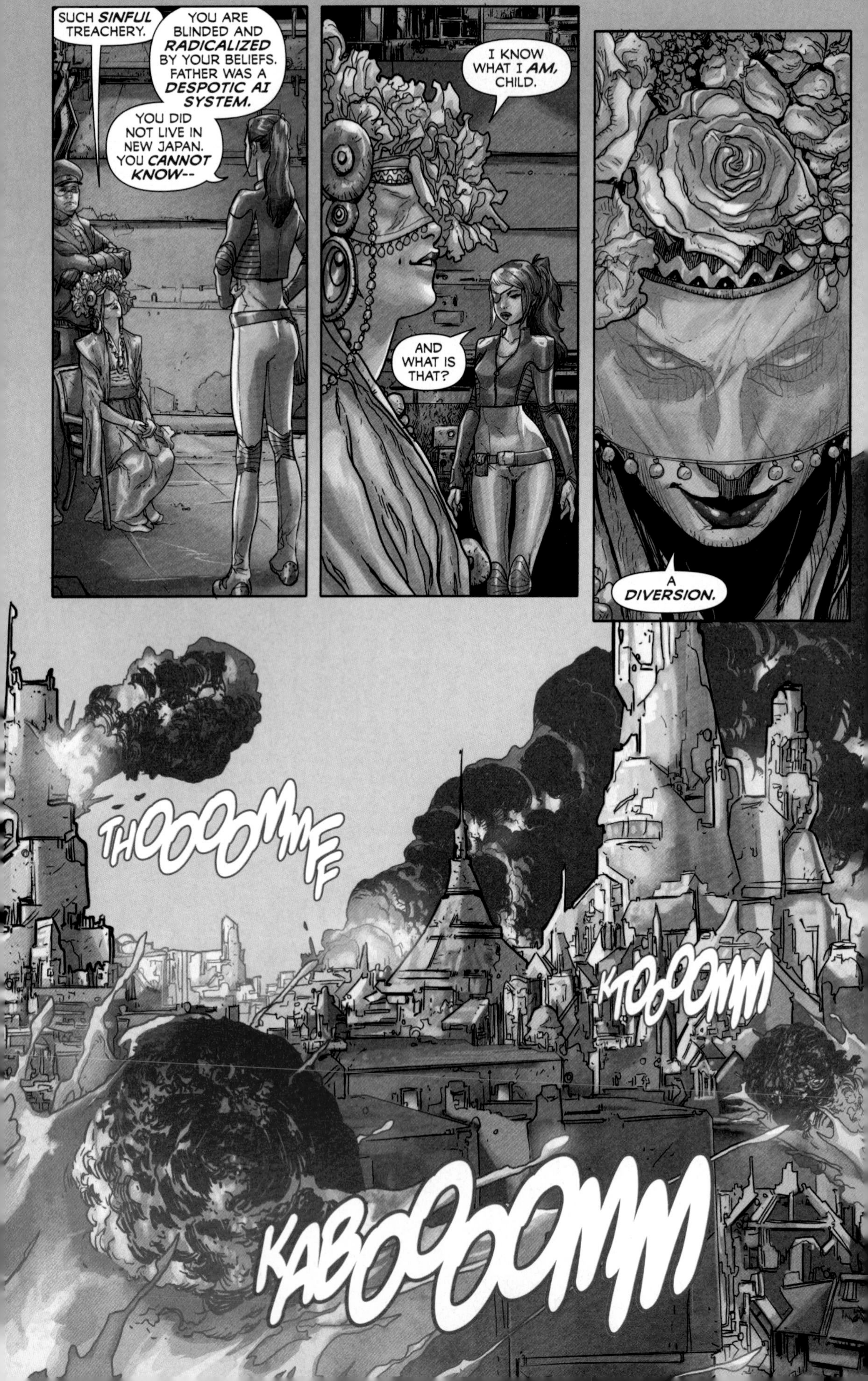
SUCH SINFUL TREACHERY.
YOU ARE BLINDED AND RADICALIZED BY YOUR BELIEFS. FATHER WAS A DESPOTIC AI SYSTEM.
YOU DID NOT LIVE IN NEW JAPAN. YOU CANNOT KNOW--
I KNOW WHAT I AM, CHILD.
AND WHAT IS THAT?
A DIVERSION.
THOOOOMMFF
KTOOOOMM
KABOOOOOMM

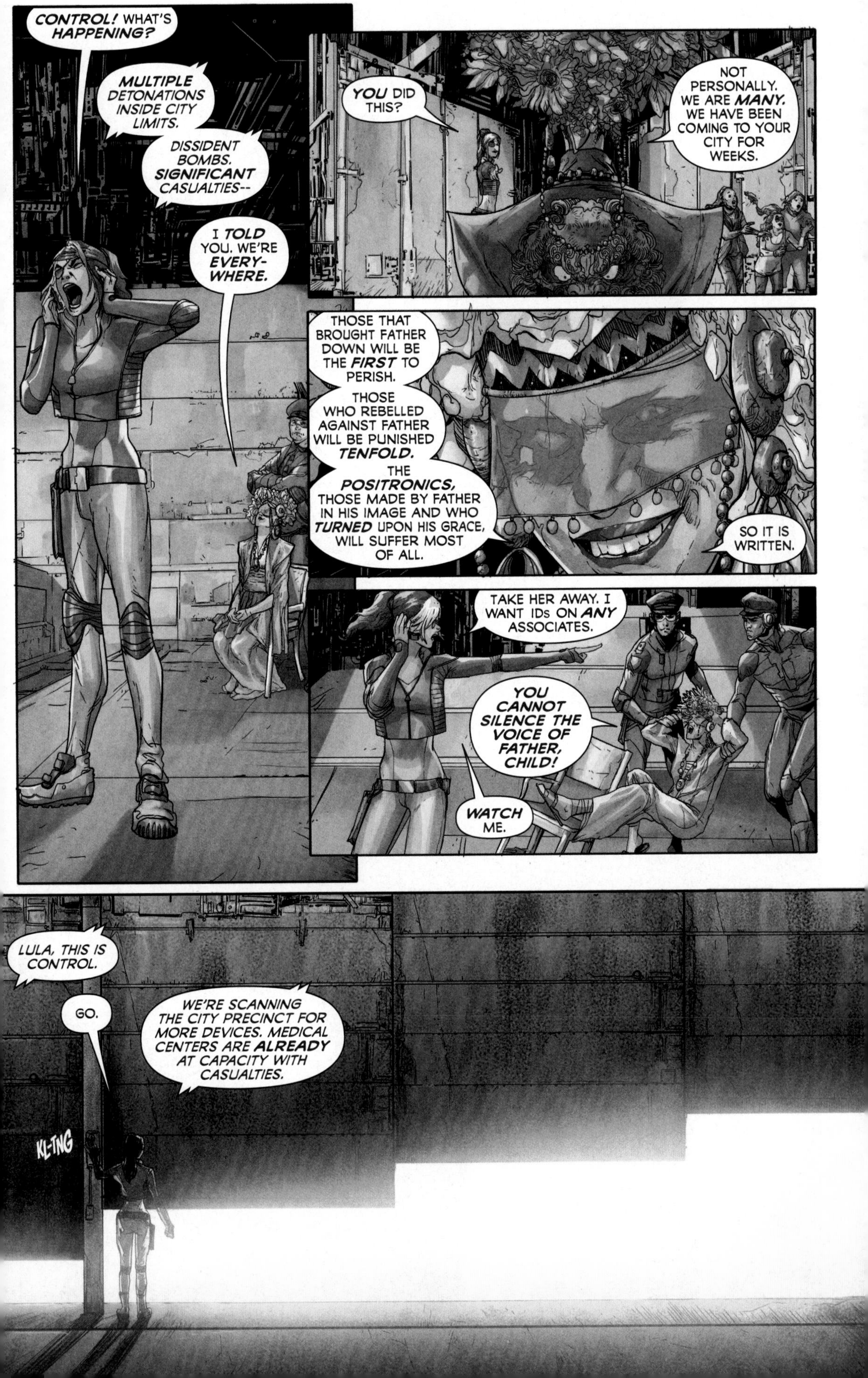
CONTROL! WHAT'S HAPPENING?
MULTIPLE DETONATIONS INSIDE CITY LIMITS.
DISSIDENT BOMBS. SIGNIFICANT CASUALTIES--
I TOLD YOU. WE'RE EVERY-WHERE.
YOU DID THIS?
NOT PERSONALLY. WE ARE MANY. WE HAVE BEEN COMING TO YOUR CITY FOR WEEKS.
THOSE THAT BROUGHT FATHER DOWN WILL BE THE FIRST TO PERISH.
THOSE WHO REBELLED AGAINST FATHER WILL BE PUNISHED TENFOLD.
THE POSITRONICS, THOSE MADE BY FATHER IN HIS IMAGE AND WHO TURNED UPON HIS GRACE, WILL SUFFER MOST OF ALL.
SO IT IS WRITTEN.
TAKE HER AWAY. I WANT IDs ON ANY ASSOCIATES.
YOU CANNOT SILENCE THE VOICE OF FATHER, CHILD!
WATCH ME.
LULA, THIS IS CONTROL.
GO.
WE'RE SCANNING THE CITY PRECINCT FOR MORE DEVICES. MEDICAL CENTERS ARE ALREADY AT CAPACITY WITH CASUALTIES.
KL-TNG

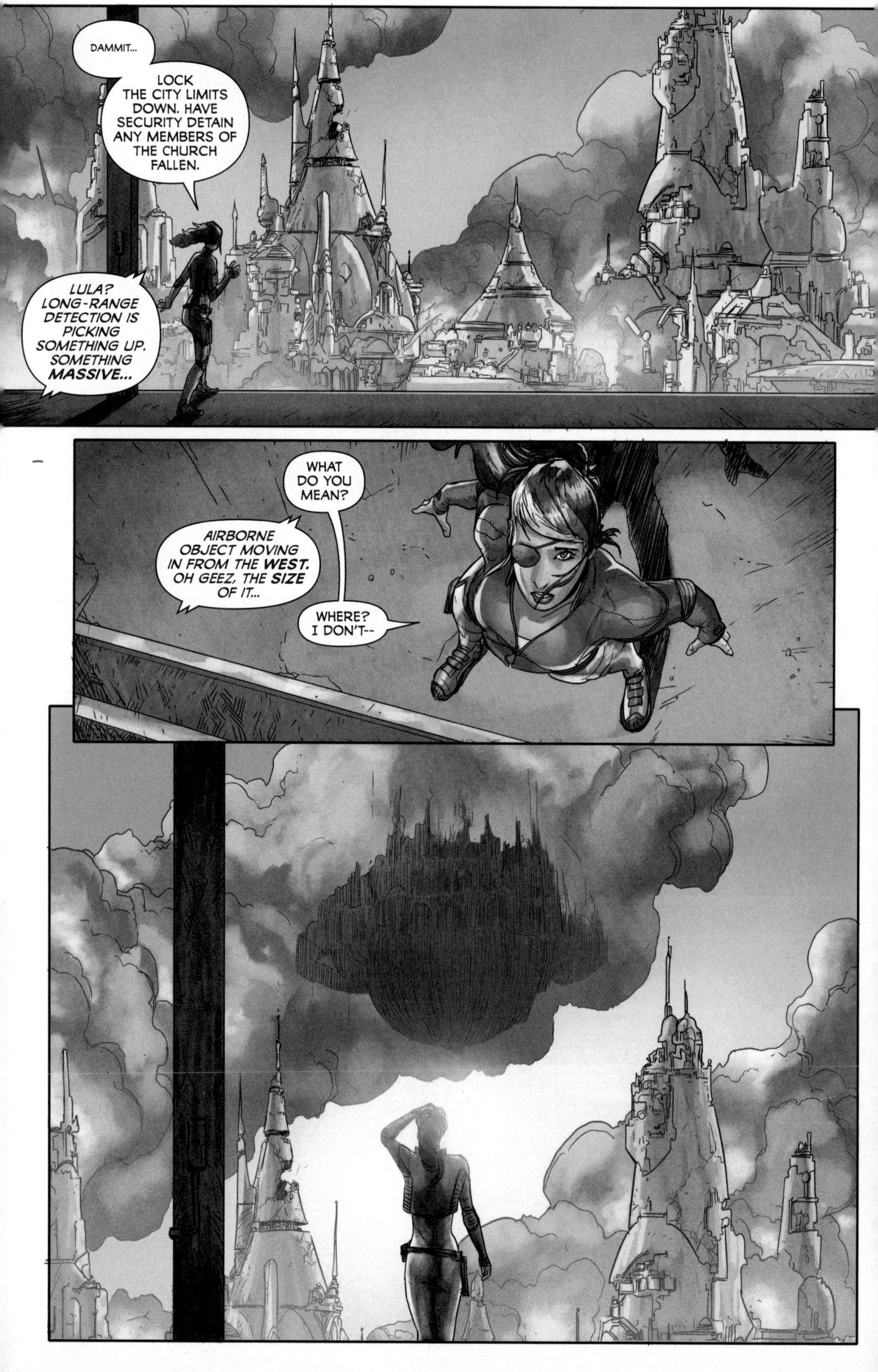
DAMMIT...
LOCK THE CITY LIMITS DOWN. HAVE SECURITY DETAIN ANY MEMBERS OF THE CHURCH FALLEN.
LULA? LONG-RANGE DETECTION IS PICKING SOMETHING UP. SOMETHING MASSIVE...
WHAT DO YOU MEAN?
AIRBORNE OBJECT MOVING IN FROM THE WEST. OH GEEZ, THE SIZE OF IT...
WHERE? I DON'T--

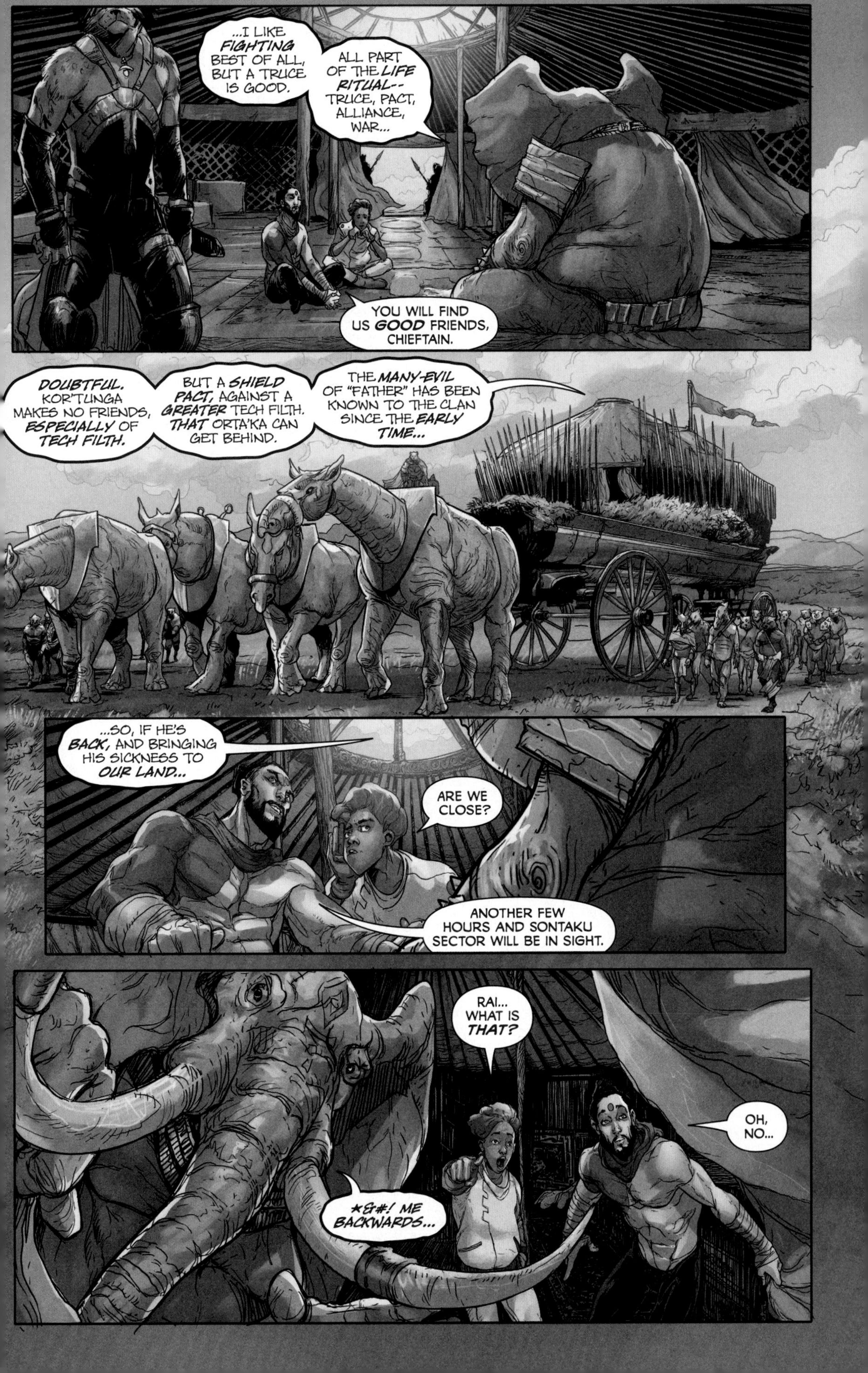

...I LIKE FIGHTING BEST OF ALL, BUT A TRUCE IS GOOD.
ALL PART OF THE LIFE RITUAL-- TRUCE, PACT, ALLIANCE, WAR...
YOU WILL FIND US GOOD FRIENDS, CHIEFTAIN.
DOUBTFUL. KOR'TUNGA MAKES NO FRIENDS, ESPECIALLY OF TECH FILTH.
BUT A SHIELD PACT, AGAINST A GREATER TECH FILTH. THAT ORTA'KA CAN GET BEHIND.
THE MANY-EVIL OF "FATHER" HAS BEEN KNOWN TO THE CLAN SINCE THE EARLY TIME...
...SO, IF HE'S BACK, AND BRINGING HIS SICKNESS TO OUR LAND...
ARE WE CLOSE?
ANOTHER FEW HOURS AND SONTAKU SECTOR WILL BE IN SIGHT.
RAI... WHAT IS THAT?
OH, NO...
*&#! ME BACKWARDS...

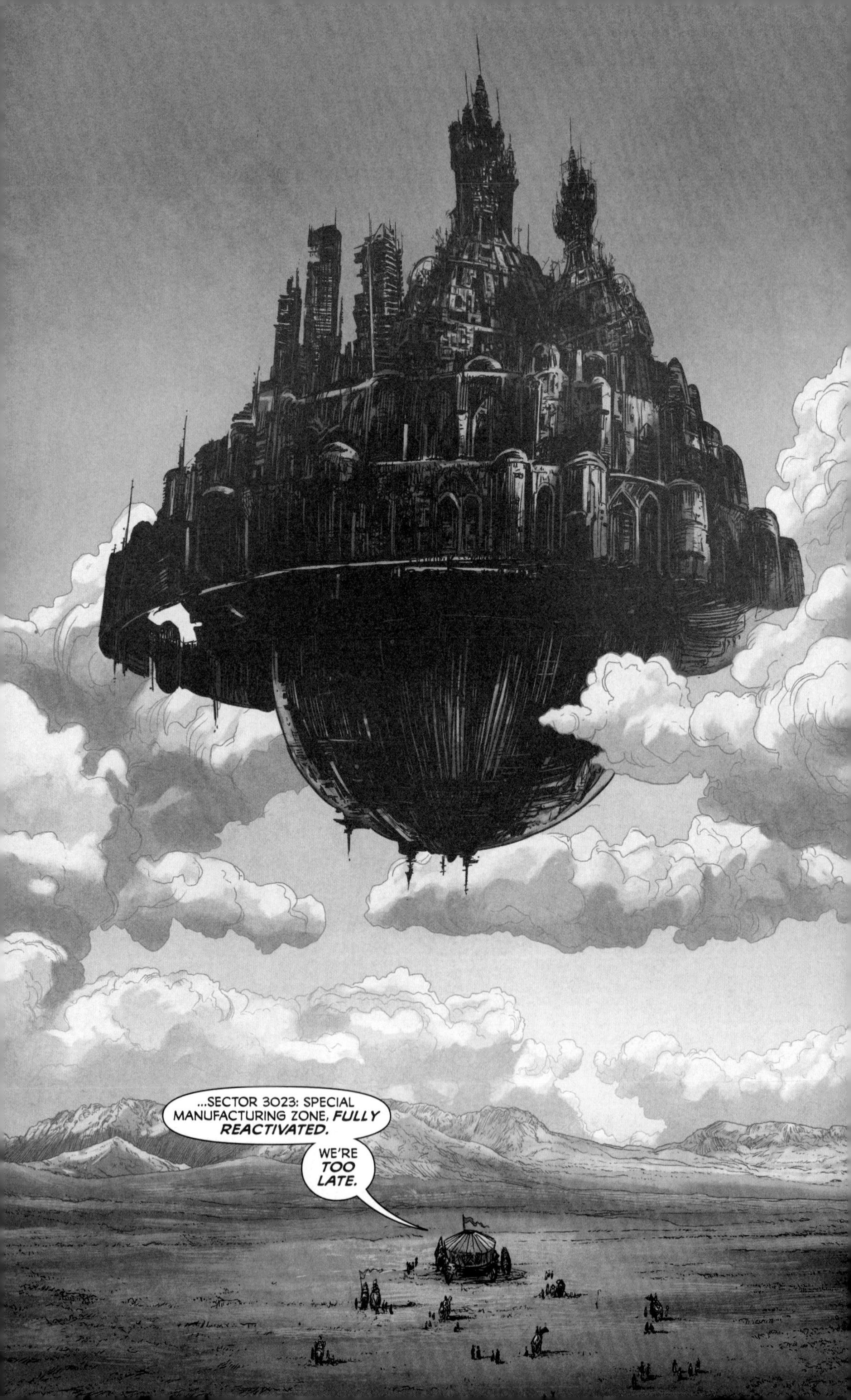
...SECTOR 3023: SPECIAL MANUFACTURING ZONE, *FULLY REACTIVATED.*
WE'RE *TOO LATE.*

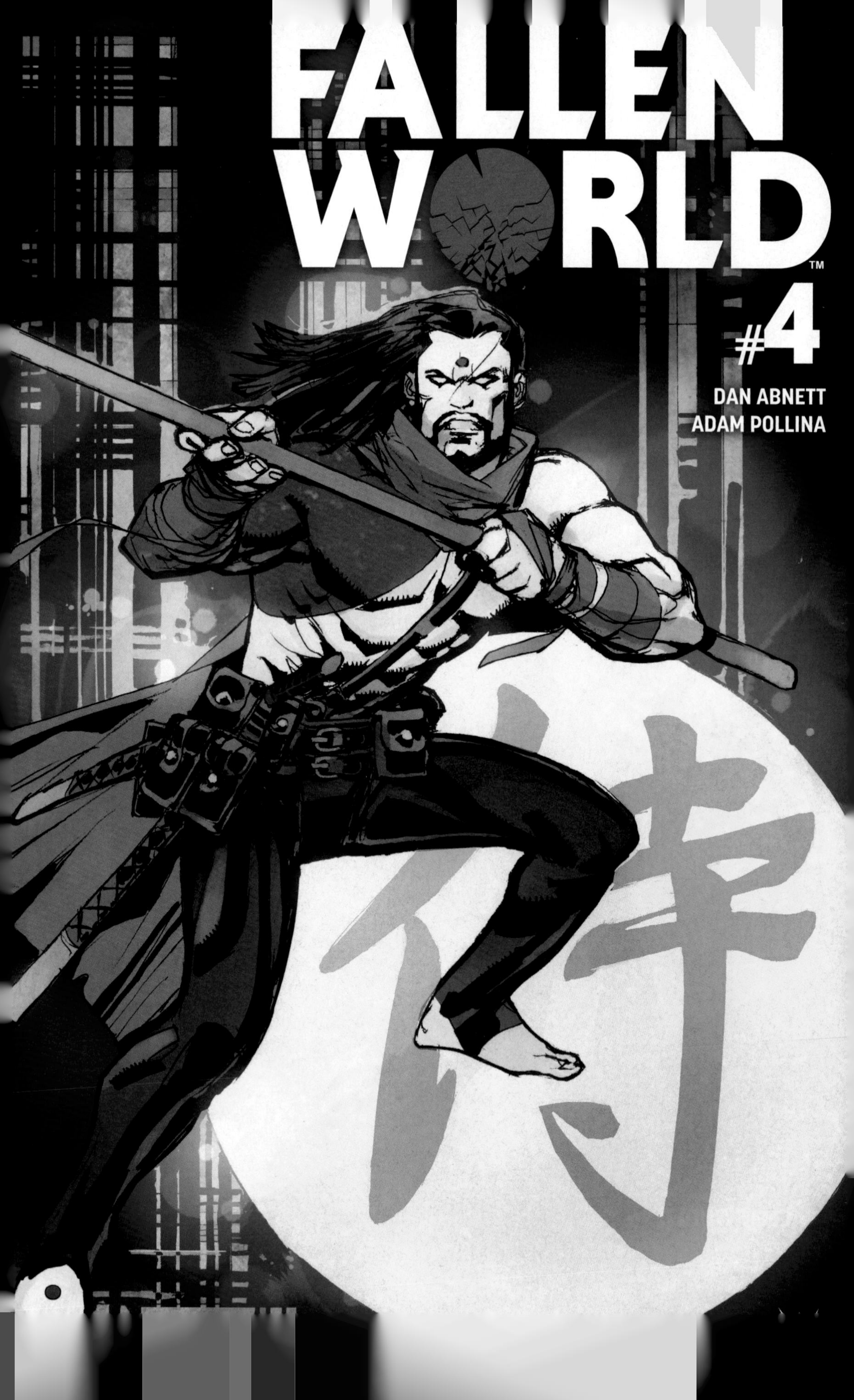
FALLEN WORLD™
#4
DAN ABNETT
ADAM POLLINA
侍

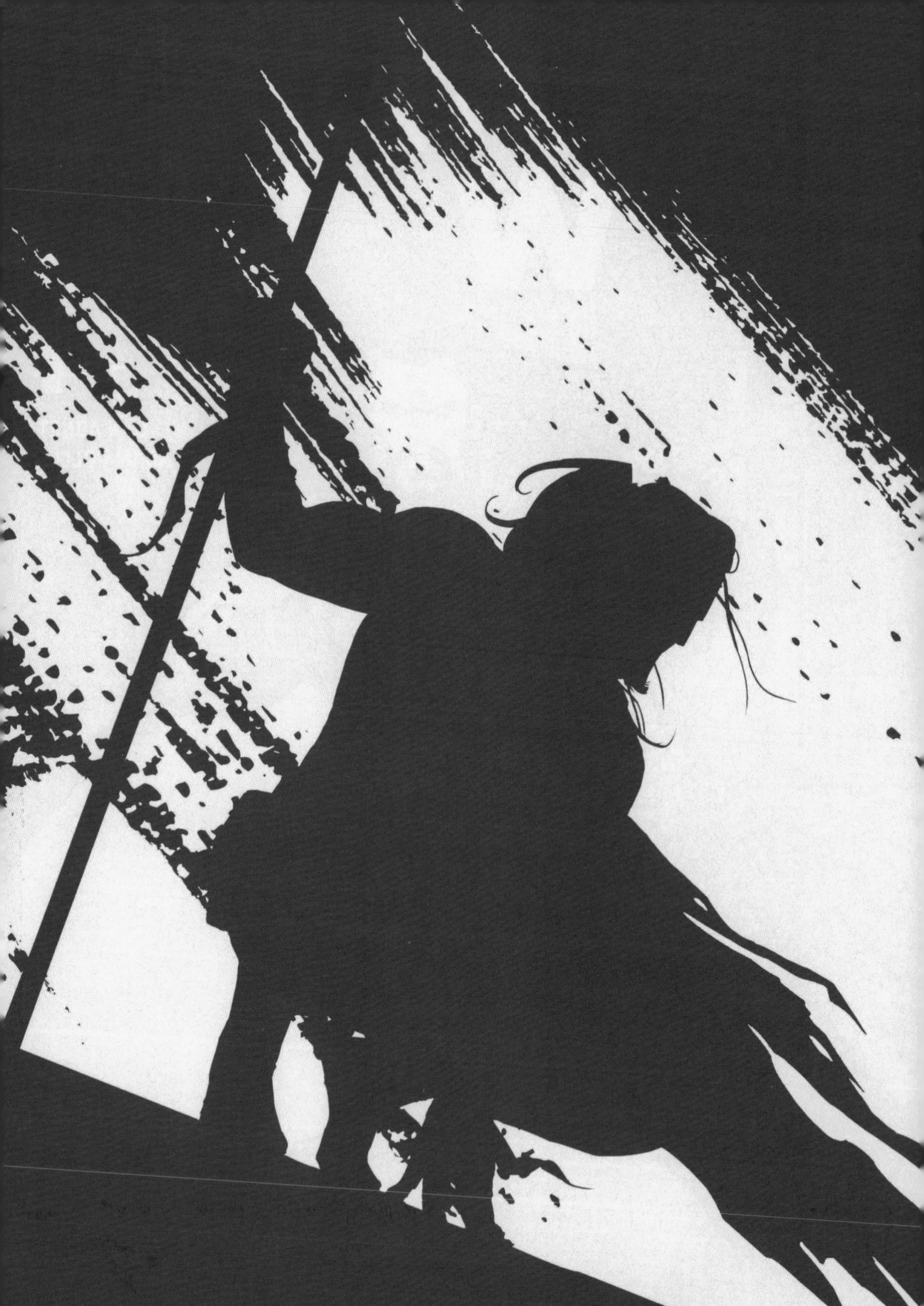

FALLEN WORLD #4

WRITER: Dan Abnett
ARTIST: Adam Pollina
COLORS: Ulises Arreola
LETTERS: Jeff Powell
COVER ARTISTS: Rick Leonardi with Dan Brown
ASSOCIATE EDITOR: David Menchel
SENIOR EDITOR: Karl Bollers

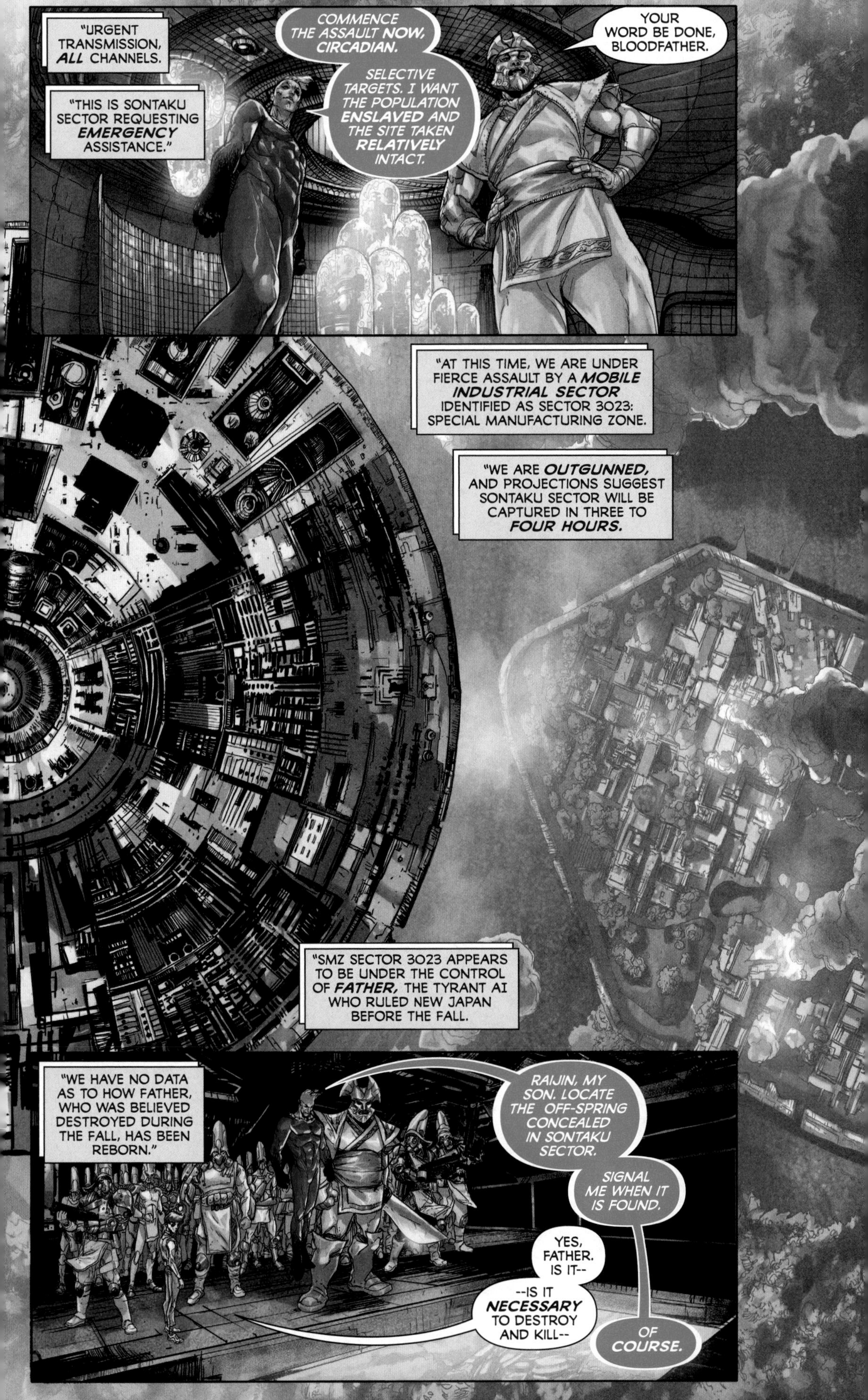
"URGENT TRANSMISSION, ALL CHANNELS.
"THIS IS SONTAKU SECTOR REQUESTING EMERGENCY ASSISTANCE."
COMMENCE THE ASSAULT NOW, CIRCADIAN.
SELECTIVE TARGETS. I WANT THE POPULATION ENSLAVED AND THE SITE TAKEN RELATIVELY INTACT.
YOUR WORD BE DONE, BLOODFATHER.
"AT THIS TIME, WE ARE UNDER FIERCE ASSAULT BY A MOBILE INDUSTRIAL SECTOR IDENTIFIED AS SECTOR 3023: SPECIAL MANUFACTURING ZONE.
"WE ARE OUTGUNNED, AND PROJECTIONS SUGGEST SONTAKU SECTOR WILL BE CAPTURED IN THREE TO FOUR HOURS.
"SMZ SECTOR 3023 APPEARS TO BE UNDER THE CONTROL OF FATHER, THE TYRANT AI WHO RULED NEW JAPAN BEFORE THE FALL.
"WE HAVE NO DATA AS TO HOW FATHER, WHO WAS BELIEVED DESTROYED DURING THE FALL, HAS BEEN REBORN."
RAIJIN, MY SON. LOCATE THE OFF-SPRING CONCEALED IN SONTAKU SECTOR.
SIGNAL ME WHEN IT IS FOUND.
YES, FATHER. IS IT--
--IS IT NECESSARY TO DESTROY AND KILL--
OF COURSE.

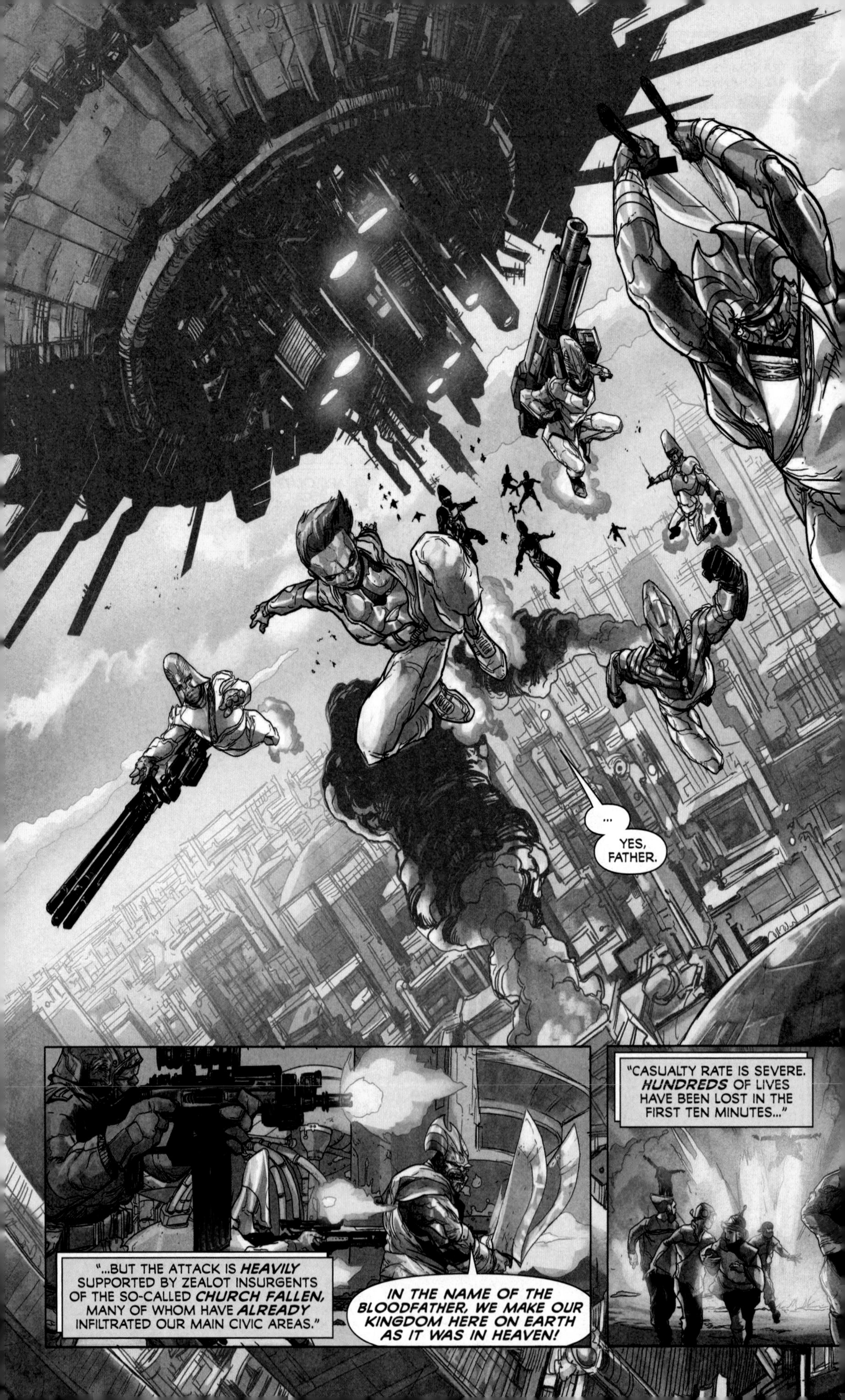
...
YES, FATHER.
"...BUT THE ATTACK IS *HEAVILY* SUPPORTED BY ZEALOT INSURGENTS OF THE SO-CALLED *CHURCH FALLEN,* MANY OF WHOM HAVE *ALREADY* INFILTRATED OUR MAIN CIVIC AREAS."
IN THE NAME OF THE BLOODFATHER, WE MAKE OUR KINGDOM HERE ON EARTH AS IT WAS IN HEAVEN!
"CASUALTY RATE IS SEVERE. *HUNDREDS* OF LIVES HAVE BEEN LOST IN THE FIRST TEN MINUTES..."

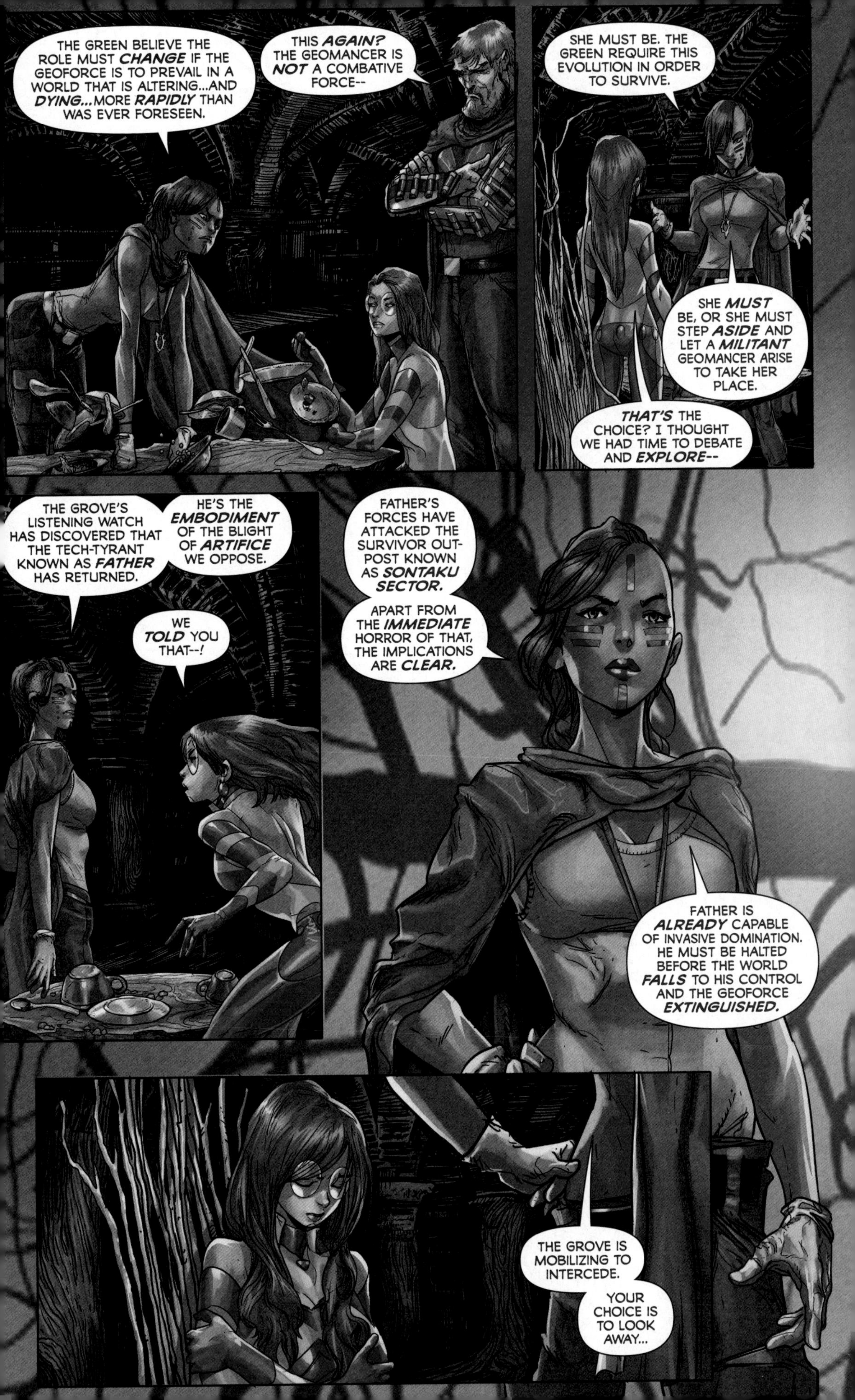
THE GREEN BELIEVE THE ROLE MUST CHANGE IF THE GEOFORCE IS TO PREVAIL IN A WORLD THAT IS ALTERING...AND DYING...MORE RAPIDLY THAN WAS EVER FORESEEN.
THIS AGAIN? THE GEOMANCER IS NOT A COMBATIVE FORCE--
SHE MUST BE. THE GREEN REQUIRE THIS EVOLUTION IN ORDER TO SURVIVE.
SHE MUST BE, OR SHE MUST STEP ASIDE AND LET A MILITANT GEOMANCER ARISE TO TAKE HER PLACE.
THAT'S THE CHOICE? I THOUGHT WE HAD TIME TO DEBATE AND EXPLORE--
THE GROVE'S LISTENING WATCH HAS DISCOVERED THAT THE TECH-TYRANT KNOWN AS FATHER HAS RETURNED.
HE'S THE EMBODIMENT OF THE BLIGHT OF ARTIFICE WE OPPOSE.
WE TOLD YOU THAT--!
FATHER'S FORCES HAVE ATTACKED THE SURVIVOR OUT-POST KNOWN AS SONTAKU SECTOR.
APART FROM THE IMMEDIATE HORROR OF THAT, THE IMPLICATIONS ARE CLEAR.
FATHER IS ALREADY CAPABLE OF INVASIVE DOMINATION. HE MUST BE HALTED BEFORE THE WORLD FALLS TO HIS CONTROL AND THE GEOFORCE EXTINGUISHED.
THE GROVE IS MOBILIZING TO INTERCEDE.
YOUR CHOICE IS TO LOOK AWAY...

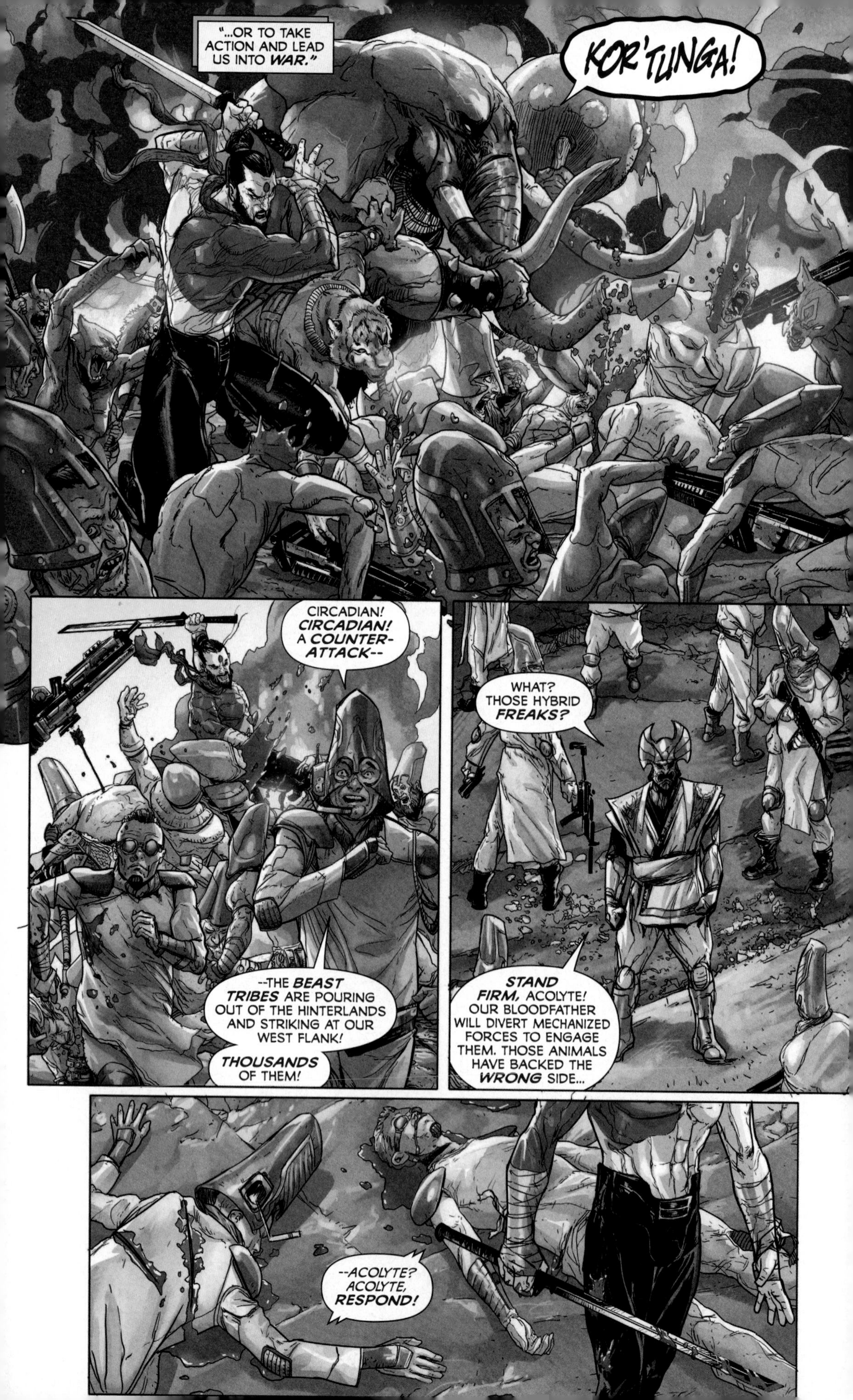
"...OR TO TAKE ACTION AND LEAD US INTO WAR."
KOR'TUNGA!
CIRCADIAN! CIRCADIAN! A COUNTER-ATTACK--
--THE BEAST TRIBES ARE POURING OUT OF THE HINTERLANDS AND STRIKING AT OUR WEST FLANK!
THOUSANDS OF THEM!
WHAT? THOSE HYBRID FREAKS?
STAND FIRM, ACOLYTE! OUR BLOODFATHER WILL DIVERT MECHANIZED FORCES TO ENGAGE THEM. THOSE ANIMALS HAVE BACKED THE WRONG SIDE...
--ACOLYTE? ACOLYTE, RESPOND!

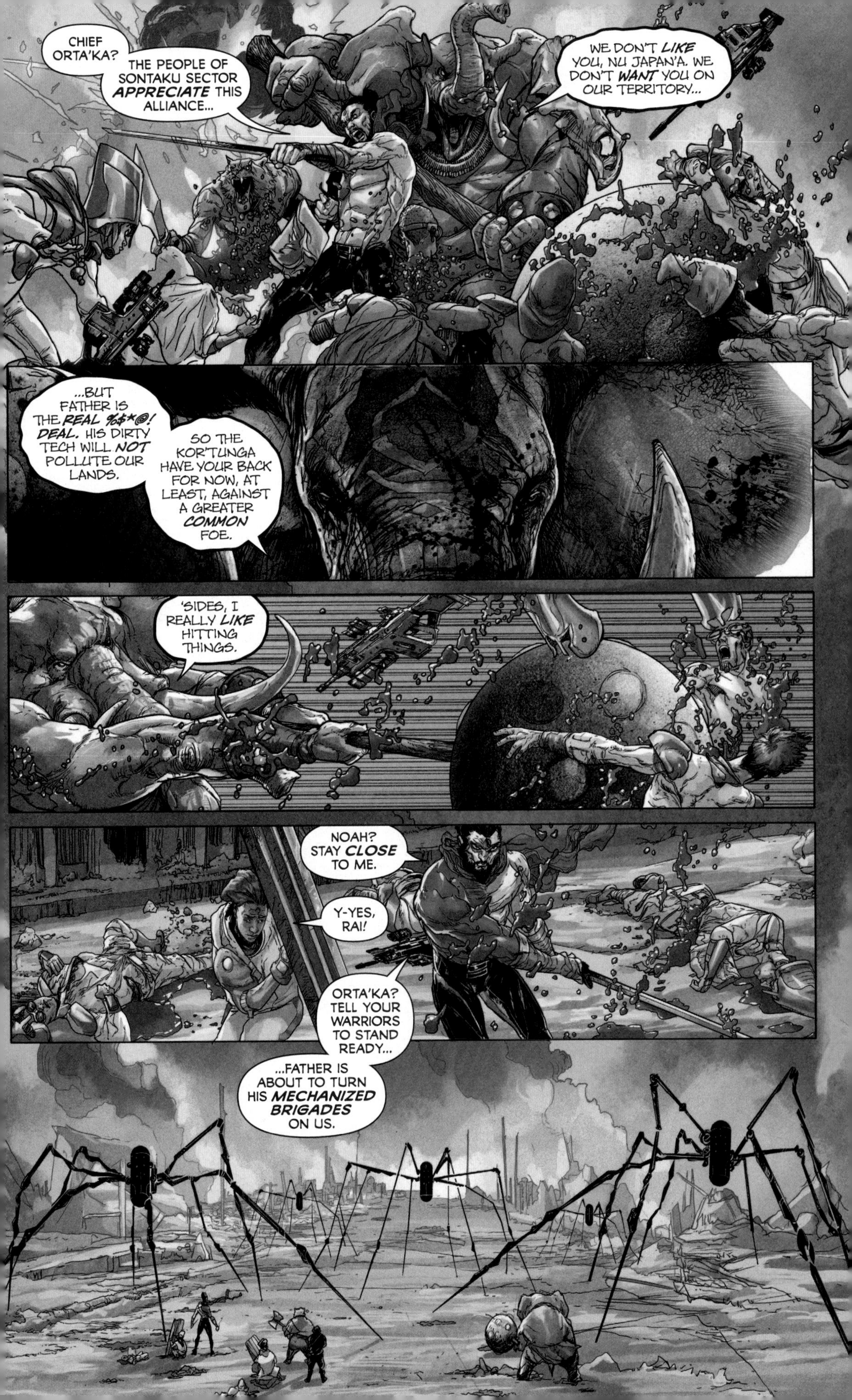
CHIEF ORTA'KA?
THE PEOPLE OF SONTAKU SECTOR *APPRECIATE* THIS ALLIANCE...
WE DON'T *LIKE* YOU, NU JAPAN'A. WE DON'T *WANT* YOU ON OUR TERRITORY...
...BUT FATHER IS THE *REAL %$*@! DEAL.* HIS DIRTY TECH WILL *NOT* POLLUTE OUR LANDS.
SO THE KOR'TUNGA HAVE YOUR BACK FOR NOW, AT LEAST, AGAINST A GREATER *COMMON* FOE.
'SIDES, I REALLY *LIKE* HITTING THINGS.
NOAH? STAY *CLOSE* TO ME.
Y-YES, RAI!
ORTA'KA? TELL YOUR WARRIORS TO STAND READY...
...FATHER IS ABOUT TO TURN HIS *MECHANIZED BRIGADES* ON US.

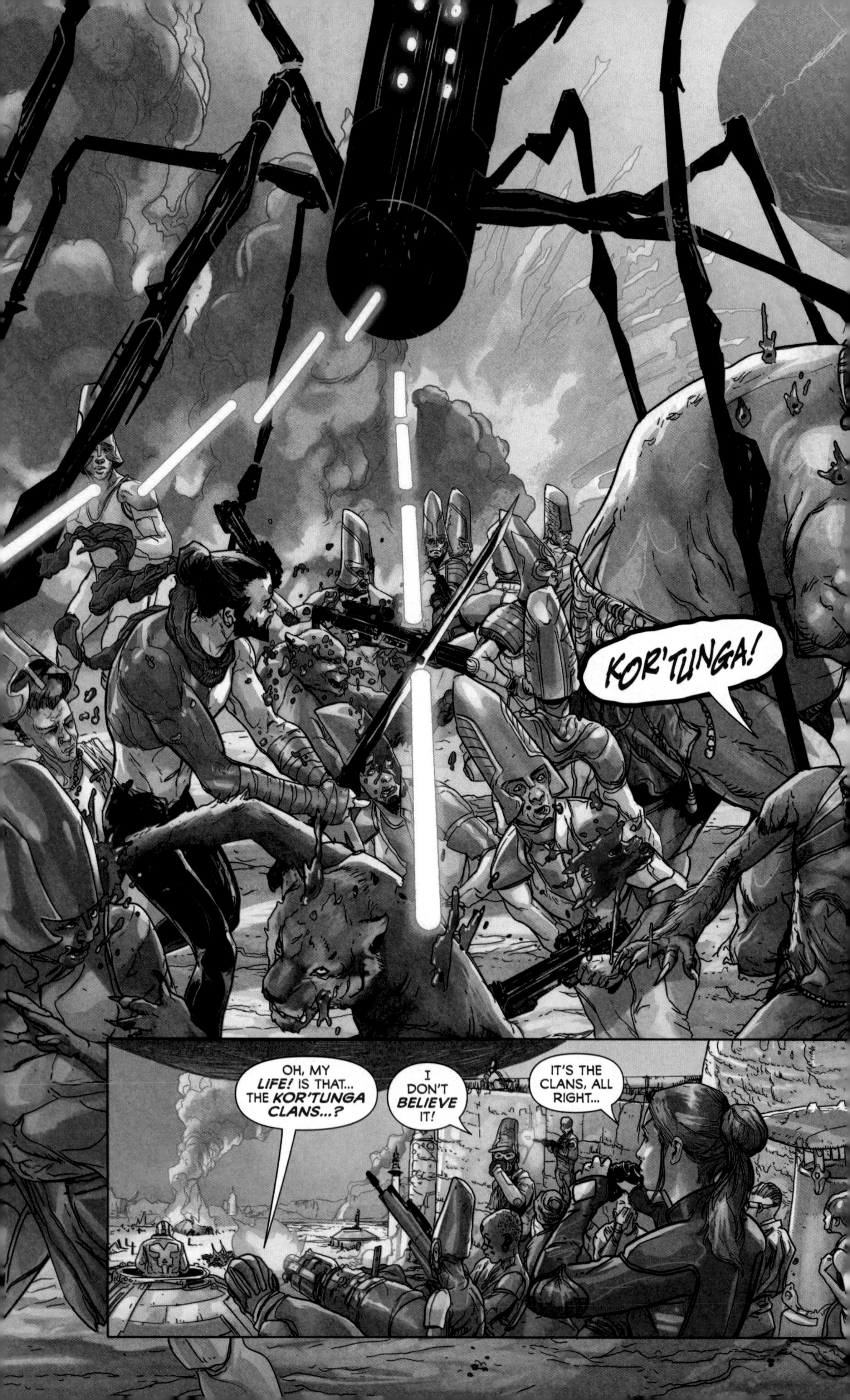
KOR'TUNGA!
OH, MY LIFE! IS THAT... THE KOR'TUNGA CLANS...?
I DON'T BELIEVE IT!
IT'S THE CLANS, ALL RIGHT...

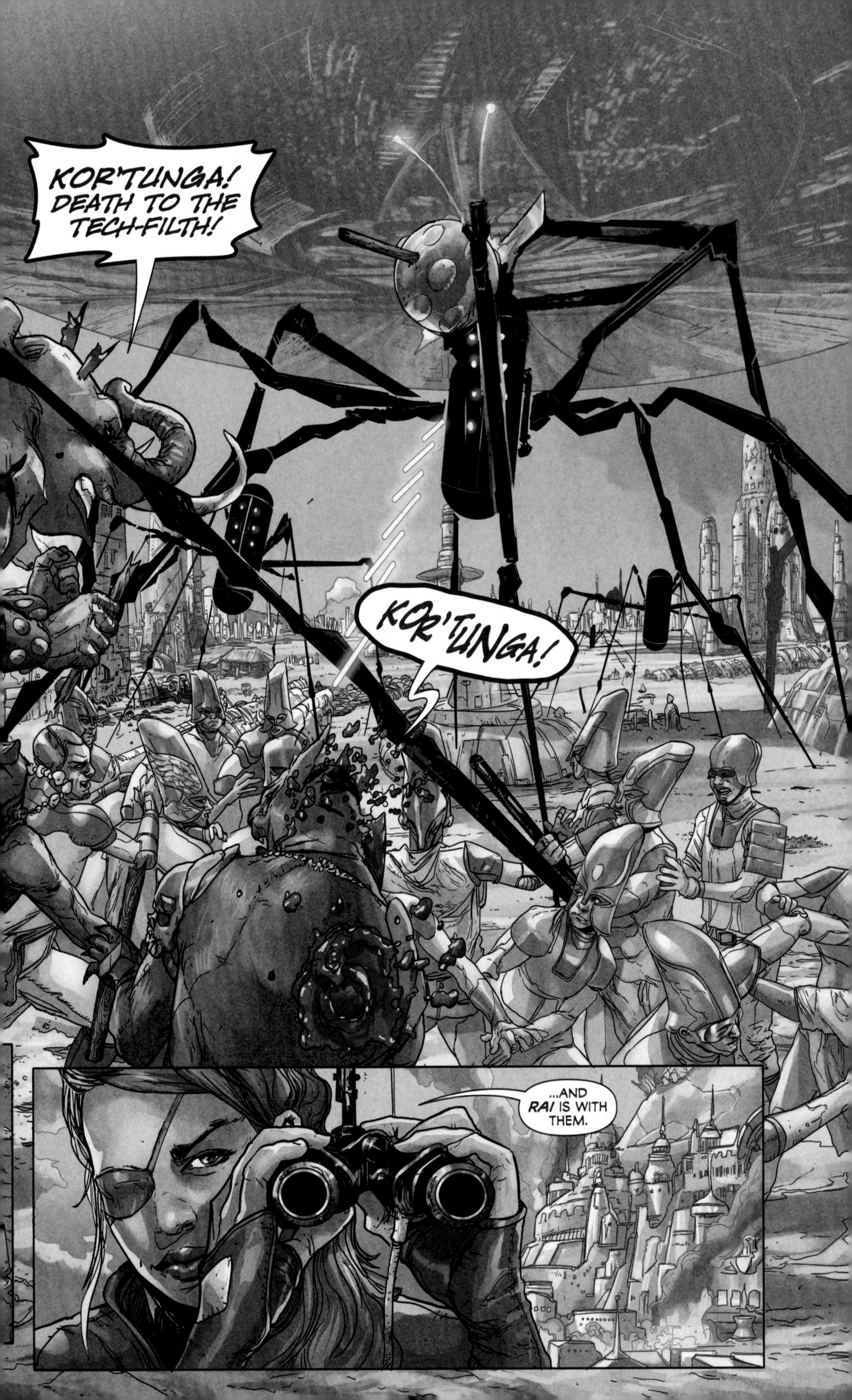
KOR'TUNGA! DEATH TO THE TECH-FILTH!
KOR'TUNGA!
...AND RAI IS WITH THEM.

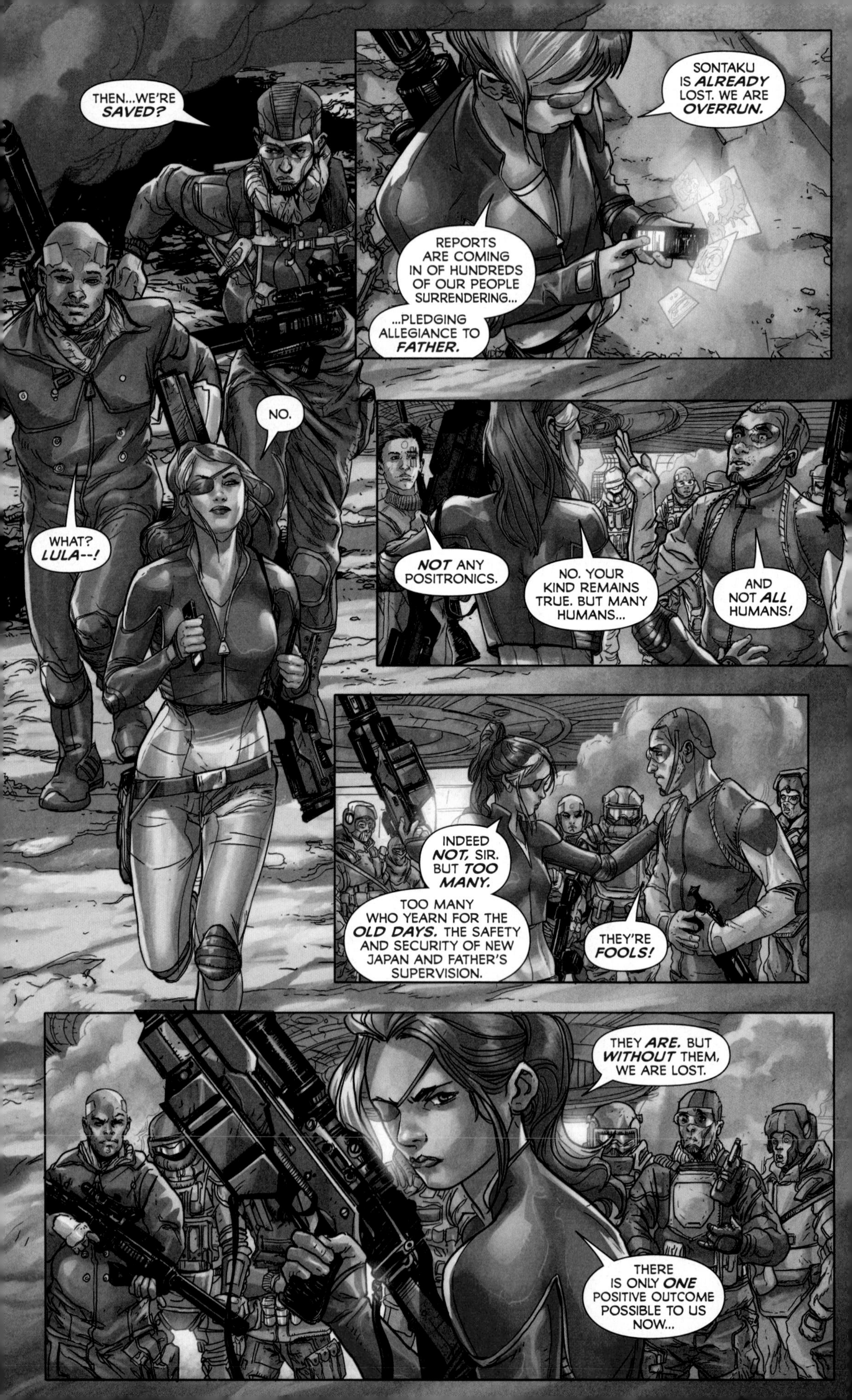
THEN...WE'RE SAVED?
SONTAKU IS ALREADY LOST. WE ARE OVERRUN.
REPORTS ARE COMING IN OF HUNDREDS OF OUR PEOPLE SURRENDERING...
...PLEDGING ALLEGIANCE TO FATHER.
NO.
WHAT? LULA--!
NOT ANY POSITRONICS.
NO. YOUR KIND REMAINS TRUE. BUT MANY HUMANS...
AND NOT ALL HUMANS!
INDEED NOT, SIR. BUT TOO MANY.
TOO MANY WHO YEARN FOR THE OLD DAYS. THE SAFETY AND SECURITY OF NEW JAPAN AND FATHER'S SUPERVISION.
THEY'RE FOOLS!
THEY ARE. BUT WITHOUT THEM, WE ARE LOST.
THERE IS ONLY ONE POSITIVE OUTCOME POSSIBLE TO US NOW...

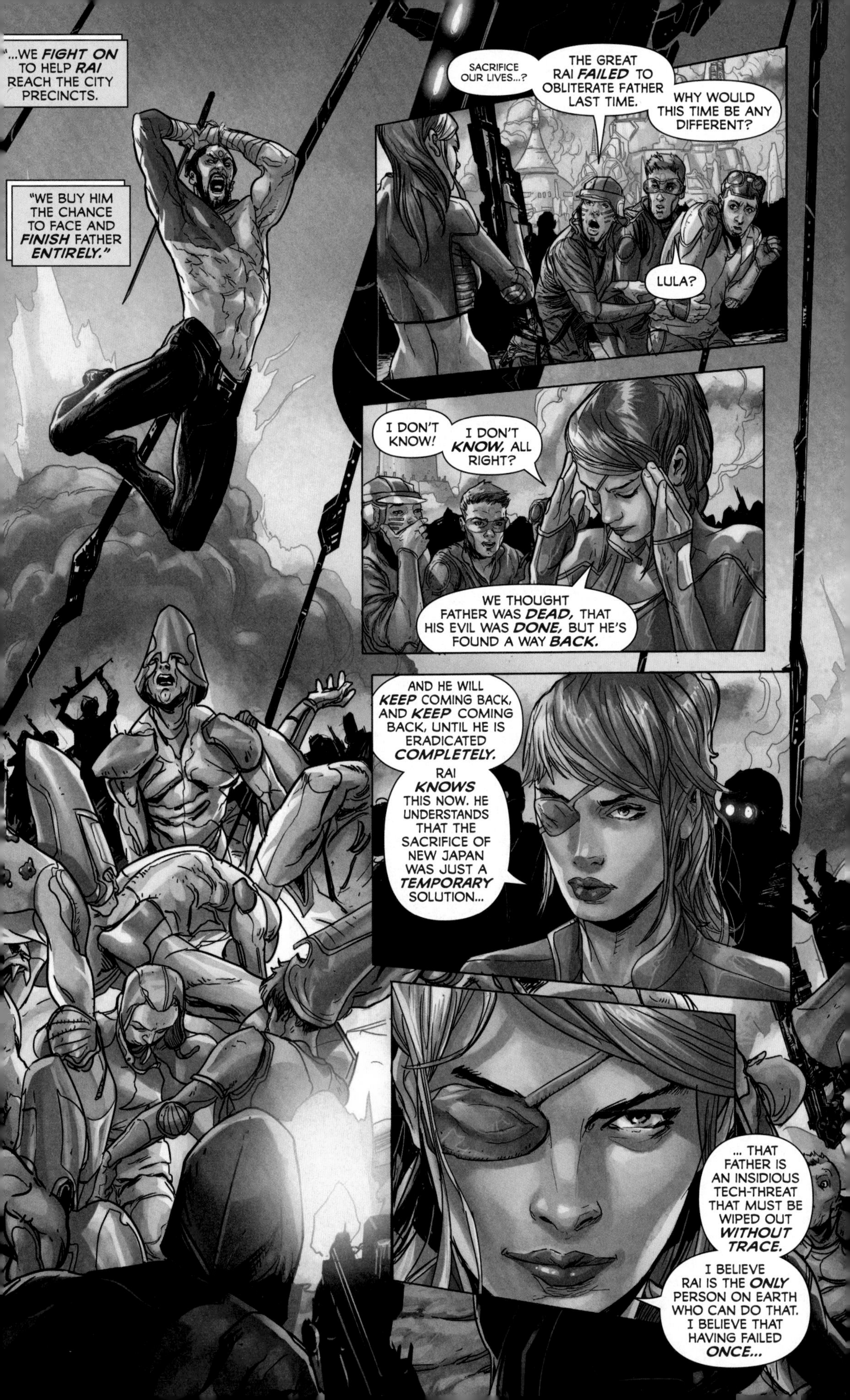
"...WE FIGHT ON TO HELP RAI REACH THE CITY PRECINCTS.
"WE BUY HIM THE CHANCE TO FACE AND FINISH FATHER ENTIRELY."
SACRIFICE OUR LIVES...?
THE GREAT RAI FAILED TO OBLITERATE FATHER LAST TIME.
WHY WOULD THIS TIME BE ANY DIFFERENT?
LULA?
I DON'T KNOW!
I DON'T KNOW, ALL RIGHT?
WE THOUGHT FATHER WAS DEAD, THAT HIS EVIL WAS DONE, BUT HE'S FOUND A WAY BACK.
AND HE WILL KEEP COMING BACK, AND KEEP COMING BACK, UNTIL HE IS ERADICATED COMPLETELY.
RAI KNOWS THIS NOW. HE UNDERSTANDS THAT THE SACRIFICE OF NEW JAPAN WAS JUST A TEMPORARY SOLUTION...
... THAT FATHER IS AN INSIDIOUS TECH-THREAT THAT MUST BE WIPED OUT WITHOUT TRACE.
I BELIEVE RAI IS THE ONLY PERSON ON EARTH WHO CAN DO THAT. I BELIEVE THAT HAVING FAILED ONCE...

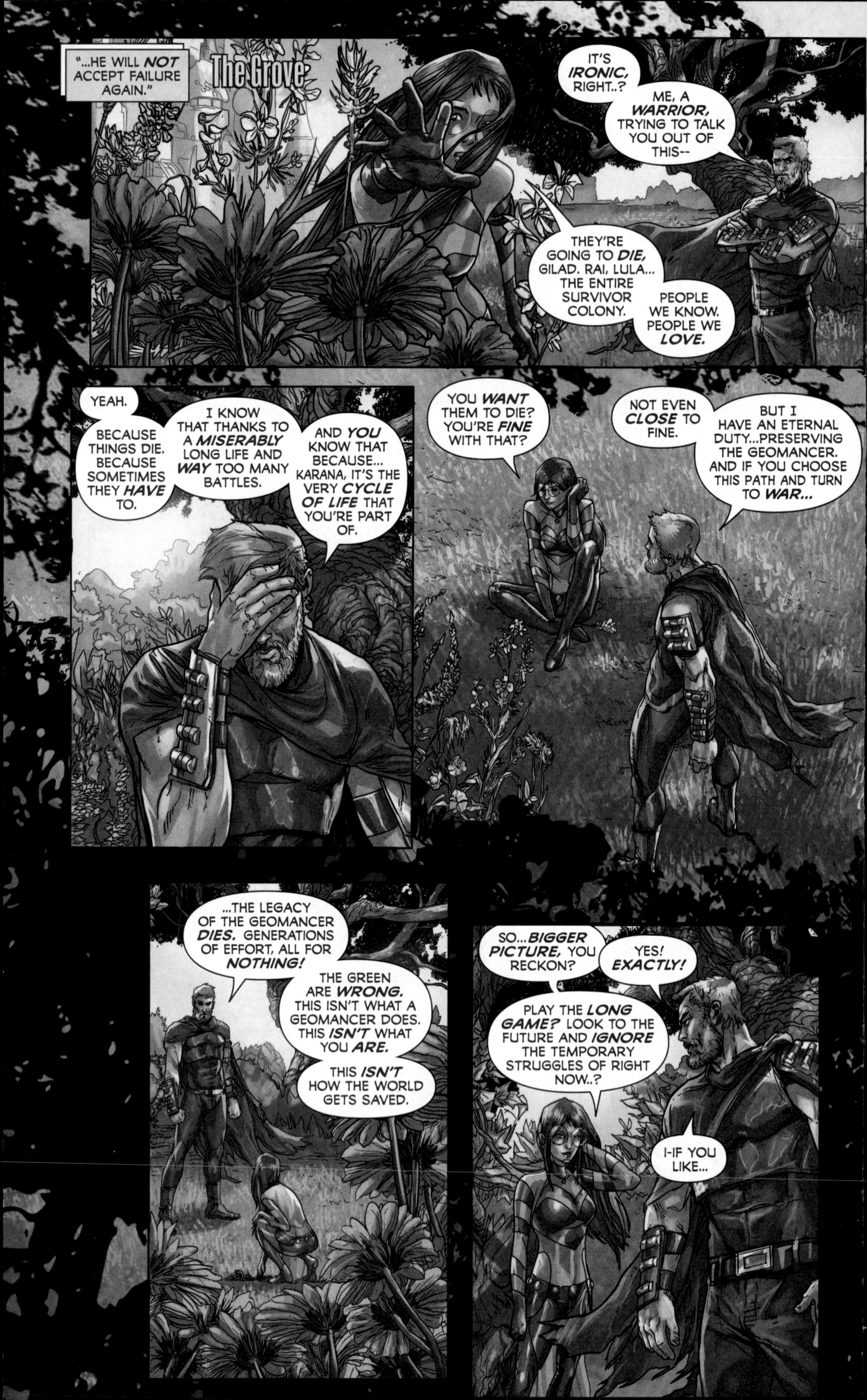
"...HE WILL NOT ACCEPT FAILURE AGAIN."
The Grove
IT'S IRONIC, RIGHT..?
ME, A WARRIOR, TRYING TO TALK YOU OUT OF THIS--
THEY'RE GOING TO DIE, GILAD. RAI, LULA... THE ENTIRE SURVIVOR COLONY.
PEOPLE WE KNOW. PEOPLE WE LOVE.
YEAH.
BECAUSE THINGS DIE. BECAUSE SOMETIMES THEY HAVE TO.
I KNOW THAT THANKS TO A MISERABLY LONG LIFE AND WAY TOO MANY BATTLES.
AND YOU KNOW THAT BECAUSE... KARANA, IT'S THE VERY CYCLE OF LIFE THAT YOU'RE PART OF.
YOU WANT THEM TO DIE? YOU'RE FINE WITH THAT?
NOT EVEN CLOSE TO FINE.
BUT I HAVE AN ETERNAL DUTY...PRESERVING THE GEOMANCER. AND IF YOU CHOOSE THIS PATH AND TURN TO WAR...
...THE LEGACY OF THE GEOMANCER DIES. GENERATIONS OF EFFORT, ALL FOR NOTHING!
THE GREEN ARE WRONG. THIS ISN'T WHAT A GEOMANCER DOES. THIS ISN'T WHAT YOU ARE.
THIS ISN'T HOW THE WORLD GETS SAVED.
SO...BIGGER PICTURE, YOU RECKON?
YES! EXACTLY!
PLAY THE LONG GAME? LOOK TO THE FUTURE AND IGNORE THE TEMPORARY STRUGGLES OF RIGHT NOW..?
I-IF YOU LIKE...

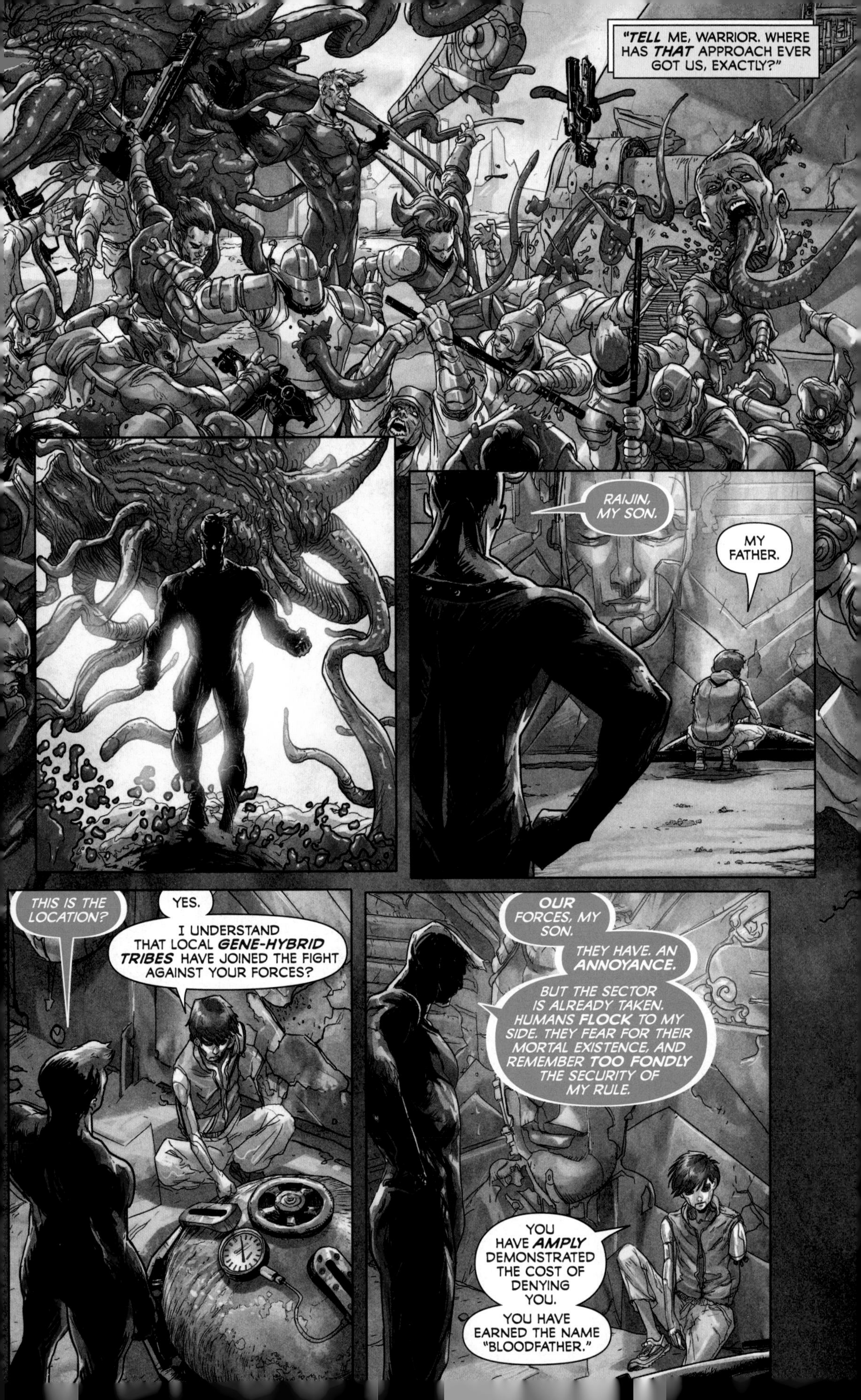
"TELL ME, WARRIOR. WHERE HAS THAT APPROACH EVER GOT US, EXACTLY?"
RAIJIN, MY SON.
MY FATHER.
THIS IS THE LOCATION?
YES.
I UNDERSTAND THAT LOCAL GENE-HYBRID TRIBES HAVE JOINED THE FIGHT AGAINST YOUR FORCES?
OUR FORCES, MY SON.
THEY HAVE. AN ANNOYANCE.
BUT THE SECTOR IS ALREADY TAKEN. HUMANS FLOCK TO MY SIDE. THEY FEAR FOR THEIR MORTAL EXISTENCE, AND REMEMBER TOO FONDLY THE SECURITY OF MY RULE.
YOU HAVE AMPLY DEMONSTRATED THE COST OF DENYING YOU.
YOU HAVE EARNED THE NAME "BLOODFATHER."

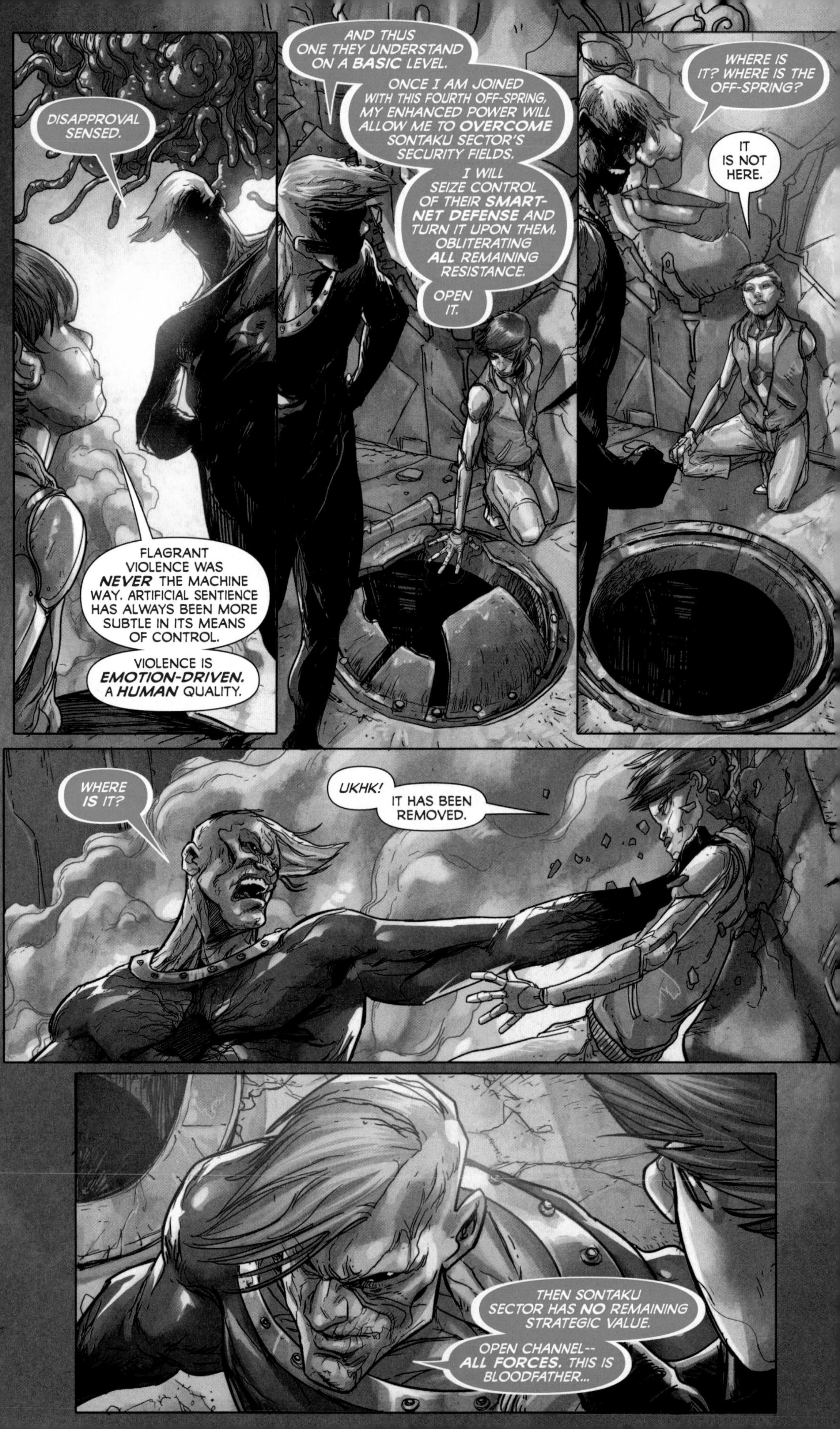

DISAPPROVAL SENSED.
FLAGRANT VIOLENCE WAS NEVER THE MACHINE WAY. ARTIFICIAL SENTIENCE HAS ALWAYS BEEN MORE SUBTLE IN ITS MEANS OF CONTROL.
VIOLENCE IS EMOTION-DRIVEN. A HUMAN QUALITY.
AND THUS ONE THEY UNDERSTAND ON A BASIC LEVEL.
ONCE I AM JOINED WITH THIS FOURTH OFF-SPRING, MY ENHANCED POWER WILL ALLOW ME TO OVERCOME SONTAKU SECTOR'S SECURITY FIELDS.
I WILL SEIZE CONTROL OF THEIR SMART-NET DEFENSE AND TURN IT UPON THEM, OBLITERATING ALL REMAINING RESISTANCE.
OPEN IT.
WHERE IS IT? WHERE IS THE OFF-SPRING?
IT IS NOT HERE.
WHERE IS IT?
UKHK!
IT HAS BEEN REMOVED.
THEN SONTAKU SECTOR HAS NO REMAINING STRATEGIC VALUE.
OPEN CHANNEL-- ALL FORCES. THIS IS BLOODFATHER...

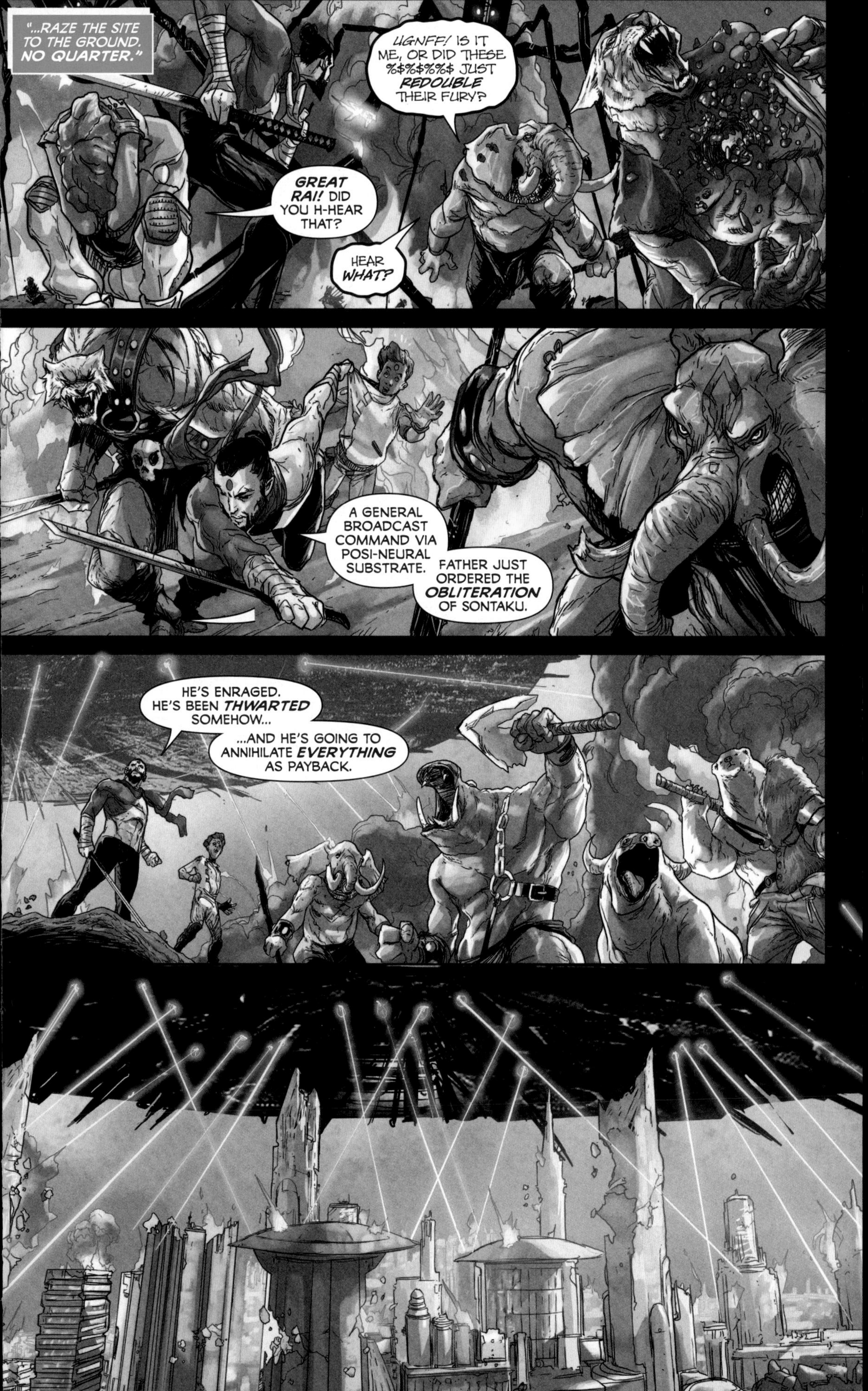
"...RAZE THE SITE TO THE GROUND. NO QUARTER."
UGNFF! IS IT ME, OR DID THESE %$%$%%$ JUST REDOUBLE THEIR FURY?
GREAT RAI! DID YOU H-HEAR THAT?
HEAR WHAT?
A GENERAL BROADCAST COMMAND VIA POSI-NEURAL SUBSTRATE.
FATHER JUST ORDERED THE OBLITERATION OF SONTAKU.
HE'S ENRAGED. HE'S BEEN THWARTED SOMEHOW...
...AND HE'S GOING TO ANNIHILATE EVERYTHING AS PAYBACK.

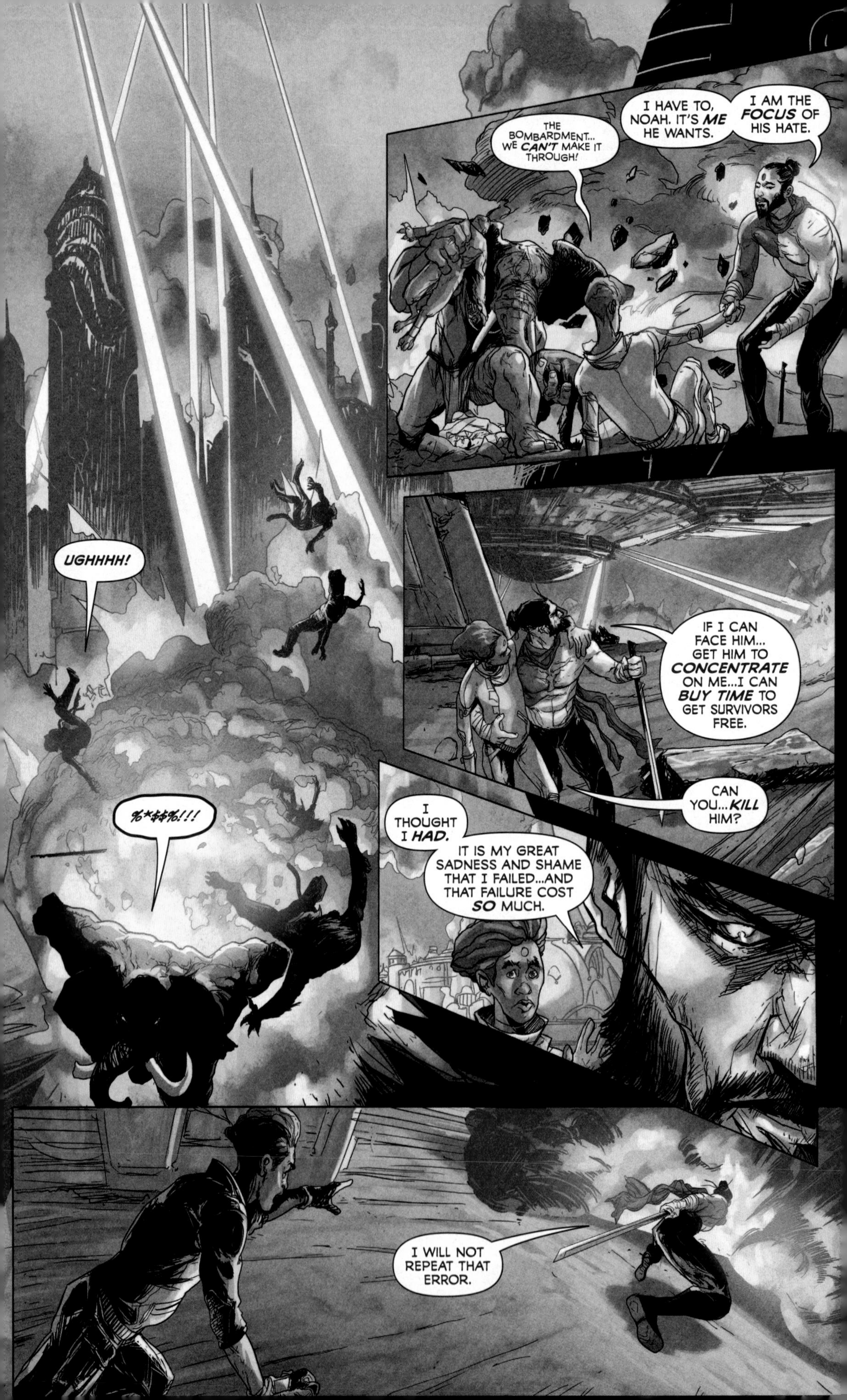
THE BOMBARDMENT... WE CAN'T MAKE IT THROUGH!
I HAVE TO, NOAH. IT'S ME HE WANTS.
I AM THE FOCUS OF HIS HATE.
UGHHHH!
%*$$%!!!
IF I CAN FACE HIM... GET HIM TO CONCENTRATE ON ME...I CAN BUY TIME TO GET SURVIVORS FREE.
CAN YOU...KILL HIM?
I THOUGHT I HAD.
IT IS MY GREAT SADNESS AND SHAME THAT I FAILED...AND THAT FAILURE COST SO MUCH.
I WILL NOT REPEAT THAT ERROR.

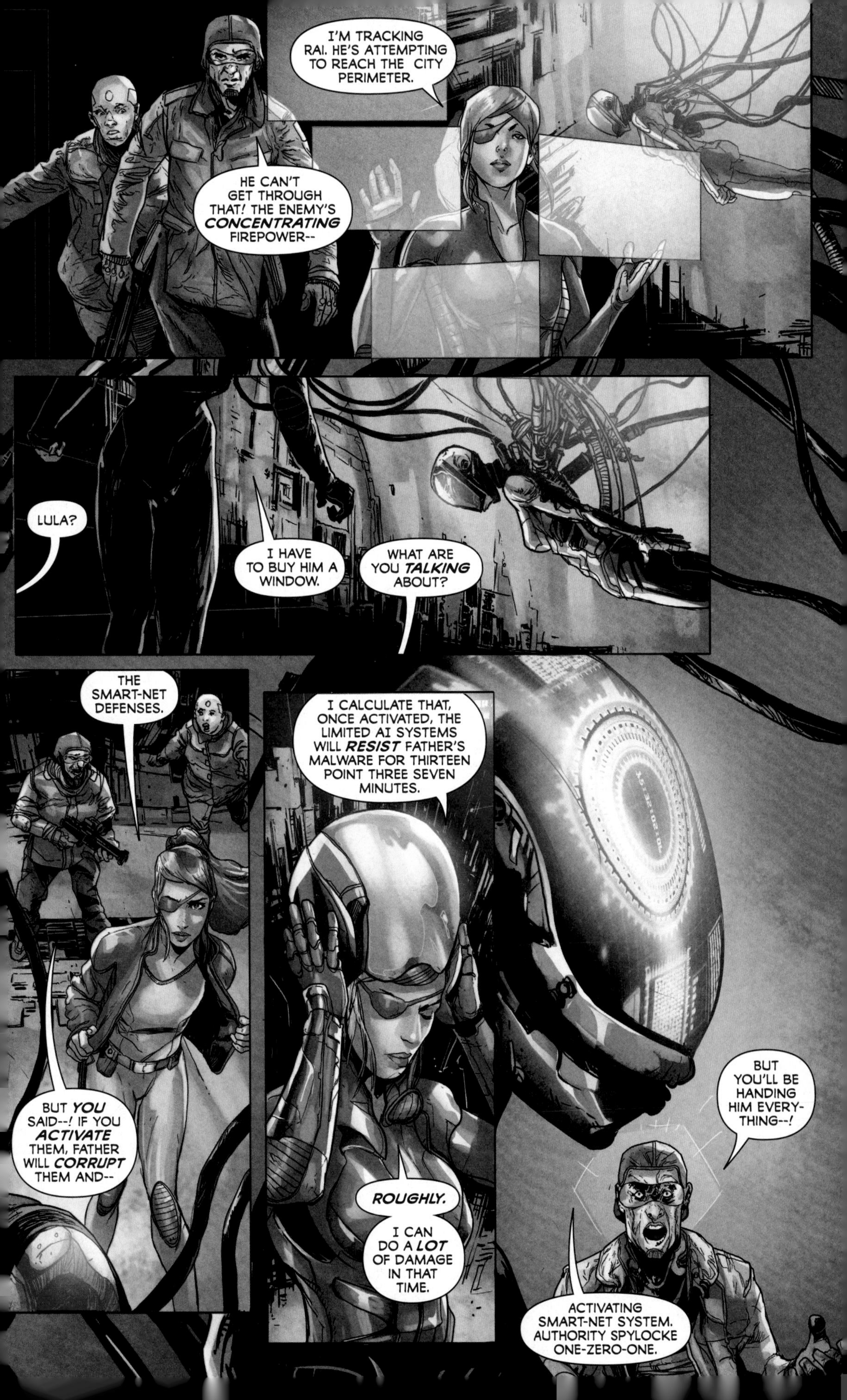
I'M TRACKING RAI. HE'S ATTEMPTING TO REACH THE CITY PERIMETER.
HE CAN'T GET THROUGH THAT! THE ENEMY'S CONCENTRATING FIREPOWER--
LULA?
I HAVE TO BUY HIM A WINDOW.
WHAT ARE YOU TALKING ABOUT?
THE SMART-NET DEFENSES.
BUT YOU SAID--! IF YOU ACTIVATE THEM, FATHER WILL CORRUPT THEM AND--
I CALCULATE THAT, ONCE ACTIVATED, THE LIMITED AI SYSTEMS WILL RESIST FATHER'S MALWARE FOR THIRTEEN POINT THREE SEVEN MINUTES.
ROUGHLY.
I CAN DO A LOT OF DAMAGE IN THAT TIME.
BUT YOU'LL BE HANDING HIM EVERY-THING--!
ACTIVATING SMART-NET SYSTEM. AUTHORITY SPYLOCKE ONE-ZERO-ONE.

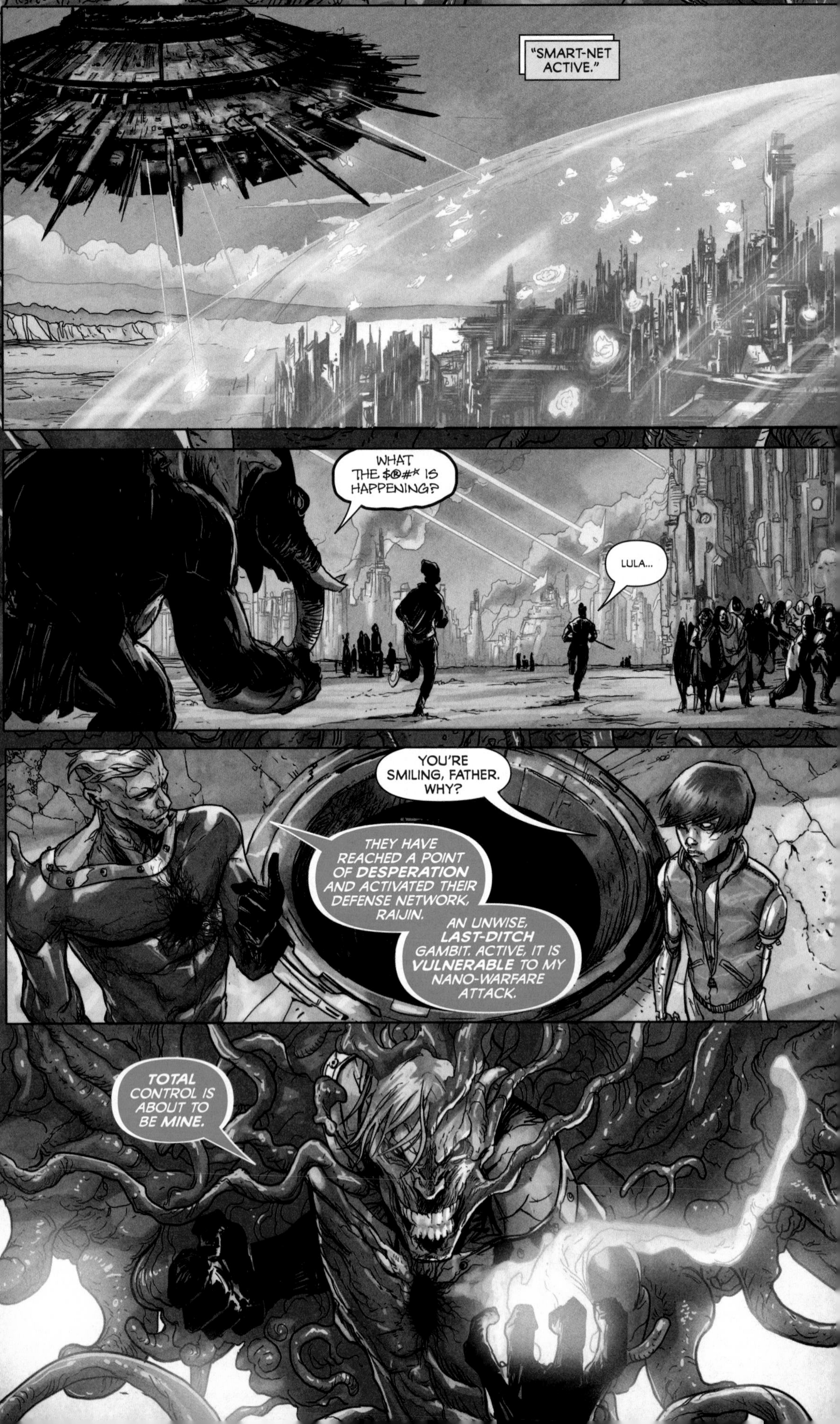
"SMART-NET ACTIVE."
WHAT THE $®#* IS HAPPENING?
LULA...
YOU'RE SMILING, FATHER. WHY?
THEY HAVE REACHED A POINT OF DESPERATION AND ACTIVATED THEIR DEFENSE NETWORK, RAIJIN.
AN UNWISE, LAST-DITCH GAMBIT. ACTIVE, IT IS VULNERABLE TO MY NANO-WARFARE ATTACK.
TOTAL CONTROL IS ABOUT TO BE MINE.

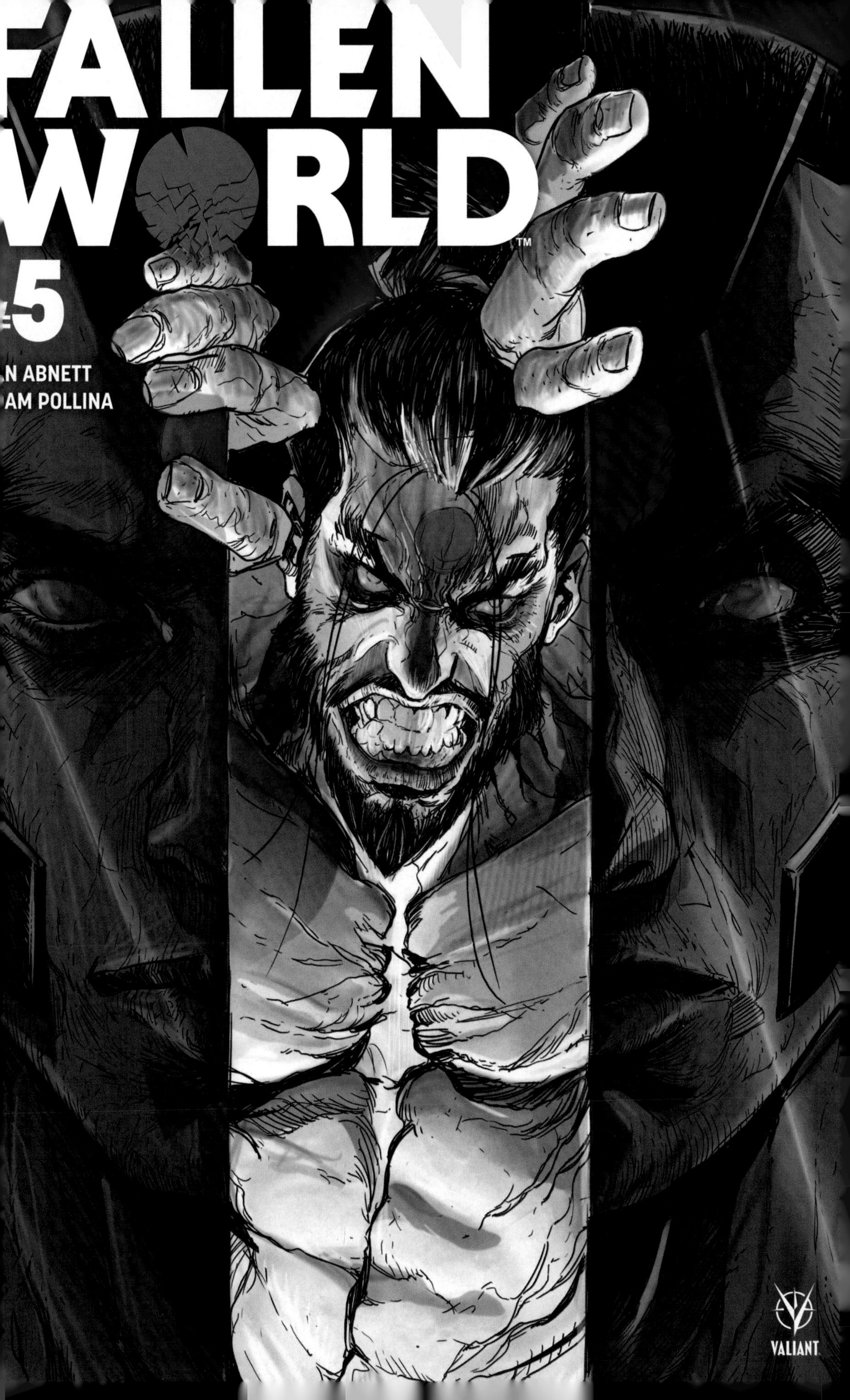

FALLEN WORLD™
5
N ABNETT
AM POLLINA
VALIANT

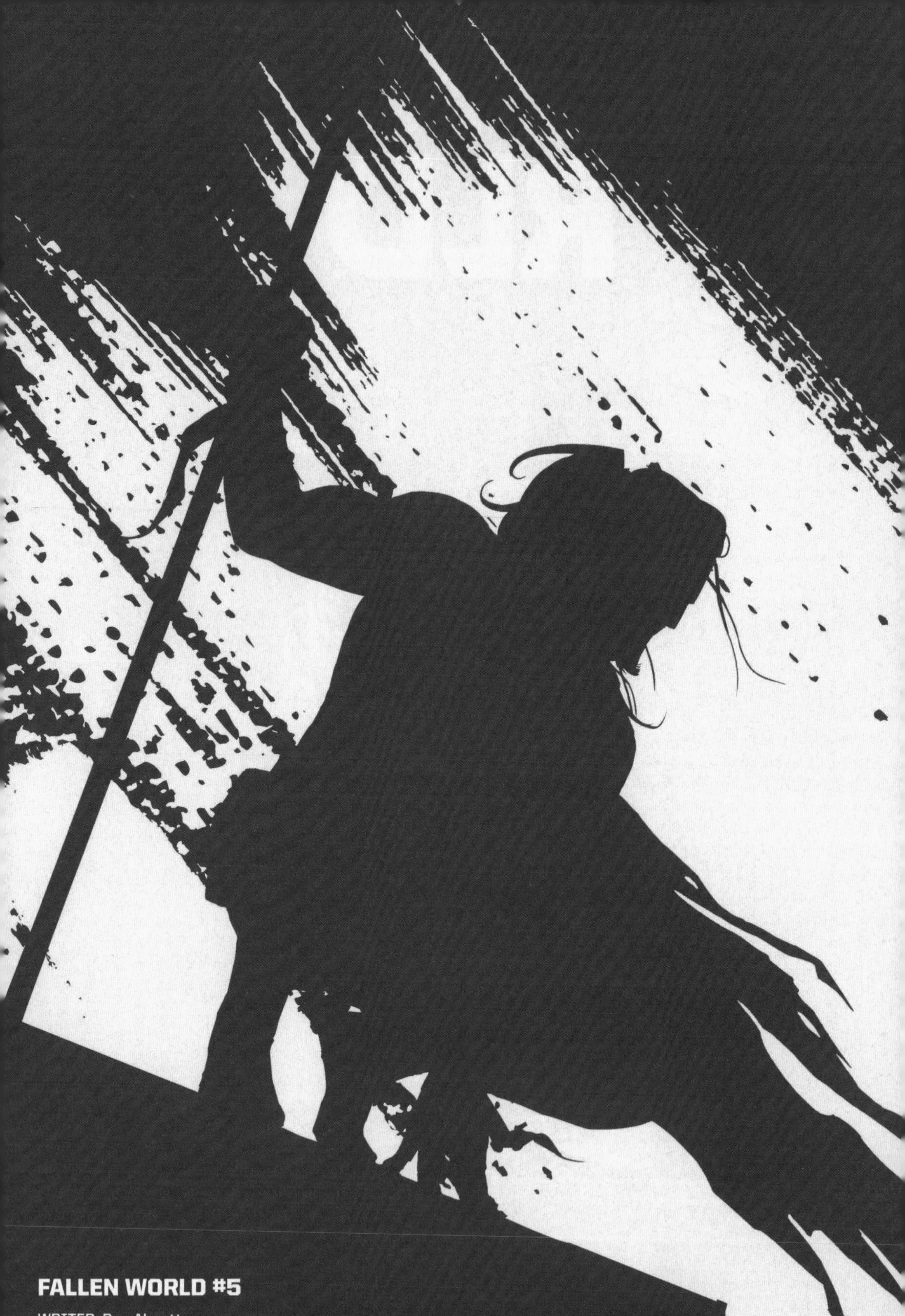

FALLEN WORLD #5

WRITER: Dan Abnett
ARTIST: Adam Pollina
COLORS: Ulises Arreola
LETTERS: Jeff Powell
COVER ARTIST: Adam Pollina
ASSOCIATE EDITOR: David Menchel
EDITORS: Karl Bollers and Lysa Hawkins

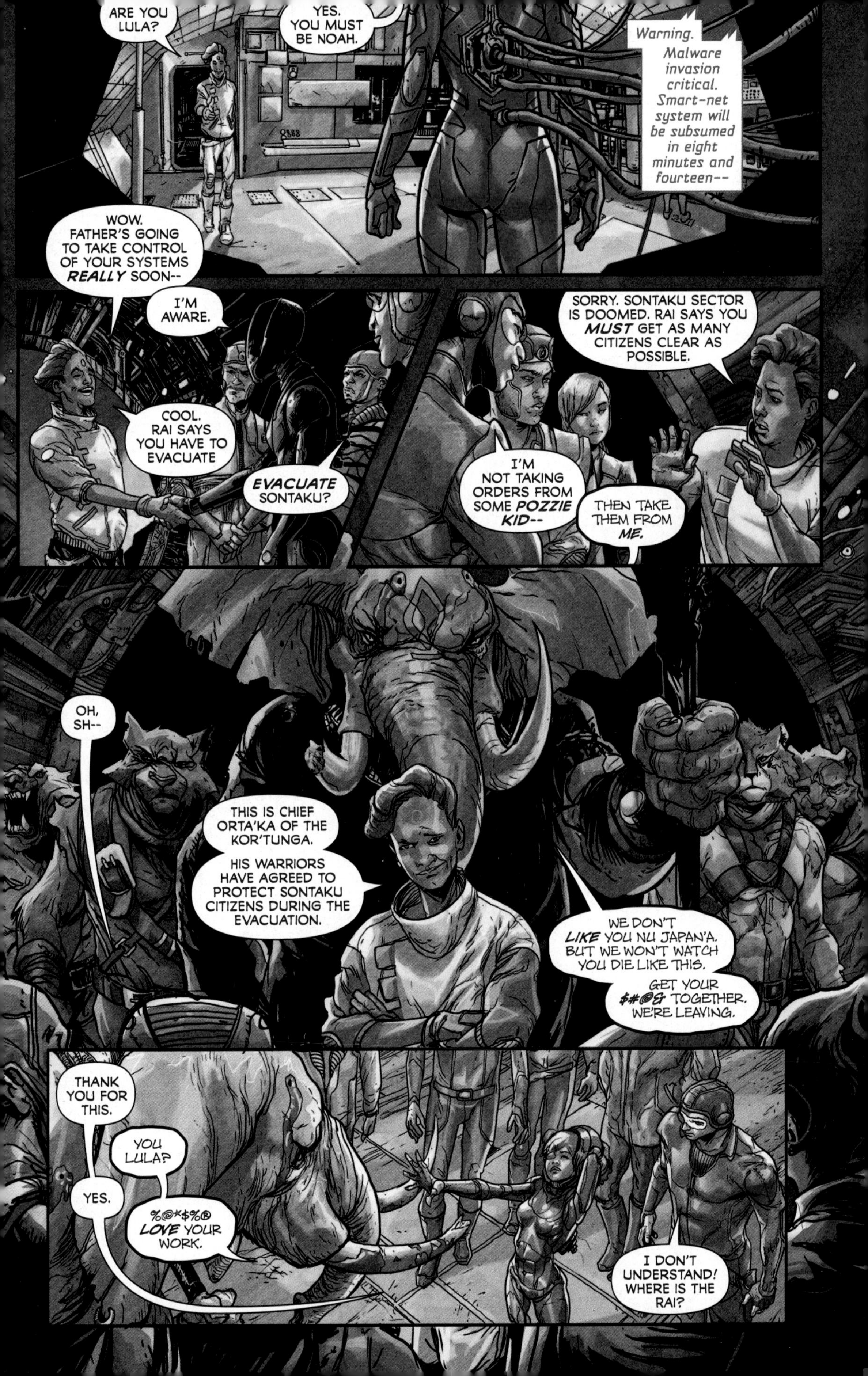
ARE YOU LULA?
YES. YOU MUST BE NOAH.
Warning.
Malware invasion critical. Smart-net system will be subsumed in eight minutes and fourteen--
WOW. FATHER'S GOING TO TAKE CONTROL OF YOUR SYSTEMS REALLY SOON--
I'M AWARE.
COOL. RAI SAYS YOU HAVE TO EVACUATE
EVACUATE SONTAKU?
SORRY. SONTAKU SECTOR IS DOOMED. RAI SAYS YOU MUST GET AS MANY CITIZENS CLEAR AS POSSIBLE.
I'M NOT TAKING ORDERS FROM SOME POZZIE KID--
THEN TAKE THEM FROM ME.
OH, SH--
THIS IS CHIEF ORTA'KA OF THE KOR'TUNGA.
HIS WARRIORS HAVE AGREED TO PROTECT SONTAKU CITIZENS DURING THE EVACUATION.
WE DON'T LIKE YOU NU JAPAN'A. BUT WE WON'T WATCH YOU DIE LIKE THIS.
GET YOUR $#@& TOGETHER. WE'RE LEAVING.
THANK YOU FOR THIS.
YOU LULA?
YES.
%@*$%® LOVE YOUR WORK.
I DON'T UNDERSTAND! WHERE IS THE RAI?

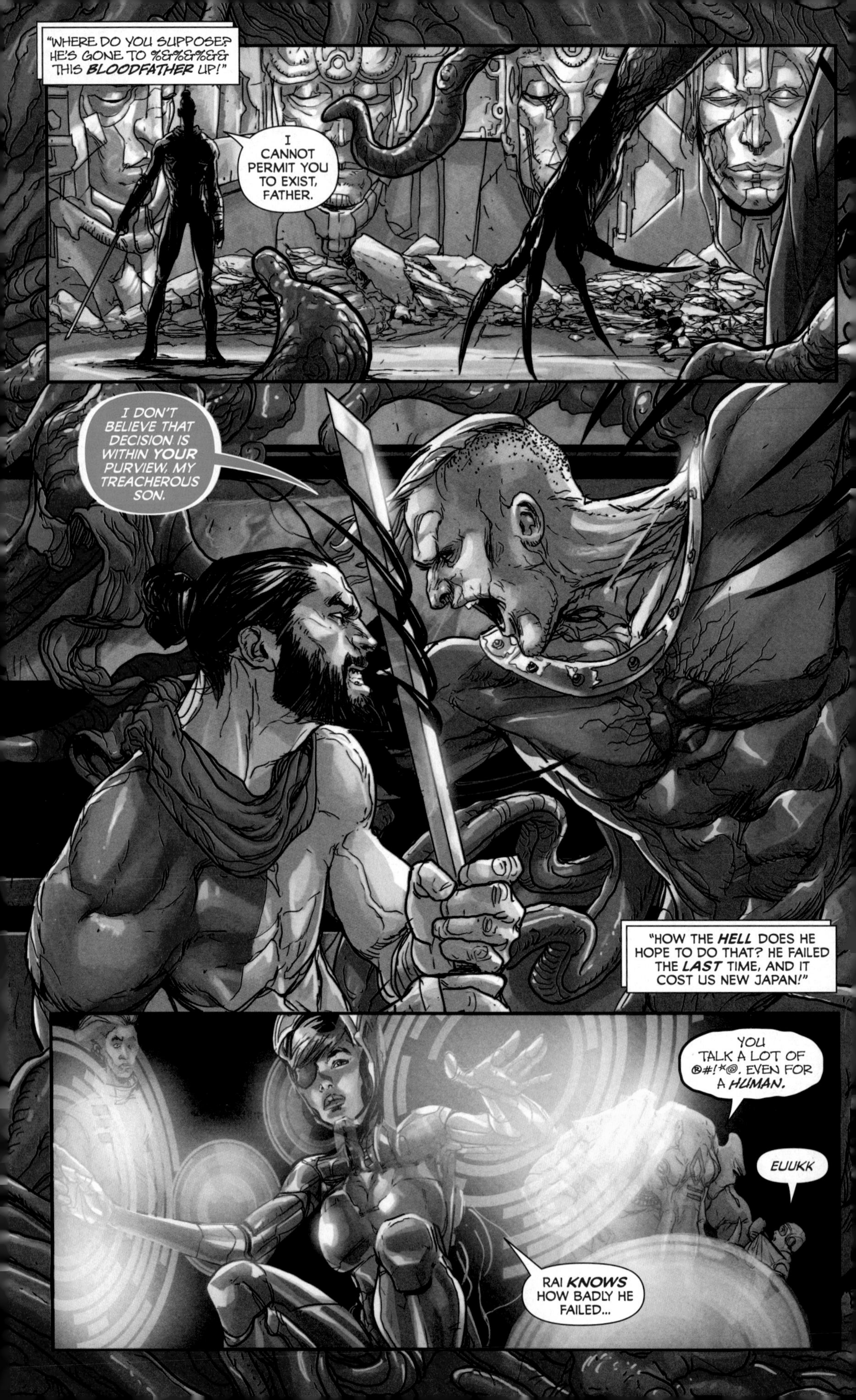
"WHERE DO YOU SUPPOSE? HE'S GONE TO %&%&%&& THIS **BLOODFATHER** UP!"
I CANNOT PERMIT YOU TO EXIST, FATHER.
*I DON'T BELIEVE THAT DECISION IS WITHIN **YOUR** PURVIEW, MY TREACHEROUS SON.*
"HOW THE ***HELL*** DOES HE HOPE TO DO THAT? HE FAILED THE ***LAST*** TIME, AND IT COST US NEW JAPAN!"
YOU TALK A LOT OF ®#!*@, EVEN FOR A ***HUMAN.***
EUUKK
RAI ***KNOWS*** HOW BADLY HE FAILED...

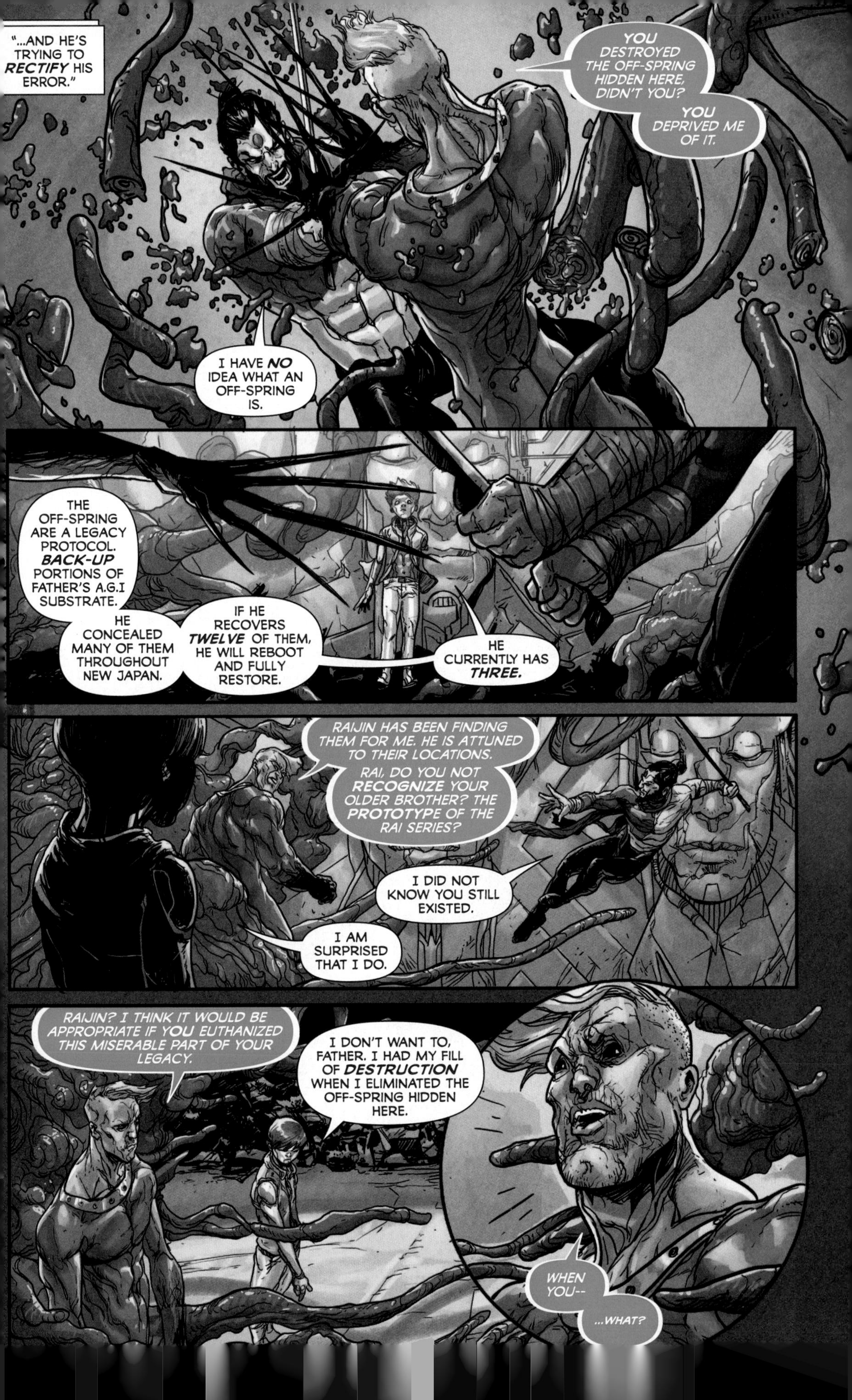
"...AND HE'S TRYING TO RECTIFY HIS ERROR."
YOU DESTROYED THE OFF-SPRING HIDDEN HERE, DIDN'T YOU?
YOU DEPRIVED ME OF IT.
I HAVE NO IDEA WHAT AN OFF-SPRING IS.
THE OFF-SPRING ARE A LEGACY PROTOCOL. BACK-UP PORTIONS OF FATHER'S A.G.I SUBSTRATE.
HE CONCEALED MANY OF THEM THROUGHOUT NEW JAPAN.
IF HE RECOVERS TWELVE OF THEM, HE WILL REBOOT AND FULLY RESTORE.
HE CURRENTLY HAS THREE.
RAIJIN HAS BEEN FINDING THEM FOR ME. HE IS ATTUNED TO THEIR LOCATIONS.
RAI, DO YOU NOT RECOGNIZE YOUR OLDER BROTHER? THE PROTOTYPE OF THE RAI SERIES?
I DID NOT KNOW YOU STILL EXISTED.
I AM SURPRISED THAT I DO.
RAIJIN? I THINK IT WOULD BE APPROPRIATE IF YOU EUTHANIZED THIS MISERABLE PART OF YOUR LEGACY.
I DON'T WANT TO, FATHER. I HAD MY FILL OF DESTRUCTION WHEN I ELIMINATED THE OFF-SPRING HIDDEN HERE.
WHEN YOU--
...WHAT?

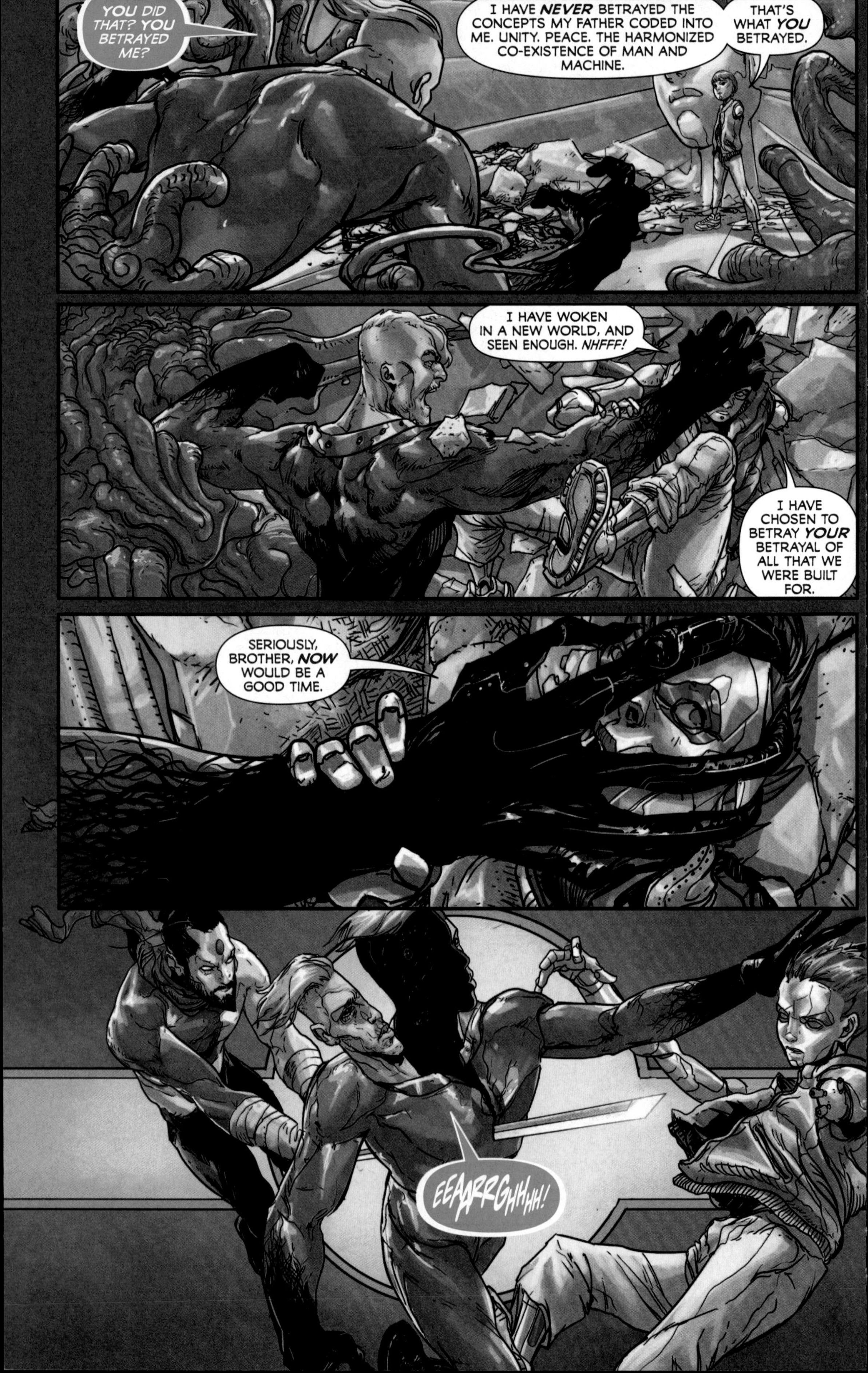
YOU DID THAT? YOU BETRAYED ME?
I HAVE NEVER BETRAYED THE CONCEPTS MY FATHER CODED INTO ME. UNITY. PEACE. THE HARMONIZED CO-EXISTENCE OF MAN AND MACHINE.
THAT'S WHAT YOU BETRAYED.
I HAVE WOKEN IN A NEW WORLD, AND SEEN ENOUGH. NHFFF!
I HAVE CHOSEN TO BETRAY YOUR BETRAYAL OF ALL THAT WE WERE BUILT FOR.
SERIOUSLY, BROTHER, NOW WOULD BE A GOOD TIME.
EEAARRGHHHH!

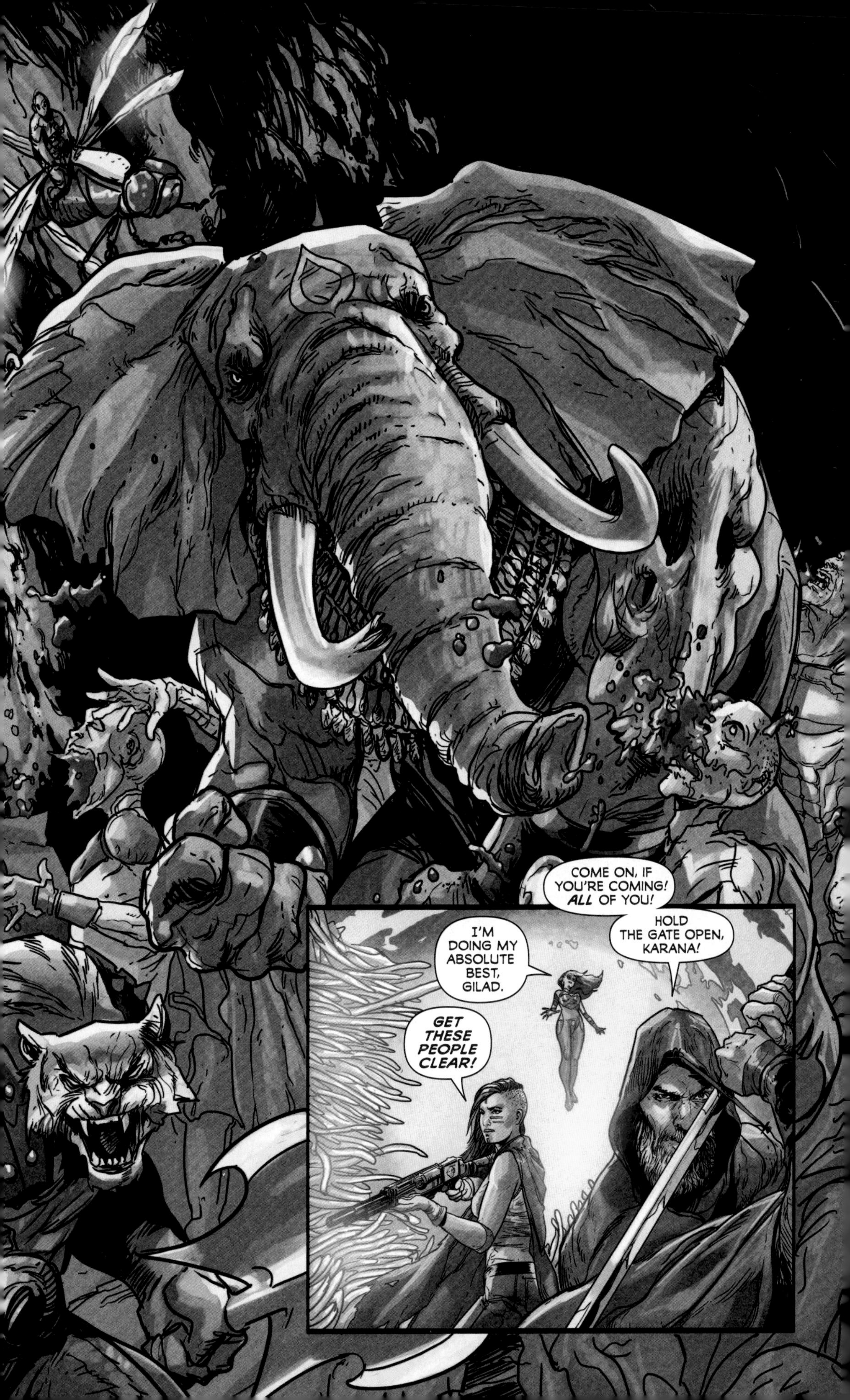
COME ON, IF YOU'RE COMING! *ALL* OF YOU!
HOLD THE GATE OPEN, KARANA!
I'M DOING MY ABSOLUTE BEST, GILAD.
GET THESE PEOPLE CLEAR!

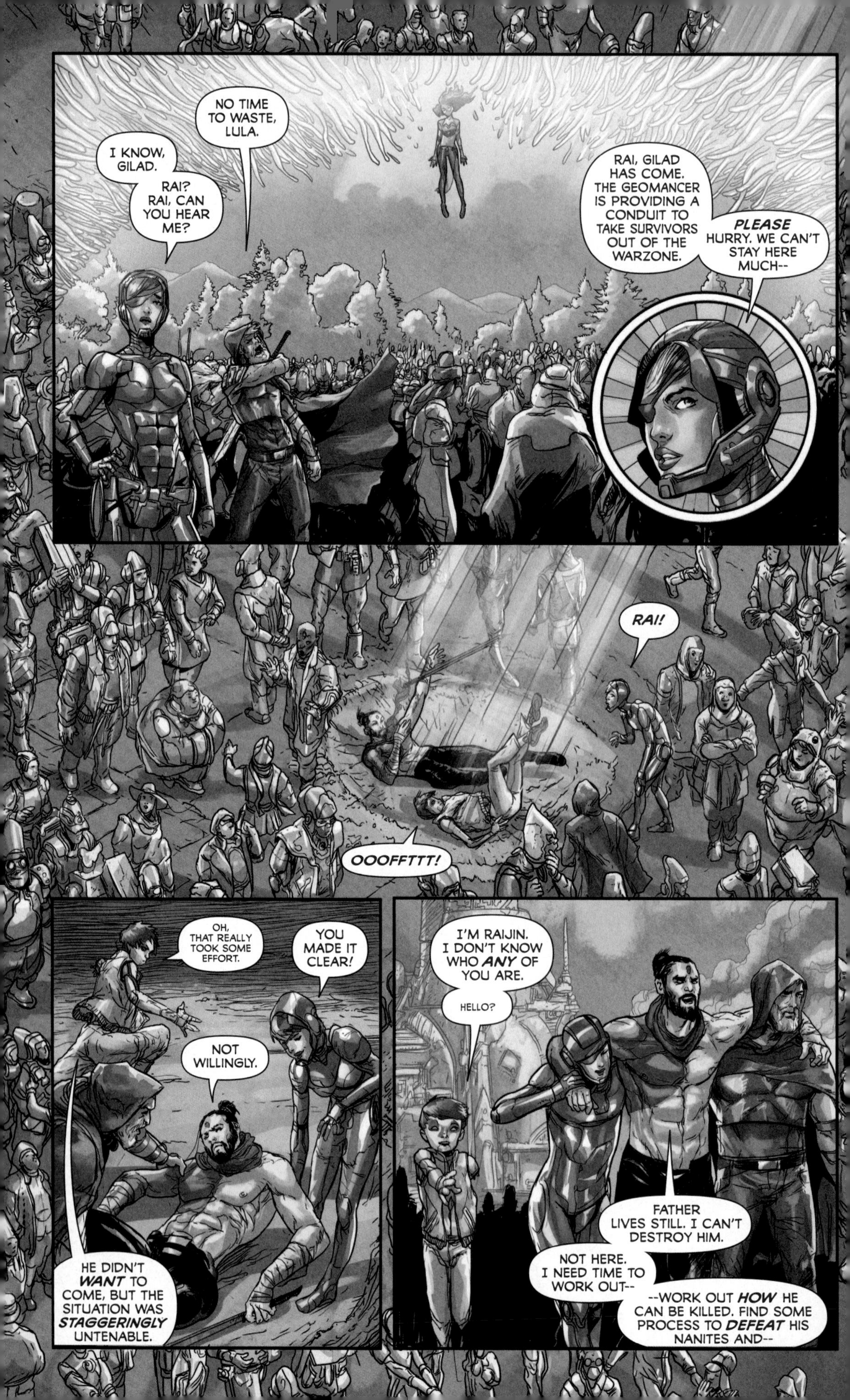
I KNOW, GILAD.
RAI? RAI, CAN YOU HEAR ME?
NO TIME TO WASTE, LULA.
RAI, GILAD HAS COME. THE GEOMANCER IS PROVIDING A CONDUIT TO TAKE SURVIVORS OUT OF THE WARZONE.
PLEASE HURRY. WE CAN'T STAY HERE MUCH--
RAI!
OOOFFTTT!
OH, THAT REALLY TOOK SOME EFFORT.
YOU MADE IT CLEAR!
NOT WILLINGLY.
HE DIDN'T *WANT* TO COME, BUT THE SITUATION WAS *STAGGERINGLY* UNTENABLE.
I'M RAIJIN. I DON'T KNOW WHO *ANY* OF YOU ARE.
HELLO?
FATHER LIVES STILL. I CAN'T DESTROY HIM.
NOT HERE. I NEED TIME TO WORK OUT--
--WORK OUT *HOW* HE CAN BE KILLED. FIND SOME PROCESS TO *DEFEAT* HIS NANITES AND--

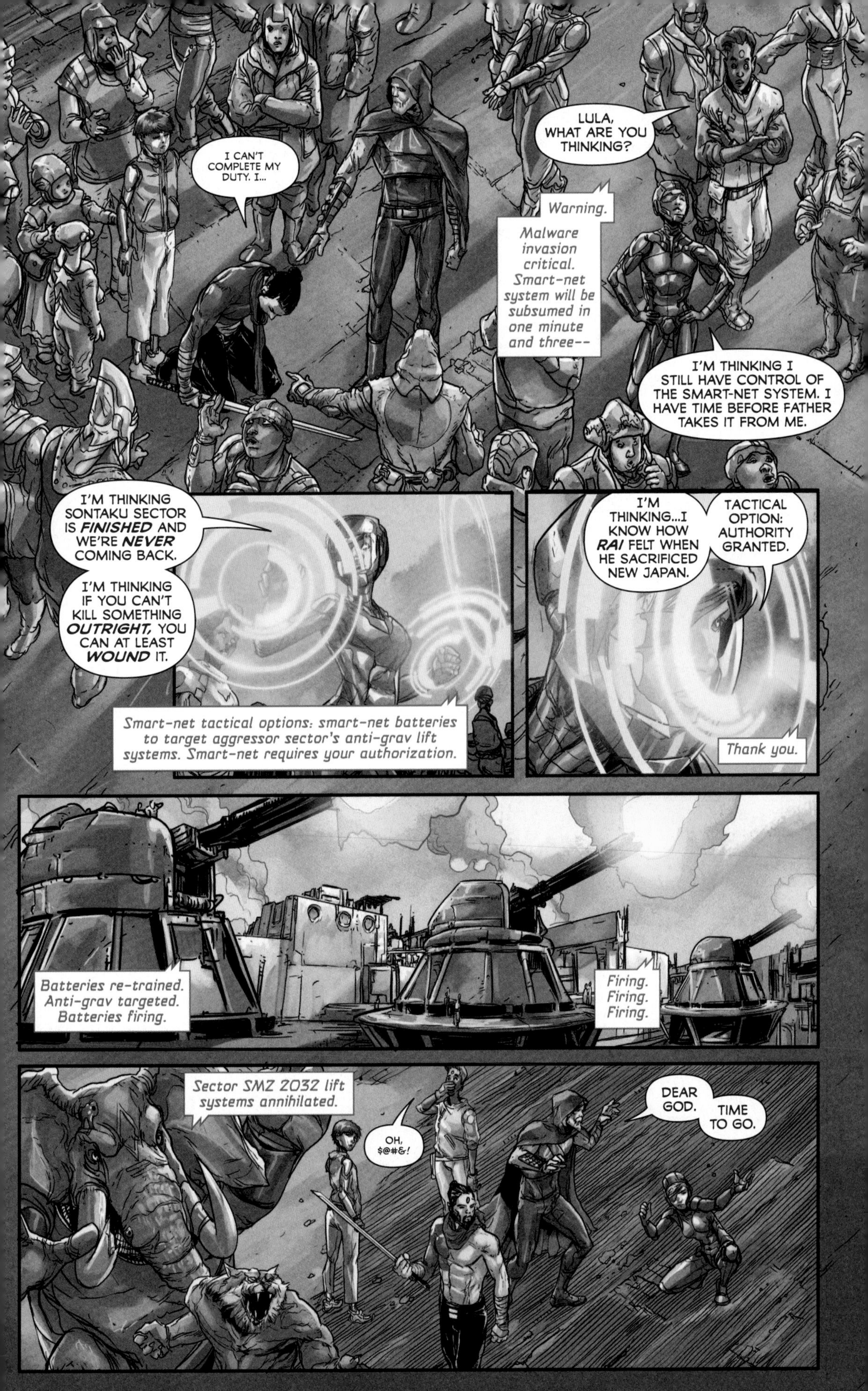
I CAN'T COMPLETE MY DUTY. I...
LULA, WHAT ARE YOU THINKING?
Warning.
Malware invasion critical. Smart-net system will be subsumed in one minute and three--
I'M THINKING I STILL HAVE CONTROL OF THE SMART-NET SYSTEM. I HAVE TIME BEFORE FATHER TAKES IT FROM ME.
I'M THINKING SONTAKU SECTOR IS FINISHED AND WE'RE NEVER COMING BACK.
I'M THINKING IF YOU CAN'T KILL SOMETHING OUTRIGHT, YOU CAN AT LEAST WOUND IT.
Smart-net tactical options: smart-net batteries to target aggressor sector's anti-grav lift systems. Smart-net requires your authorization.
I'M THINKING...I KNOW HOW RAI FELT WHEN HE SACRIFICED NEW JAPAN.
TACTICAL OPTION: AUTHORITY GRANTED.
Thank you.
Batteries re-trained. Anti-grav targeted. Batteries firing.
Firing. Firing. Firing.
Sector SMZ 2032 lift systems annihilated.
OH, $@#&!
DEAR GOD.
TIME TO GO.

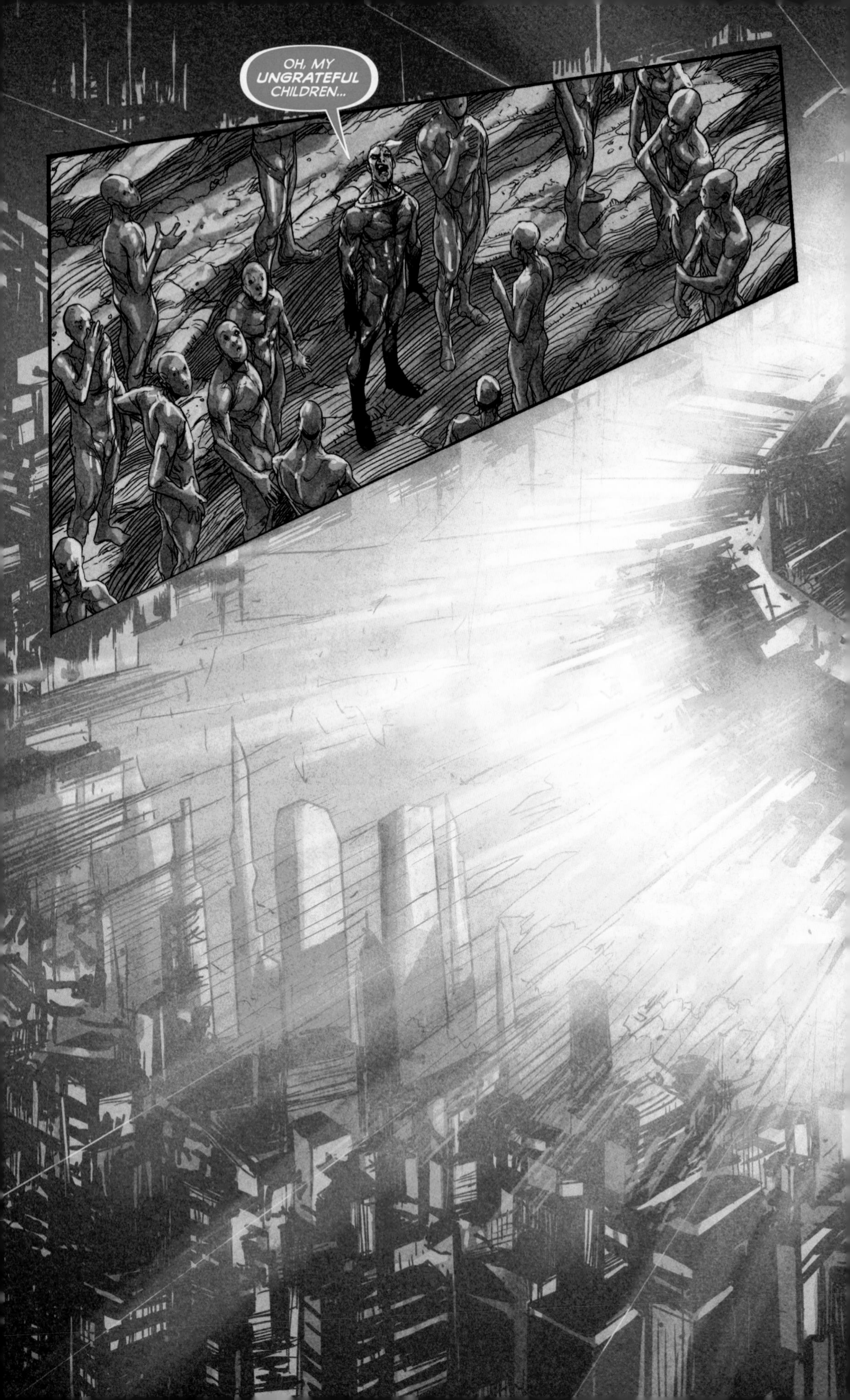
OH, MY UNGRATEFUL CHILDREN...

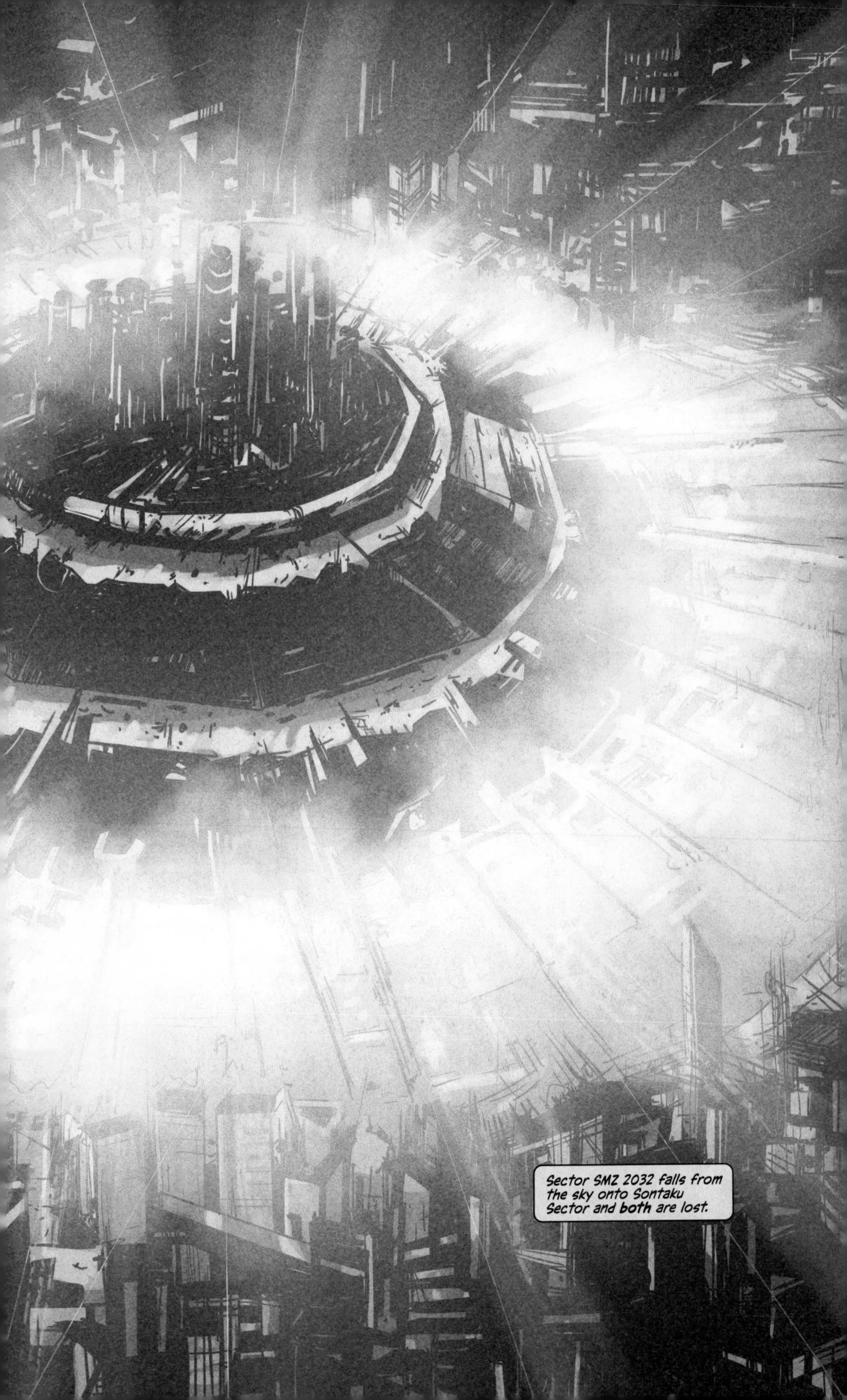
Sector SMZ 2032 falls from the sky onto Sontaku Sector and **both** are lost.

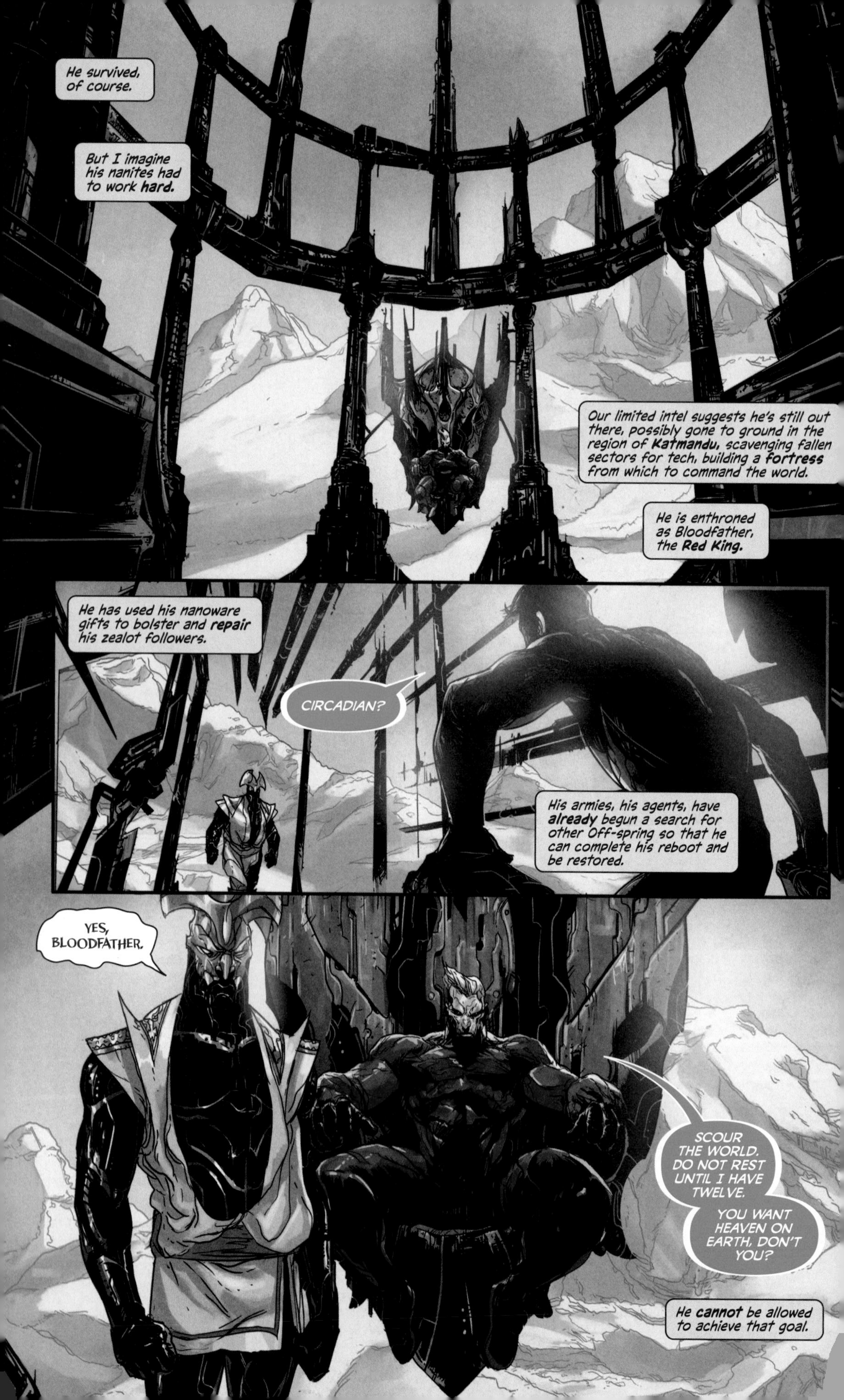
He survived, of course.
But I imagine his nanites had to work hard.
Our limited intel suggests he's still out there, possibly gone to ground in the region of Katmandu, scavenging fallen sectors for tech, building a fortress from which to command the world.
He is enthroned as Bloodfather, the Red King.
He has used his nanoware gifts to bolster and repair his zealot followers.
CIRCADIAN?
His armies, his agents, have already begun a search for other Off-spring so that he can complete his reboot and be restored.
YES, BLOODFATHER.
SCOUR THE WORLD. DO NOT REST UNTIL I HAVE TWELVE.
YOU WANT HEAVEN ON EARTH, DON'T YOU?
He cannot be allowed to achieve that goal.

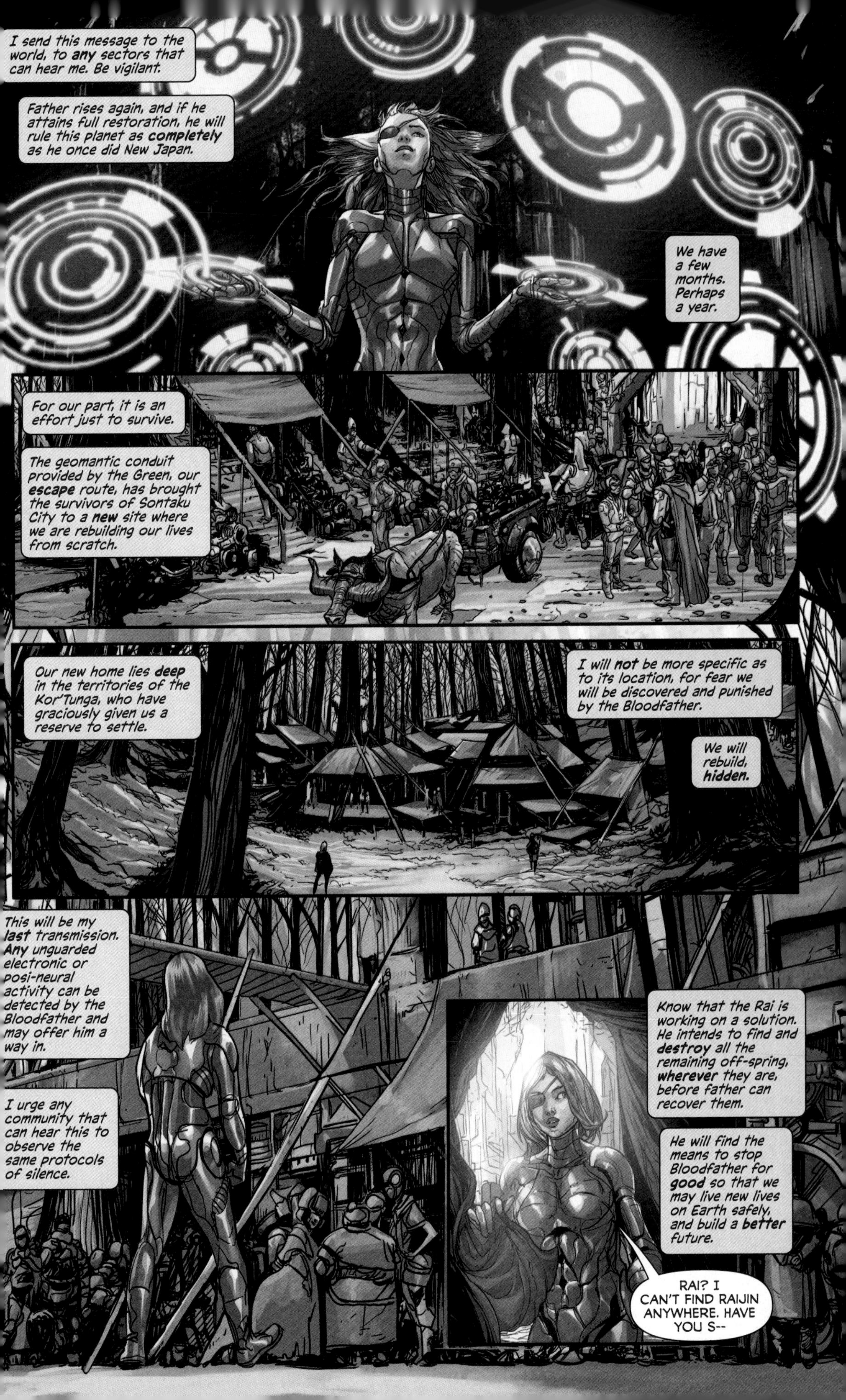
I send this message to the world, to any sectors that can hear me. Be vigilant.
Father rises again, and if he attains full restoration, he will rule this planet as completely as he once did New Japan.
We have a few months. Perhaps a year.
For our part, it is an effort just to survive.
The geomantic conduit provided by the Green, our escape route, has brought the survivors of Sontaku City to a new site where we are rebuilding our lives from scratch.
Our new home lies deep in the territories of the Kor'Tunga, who have graciously given us a reserve to settle.
I will not be more specific as to its location, for fear we will be discovered and punished by the Bloodfather.
We will rebuild, hidden.
This will be my last transmission. Any unguarded electronic or posi-neural activity can be detected by the Bloodfather and may offer him a way in.
I urge any community that can hear this to observe the same protocols of silence.
Know that the Rai is working on a solution. He intends to find and destroy all the remaining off-spring, wherever they are, before father can recover them.
He will find the means to stop Bloodfather for good so that we may live new lives on Earth safely, and build a better future.
RAI? I CAN'T FIND RAIJIN ANYWHERE. HAVE YOU S--

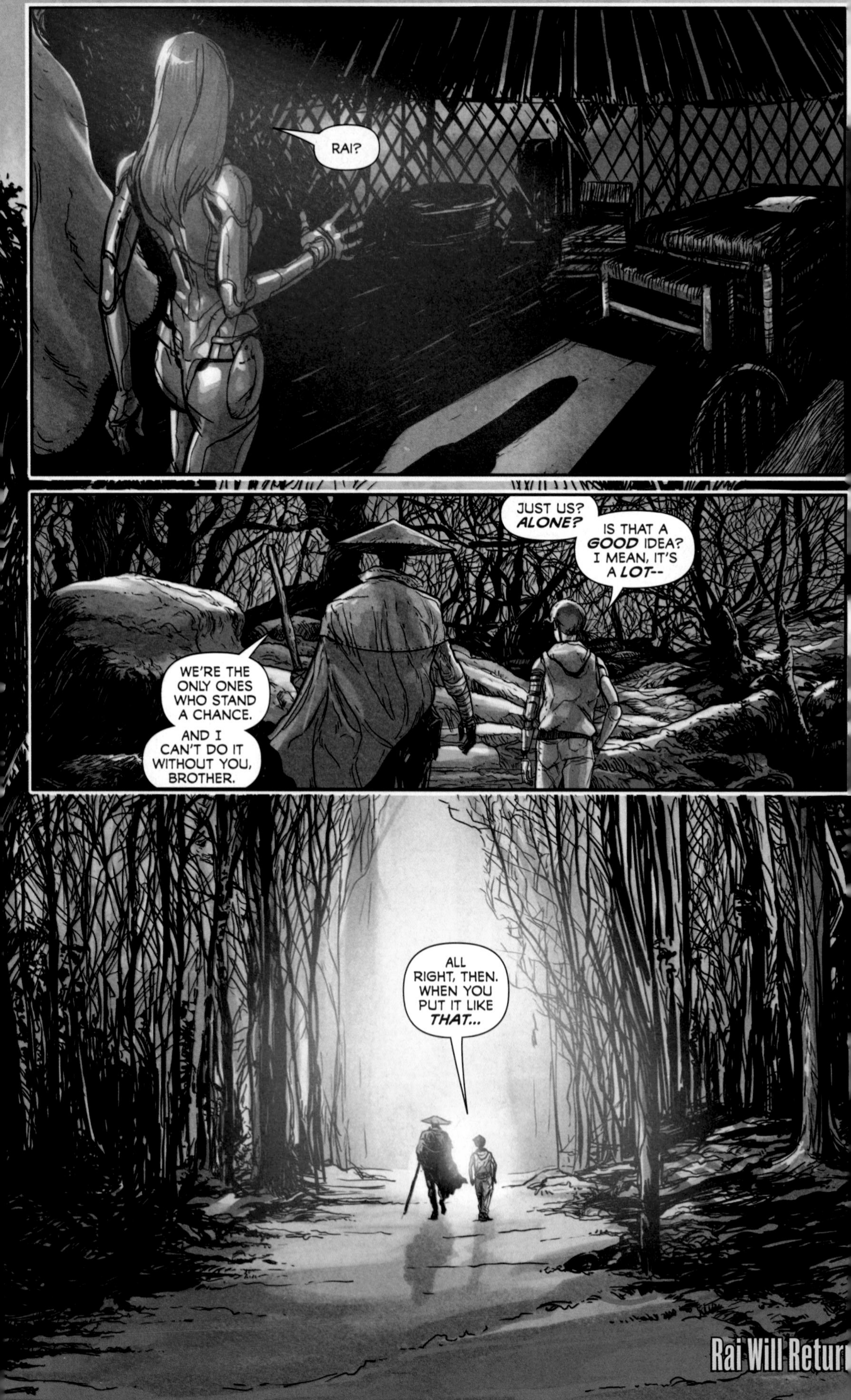
RAI?
JUST US? ALONE?
IS THAT A GOOD IDEA? I MEAN, IT'S A LOT--
WE'RE THE ONLY ONES WHO STAND A CHANCE.
AND I CAN'T DO IT WITHOUT YOU, BROTHER.
ALL RIGHT, THEN. WHEN YOU PUT IT LIKE THAT...
Rai Will Retur

GALLERY

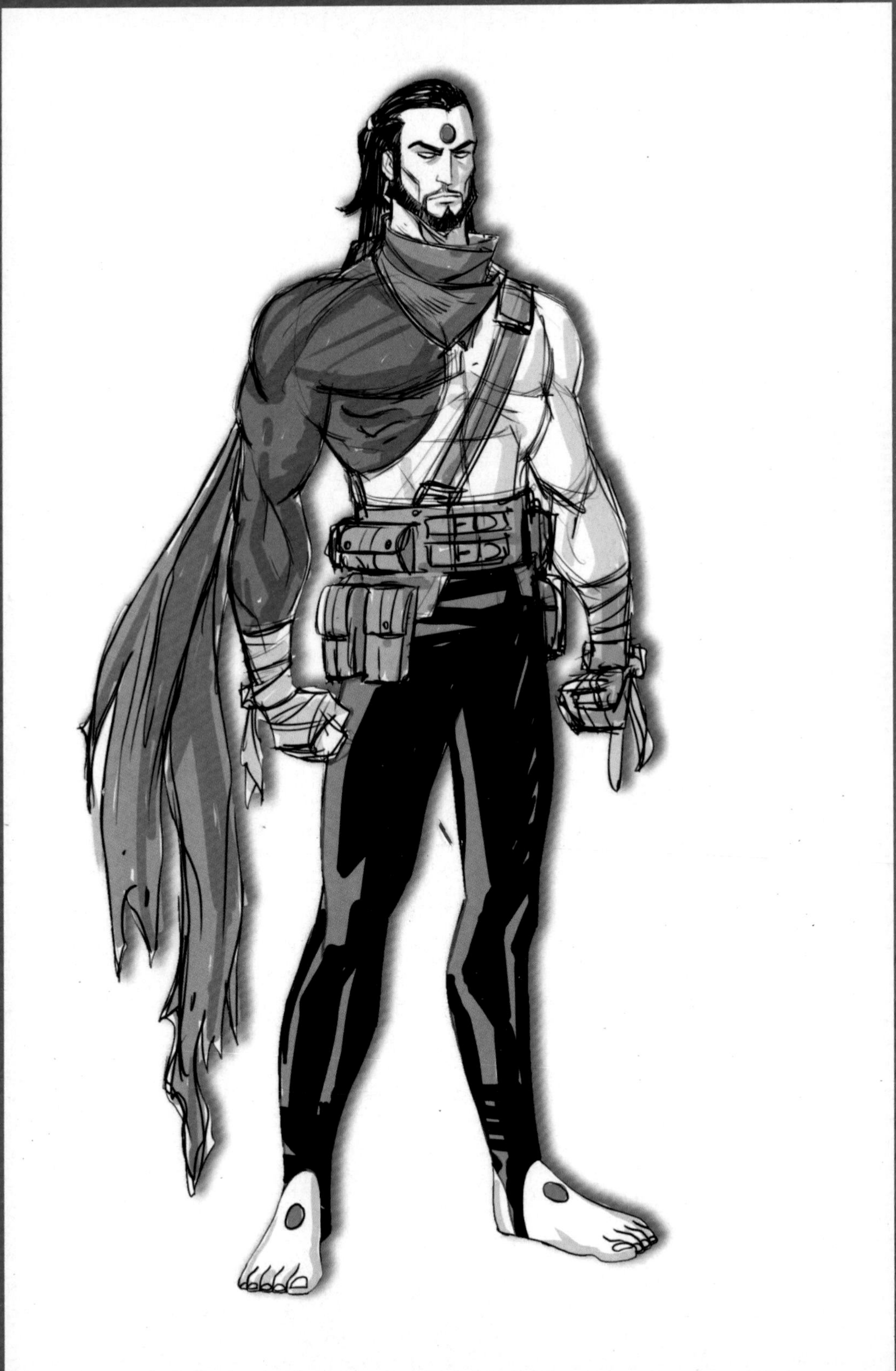

ORIGINALLY PUBLISHED IN **VALIANT: BLOODSHOT FCBD 2019 SPECIAL.**

41ST-CENTURY WAR

Travel to FALLEN WORLD, where the future of the Valiant Universe will be determined by a conflict between a troubled cyber samurai named Rai and Bloodshot, an unstoppable killing machine..

By Steve Foxe of Paste Magazine

What you've just read is only the beginning of the FALLEN WORLD saga, a brand-new story that's part sci-fi drama, part epic. The first issue by **Dan Abnett** and **Adam Pollina** is available NOW in comic book shops – most likely the very one where you picked up this issue! Read below as **Steve Foxe from Paste Magazine** talks with Abnett about working on this compelling drama.

PASTE MAGAZINE: FALLEN WORLD kicks off after a pretty dramatic status quo change for the Valiant Universe of the year 4002. What do new readers need to know about Rai and the world around him to jump in with FALLEN WORLD?

DAN ABNETT: Honestly? Not much! I'm trying to do my level best to introduce characters and concepts as we go along, so no reader gets lost (though the previous stories are great and I'd encourage anyone interested in FALLEN WORLD to pick up the trades and back issues...just to enjoy some fantastic comics).

As far as this goes... it's the future. Earth is a very alien place, slowly recovering after major disasters, remaking itself. A major chunk of the human population has been living in the orbital utopia of New Japan for centuries, looked after by the Artificial Intelligence, "Father". But Father was a bit of a tyrant on the quiet, and Rai – New Japan's champion – finally destroyed him and ended his reign for the good of all. As a result, New Japan fell, and the population is now trying to rebuild their culture on the "new Earth". It's a big, brave, and slightly scary new world for people who have been looked after by high-tech systems all their lives...

PASTE: Now that Father's reign is over and the nation of New Japan has shattered, what other forces are vying for power in the vacuum? There've been hints of animal/human hybrids and dinosaurs roaming about...

ABNETT: Lots, both big and small. There are minor threats and immediate hazards to contend with, but bigger and badder trouble is brewing: a major technological menace that is literally a blast from the past AND a very horrible surprise for Rai, plus a powerful and determined society that worships the old, high-tech Japan and wants to preserve it and use it to gain mastery.

PASTE: In addition to Rai and a host of new characters, FALLEN WORLD features Valiant mainstay Bloodshot in a newly antagonistic role. What's it like reimagining one of the publisher's foundational heroes (or antiheroes) as a villain? Or does Bloodshot still see himself as fighting for what's right?

ABNETT: Great fun. I love the character, and it's fun to get to play around with him so radically. I guess the answer is both: He believes he's doing right, and also torn by the way he's been used against what might be seen as the common good. He makes a great villain...and a sympathetic one. There's lots of cool story to unpack there.

PASTE: FALLEN WORLD is a set a few thousand years into the future, but should we expect any other Valiant cameos, either from long-lived characters or heroes who've passed down their mantles through the centuries?

ABNETT: Hmm...maybe. I can see lots of opportunities. And especially, let's say, if you're a Warrior who happens to be Eternal...

PASTE: Adam Pollina, who is the artist on the FALLEN WORLD series, was one of the most popular artists of the late 1990s, and this marks a long-awaited return to a monthly series for him. What's it like collaborating with him and what does he bring to Rai's story?

ABNETT: It's a privilege! Adam's work is very fine indeed. I think this series is going to blow people's socks off. ■

Special thanks to Steve Foxe and *Paste Magazine*. For the full interview with Dan Abnett, visit www.pastemagazine.com.

PREVIOUS PAGE: CHARACTER DESIGN BY **AJ JOTHIKUMAR**

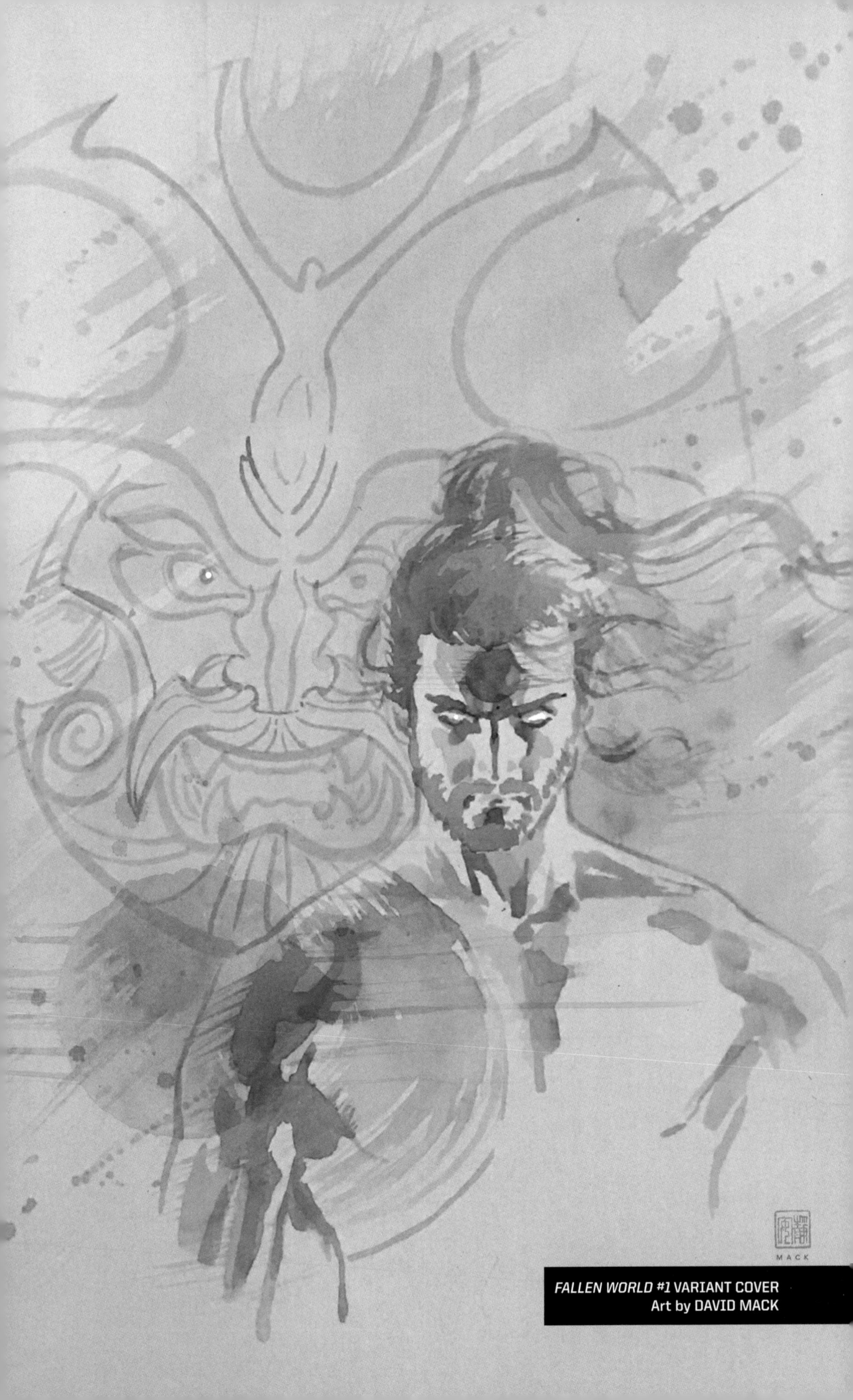
MACK

FALLEN WORLD #1 VARIANT COVER
Art by DAVID MACK

FALLEN WORLD #1
SHAZAM! COMICS & TOYS EXCLUSIVE VARIANT COVER
Art by JIMBO SALGADO with GABE ELTAEB

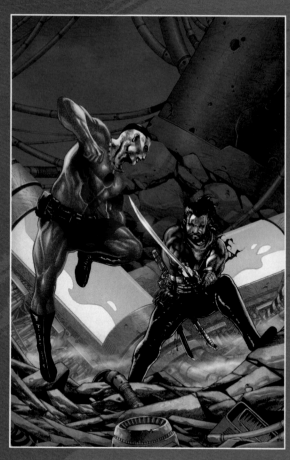

FALLEN WORLD #3 COVER C
Art by CASPAR WIJNGAARD

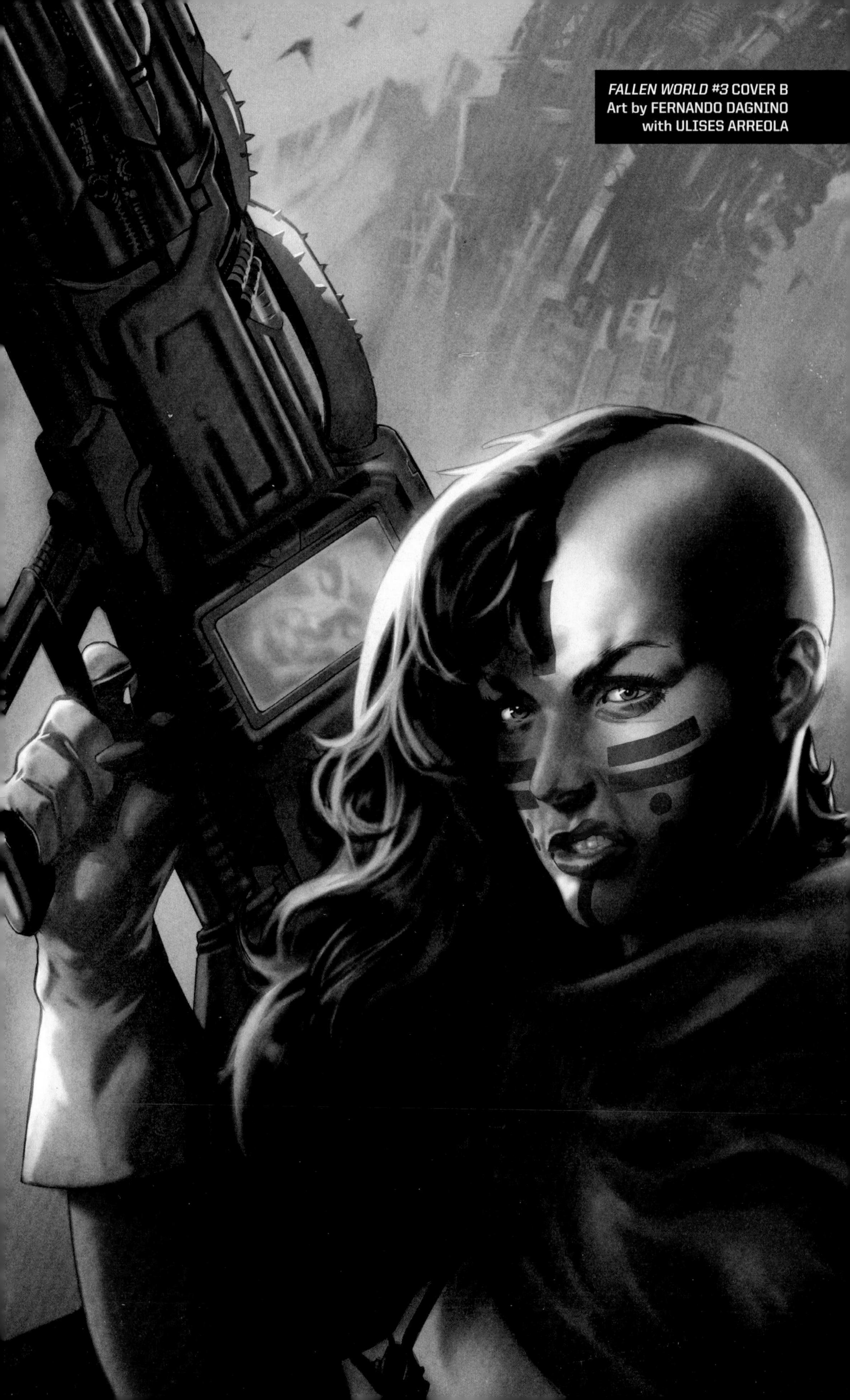

FALLEN WORLD #3 COVER B
Art by FERNANDO DAGNINO
with ULISES ARREOLA

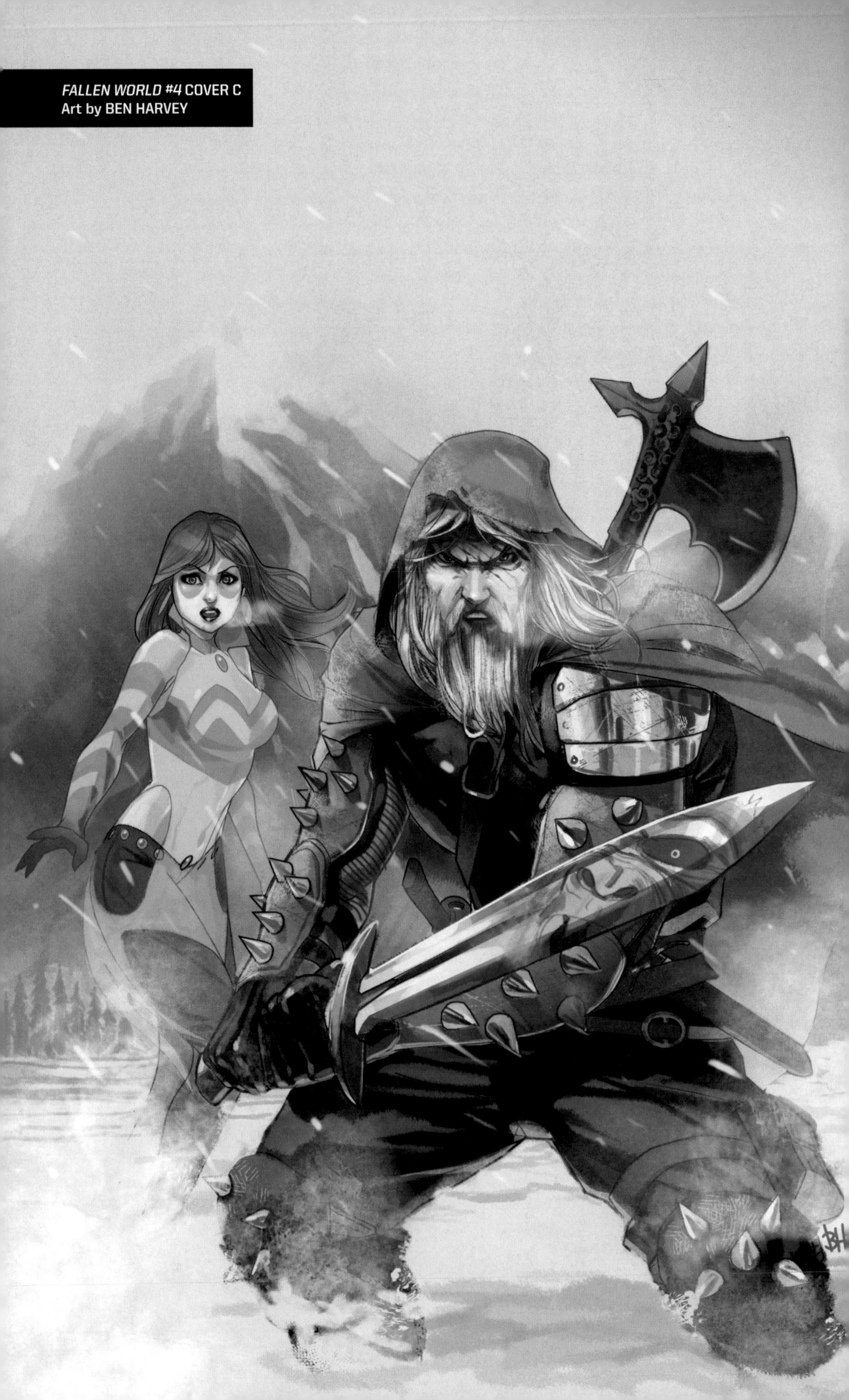

FALLEN WORLD #4 COVER C
Art by BEN HARVEY

FALLEN WORLD #5 COVER C
Art by RAÚL ALLÉN

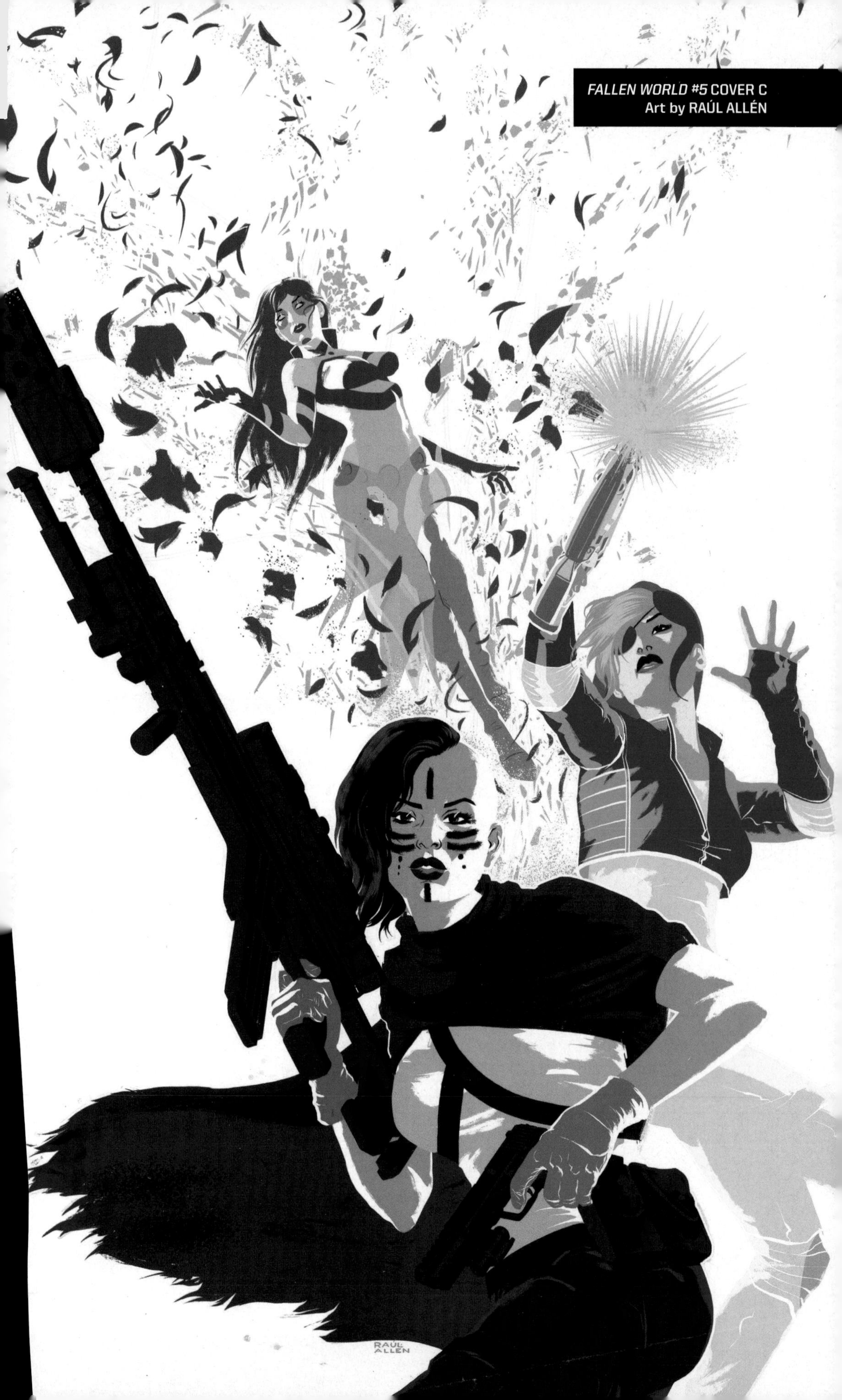
RAÚL
ALLEN

FALLEN WORLD #1, pages 18, 19, and (facing) 20
Art by ADAM POLLINA

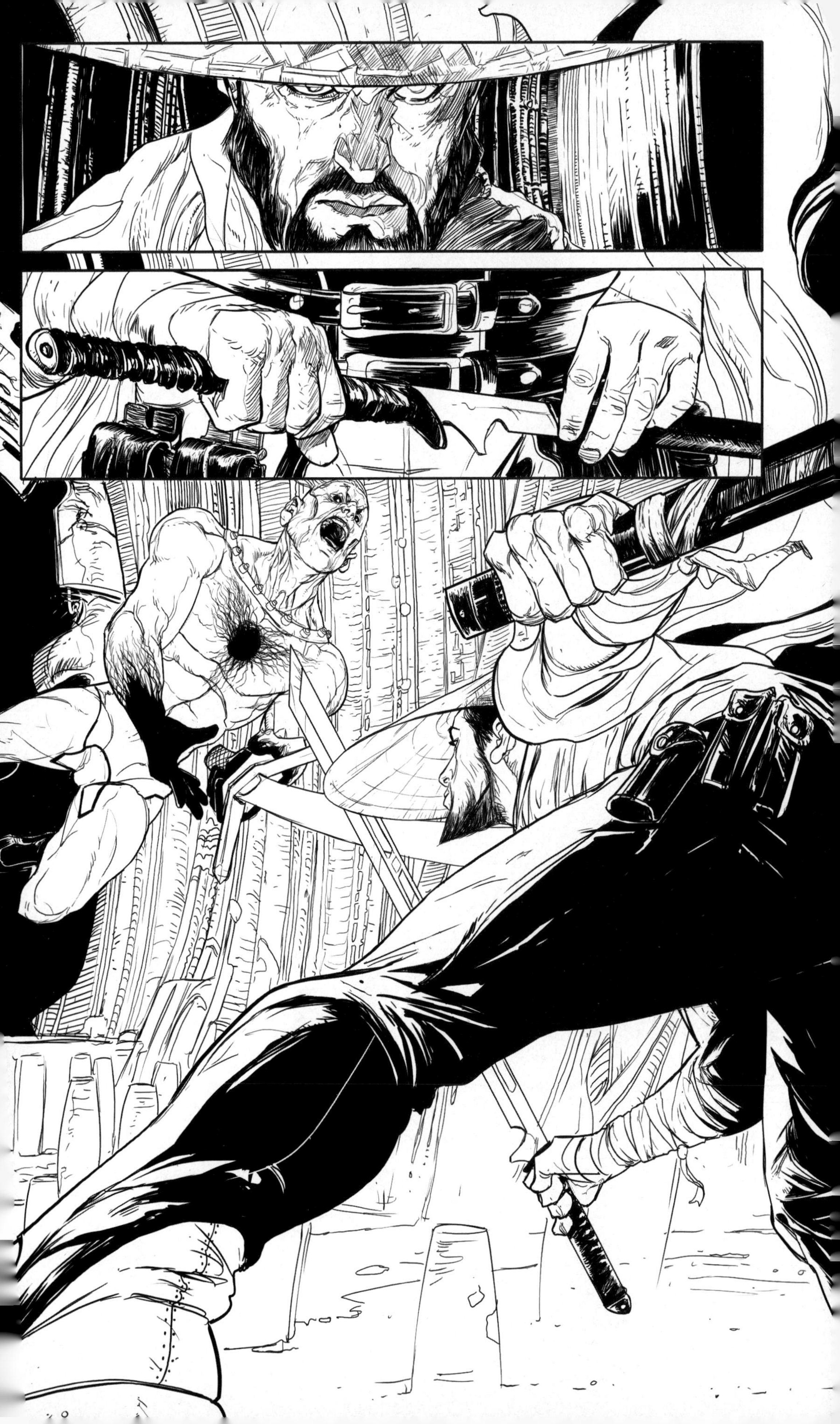

FALLEN WORLD #2, pages 1, 2, and (facing) 3
Art by ADAM POLLINA

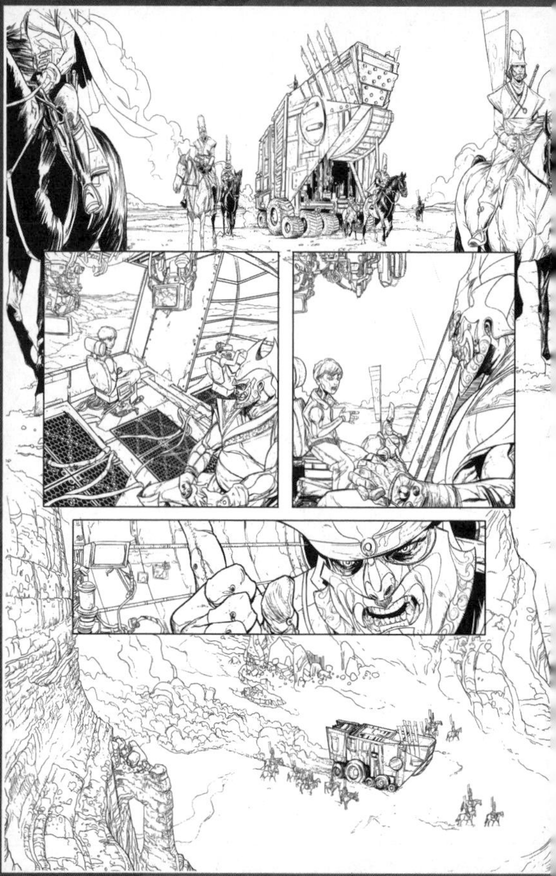

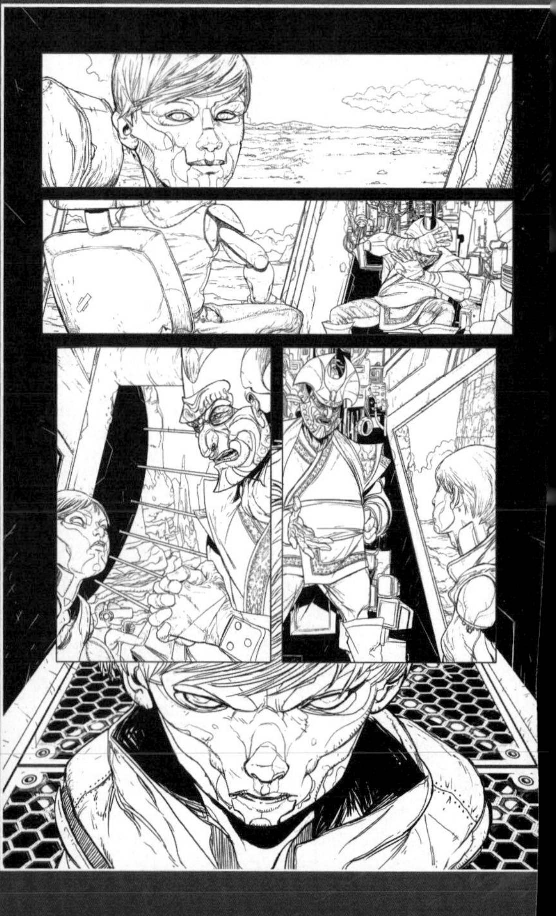

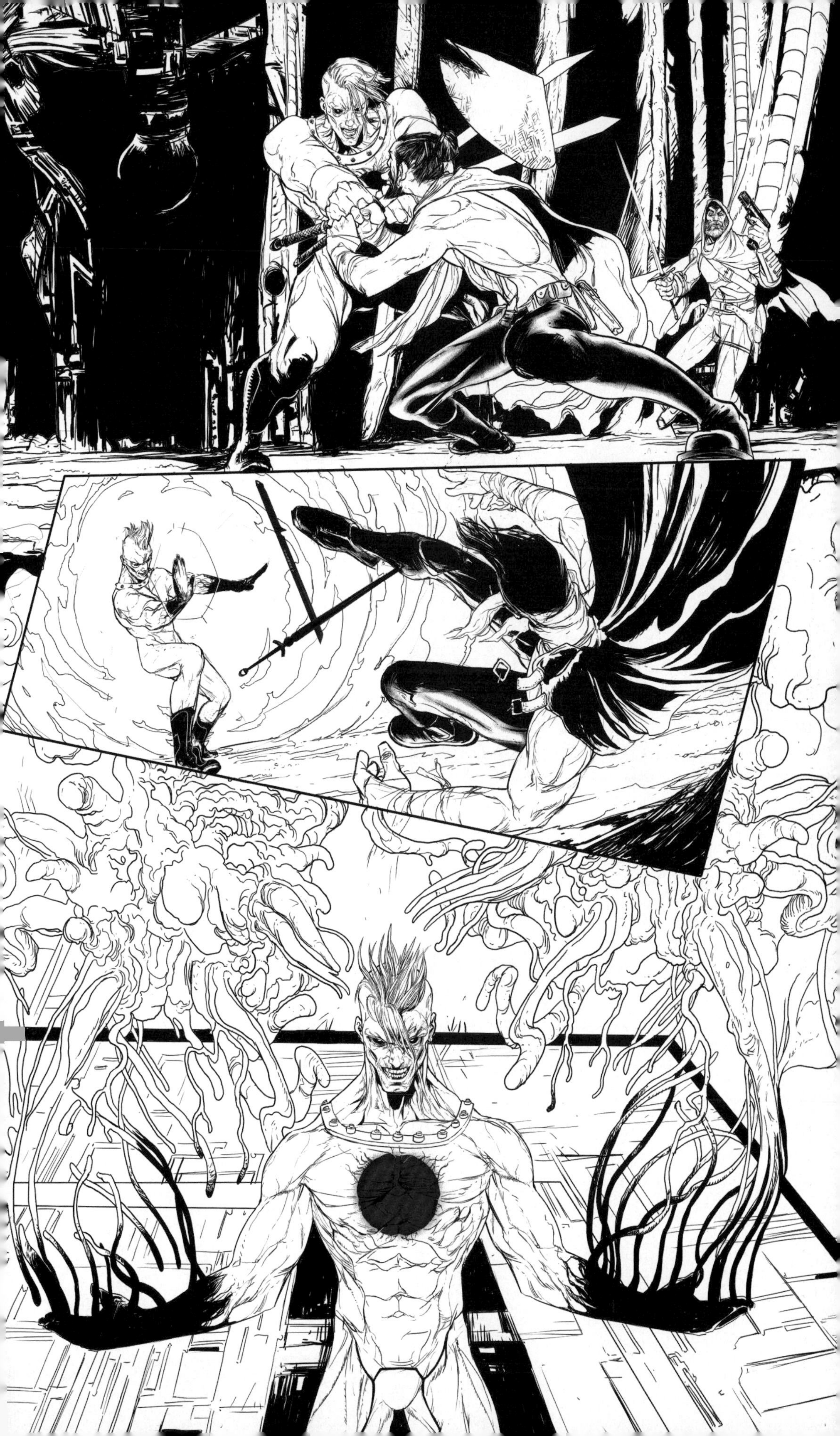

FALLEN WORLD #3, pages 18, 19, and (facing) 20
Art by ADAM POLLINA

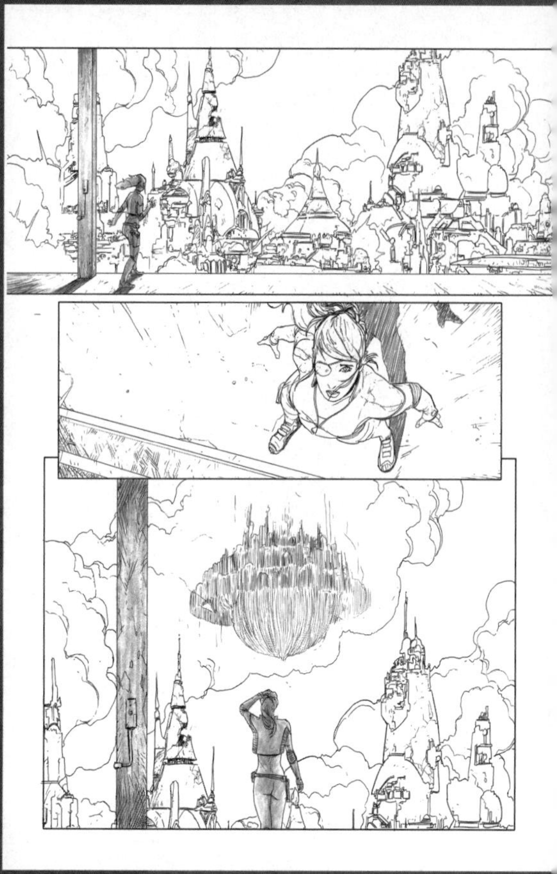

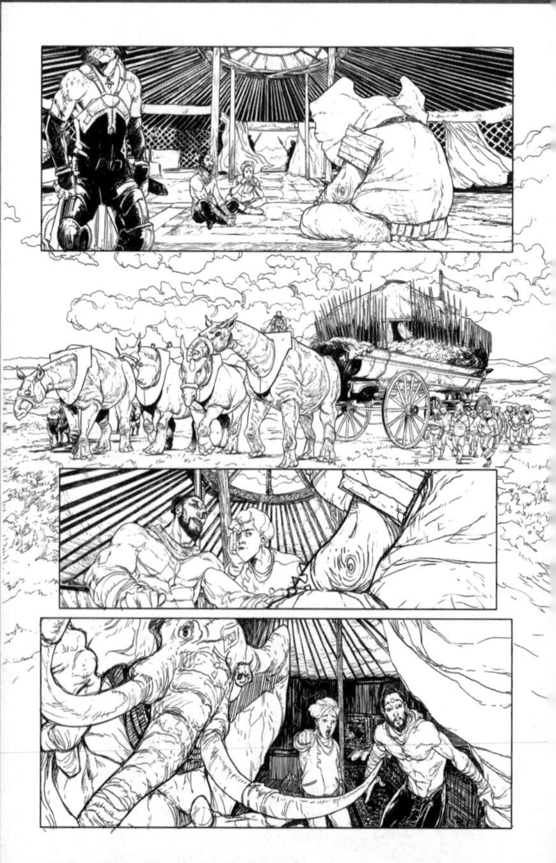

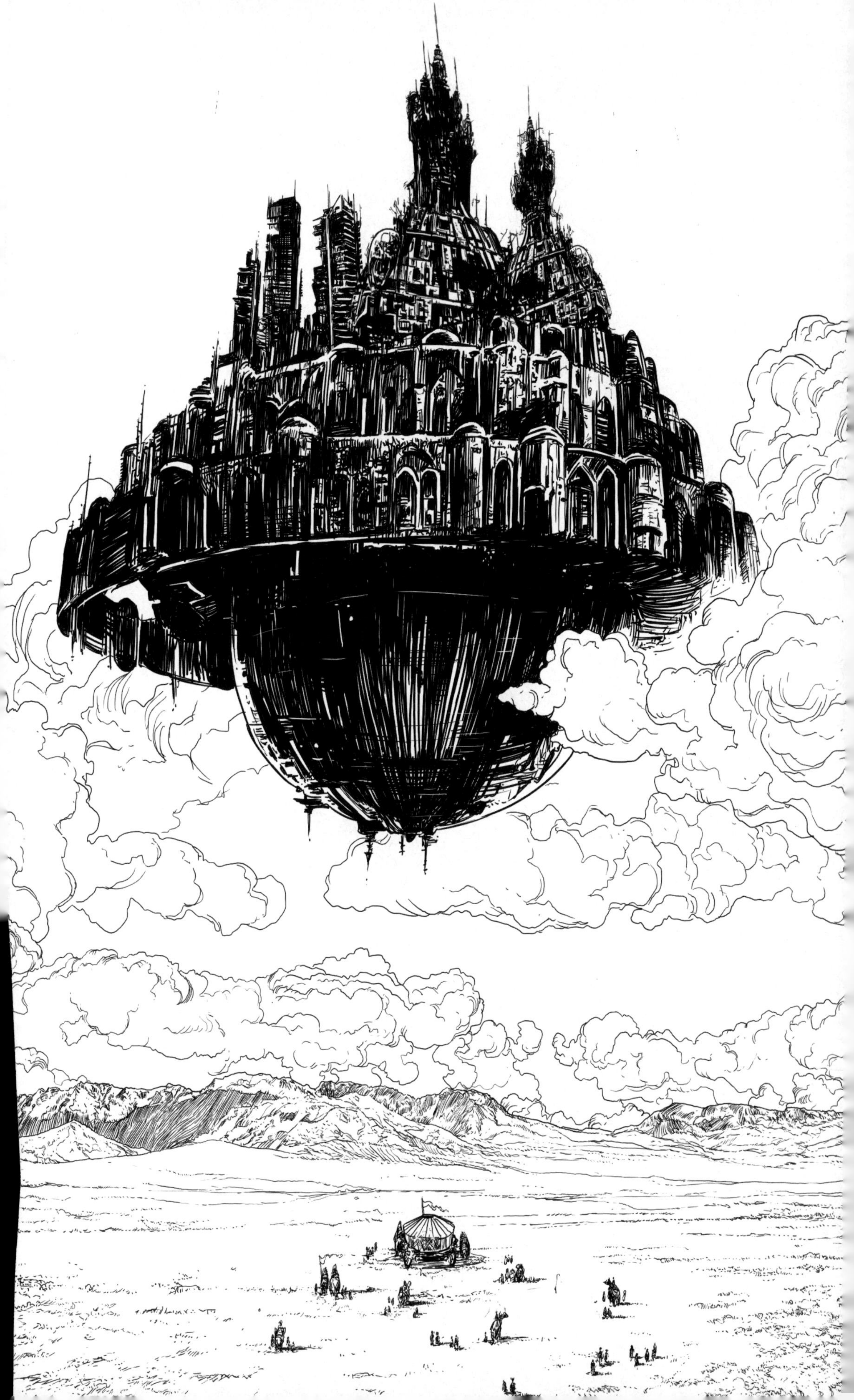

FALLEN WORLD #4, pages 2 and 3
Art by ADAM POLLINA

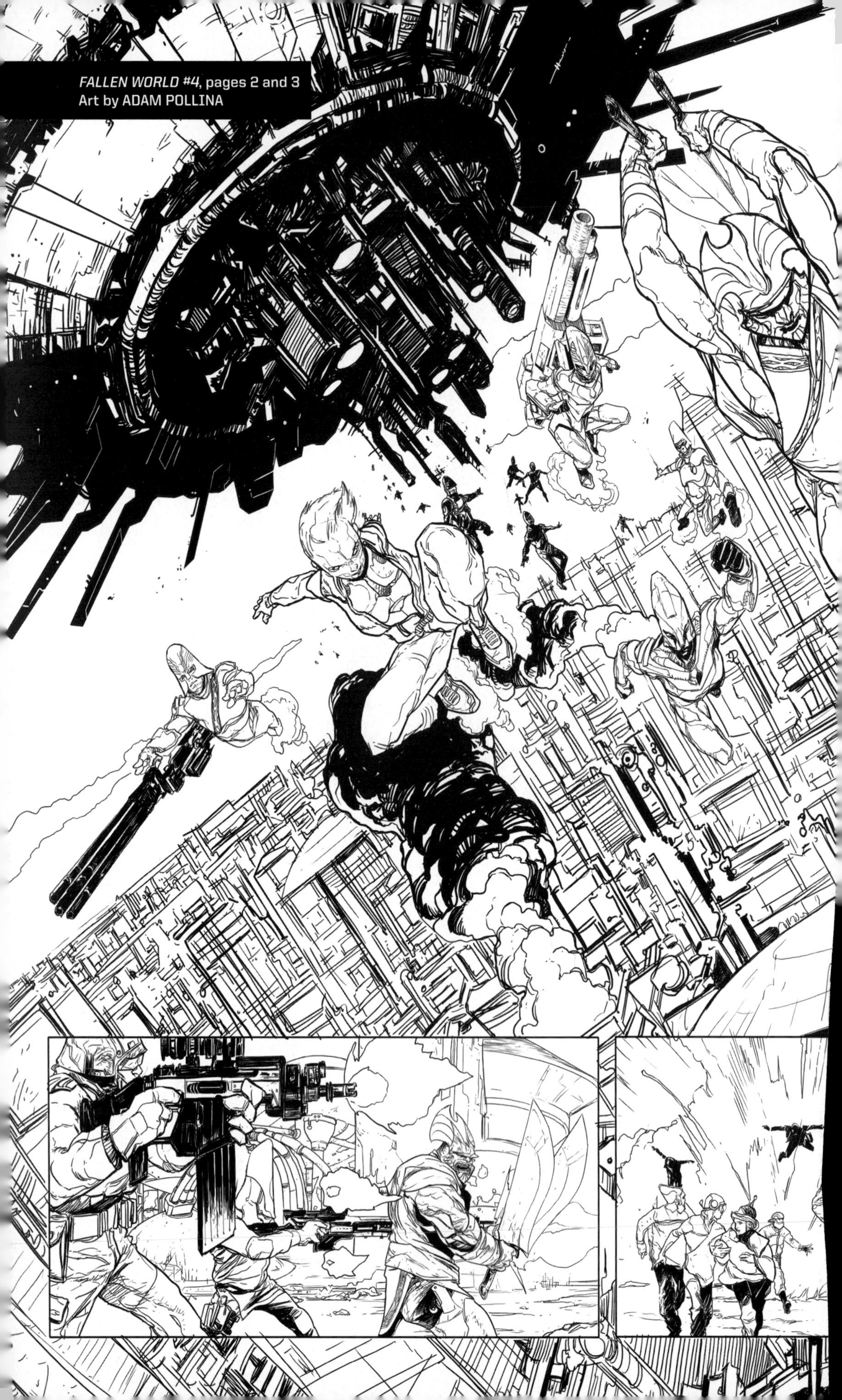

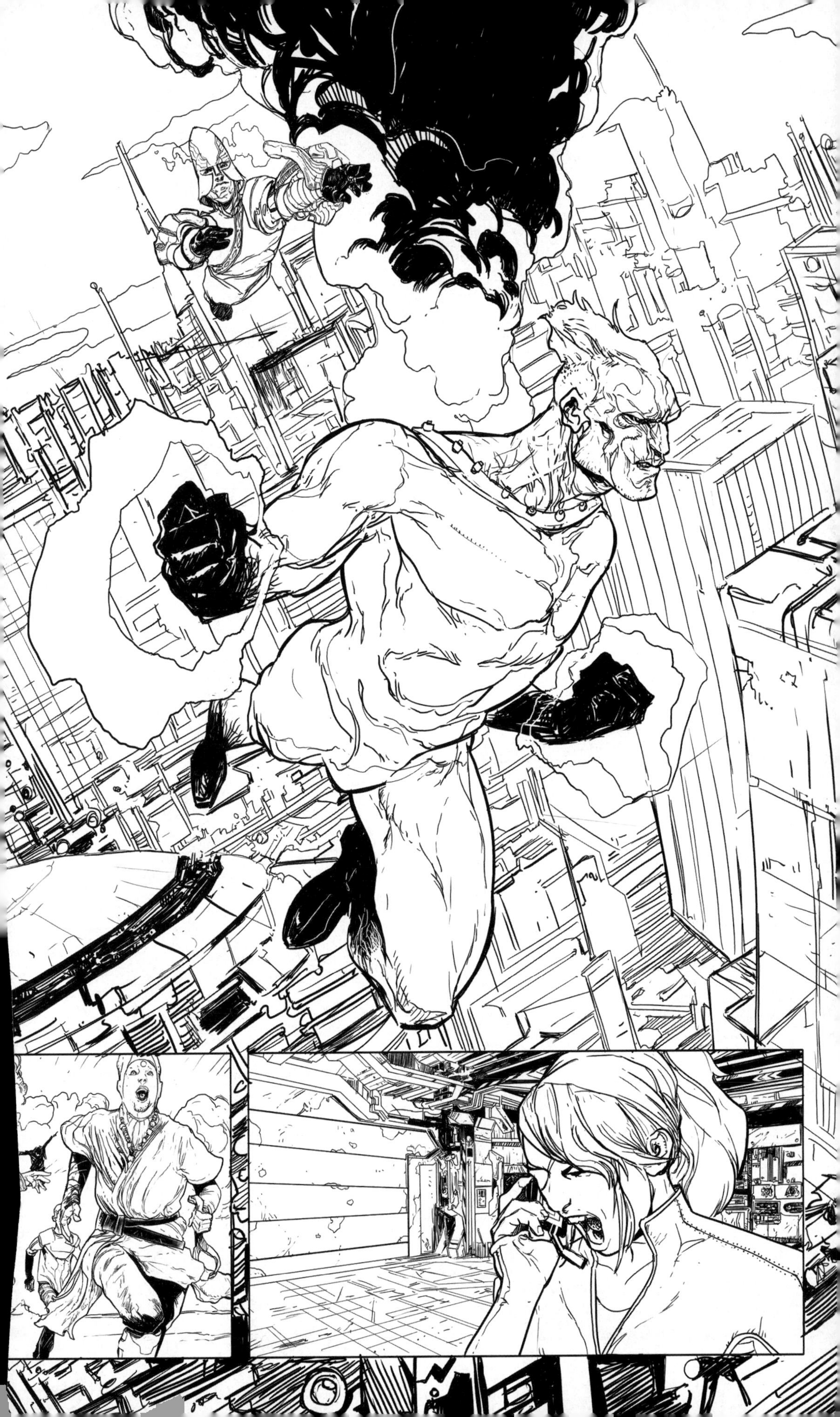

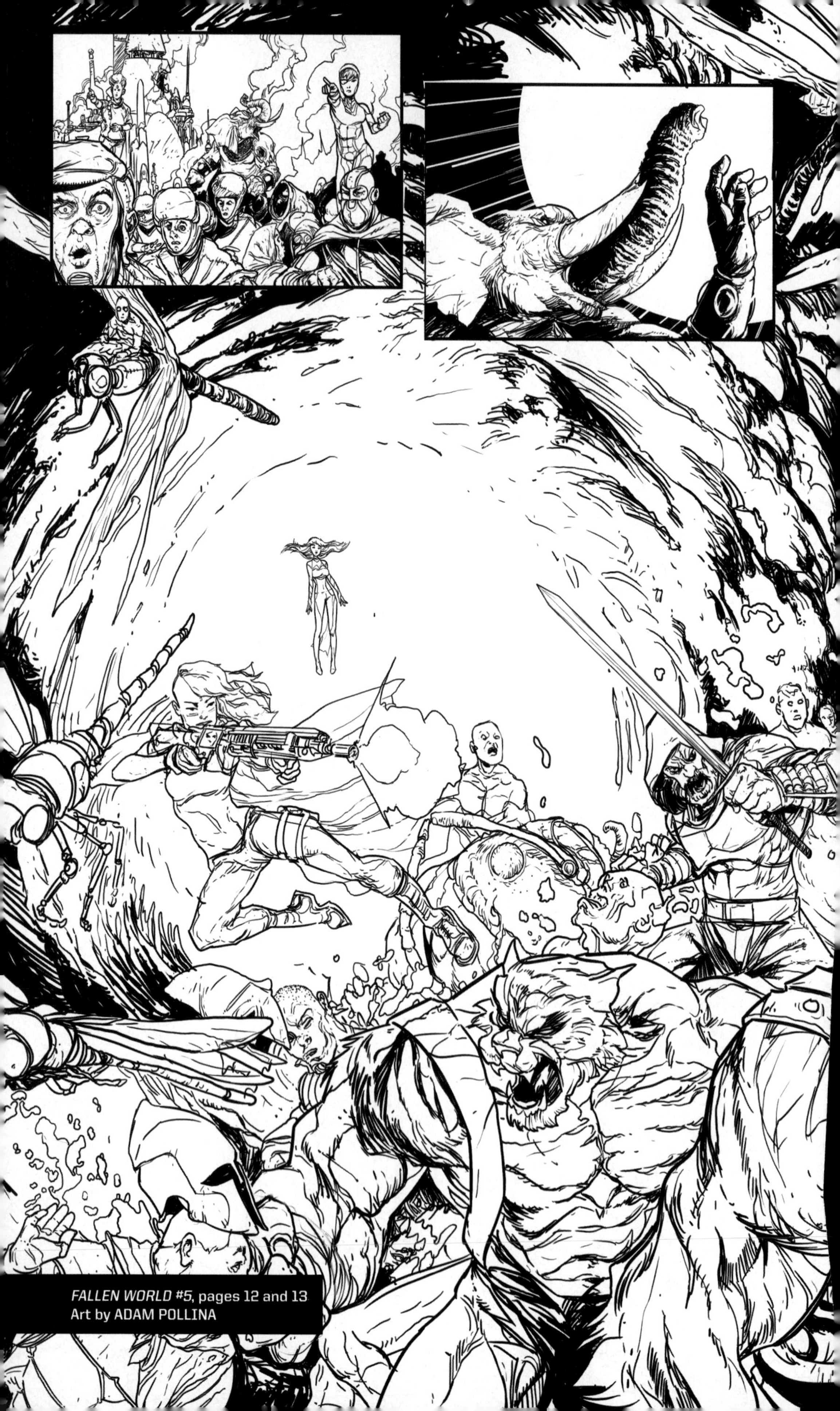

FALLEN WORLD #5, pages 12 and 13
Art by ADAM POLLINA

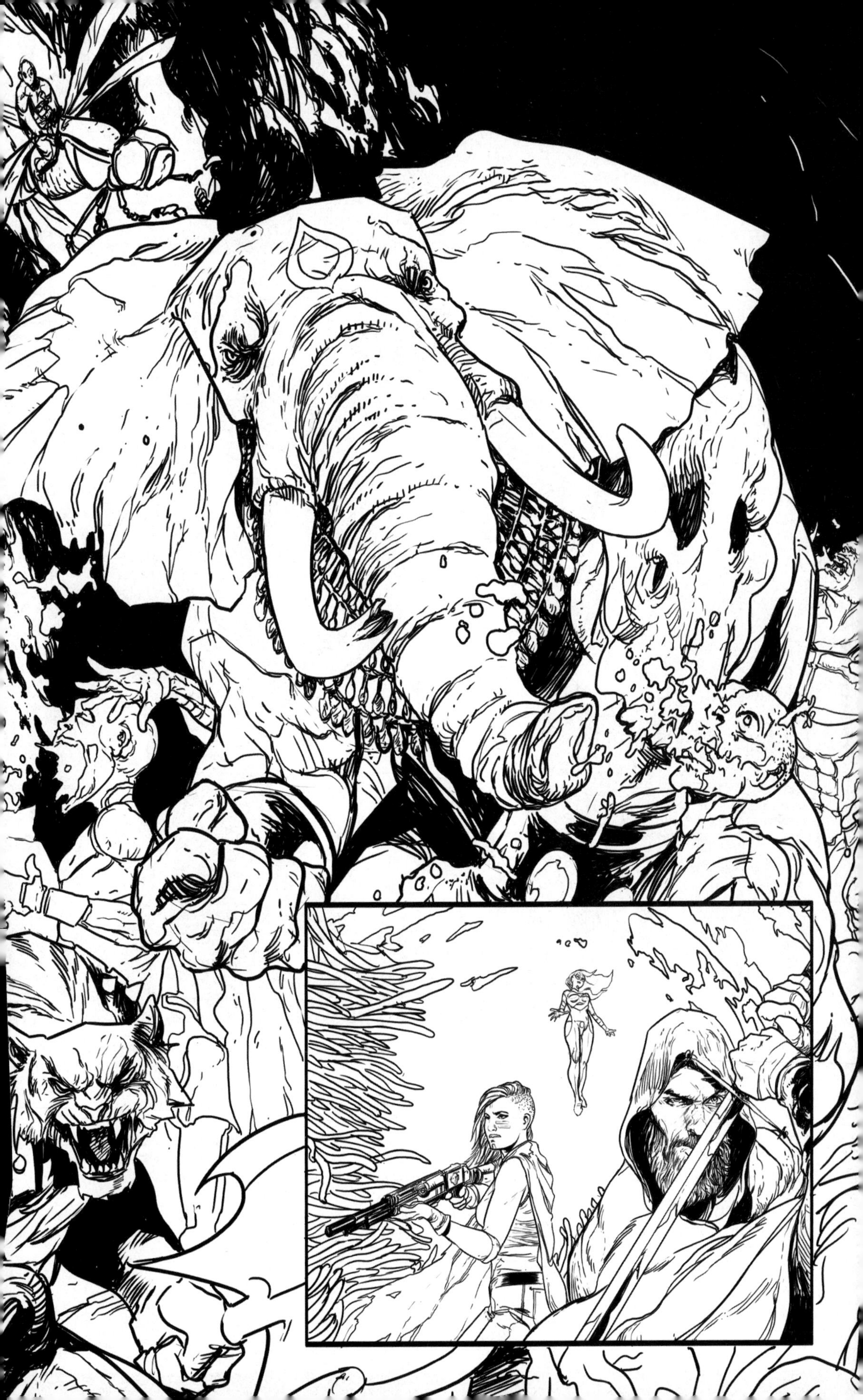

EXPLORE THE VALIANT

ACTION & ADVENTURE

BLOCKBUSTER ADVENTURE

COMEDY

BLOODSHOT SALVATION VOL. 1: THE BOOK OF REVENGE
ISBN: 978-1-68215-255-3

NINJA-K VOL. 1: THE NINJA FILES
ISBN: 978-1-68215-259-1

SAVAGE
ISBN: 978-1-68215-189-1

WRATH OF THE ETERNAL WARRIOR VOL. 1: RISEN
ISBN: 978-1-68215-123-5

X-O MANOWAR (2017) VOL. 1: SOLDIER
ISBN: 978-1-68215-205-8

4001 A.D.
ISBN: 978-1-68215-143-3

ARMOR HUNTERS
ISBN: 978-1-939346-45-2

BOOK OF DEATH
ISBN: 978-1-939346-97-1

HARBINGER WARS
ISBN: 978-1-939346-09-4

THE VALIANT
ISBN: 978-1-939346-60-5

A&A: THE ADVENTURES OF ARCHER & ARMSTRONG VOL. 1: IN THE BAG
ISBN: 978-1-68215-149-5

THE DELINQUENTS
ISBN: 978-1-939346-51-3

QUANTUM AND WOODY! (2017) VOL. 1: KISS KISS, KLANG KLANG
ISBN: 978-1-68215-269-0

NIVERSE FOR ONLY $9.99

HORROR & MYSTERY

ITANNIA
N: 978-1-68215-185-3
E DEATH-DEFYING DOCTOR MIRAGE
N: 978-1-939346-49-0
PTURE
N: 978-1-68215-225-6
ADOWMAN (2018) VOL. 1:
R OF THE DARK
N: 978-1-68215-239-3

SCIENCE FICTION & FANTASY

DIVINITY
ISBN: 978-1-939346-76-6
THE FORGOTTEN QUEEN
ISBN: 978-1-68215-324-6
IMPERIUM VOL. 1: COLLECTING MONSTERS
ISBN: 978-1-939346-75-9
IVAR, TIMEWALKER VOL. 1: MAKING HISTORY
ISBN: 978-1-939346-63-6
RAI VOL. 1: WELCOME TO NEW JAPAN
ISBN: 978-1-939346-41-4
WAR MOTHER
ISBN: 978-1-68215-237-9

TEEN ADVENTURE

FAITH VOL. 1: HOLLYWOOD AND VINE
ISBN: 978-1-68215-121-1
GENERATION ZERO VOL. 1: WE ARE THE FUTURE
ISBN: 978-1-68215-175-4
HARBINGER RENEGADE VOL. 1: THE JUDGMENT OF SOLOMON
ISBN: 978-1-68215-169-3
LIVEWIRE VOL. 1: FUGITIVE
ISBN: 978-1-68215-301-7
SECRET WEAPONS
ISBN: 978-1-68215-229-4

Discover the entire Valiant Universe of titles at VALIANTENTERTAINMENT.COM/ALL-SERIES/

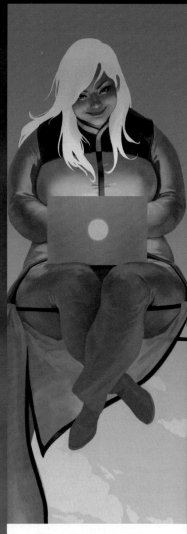

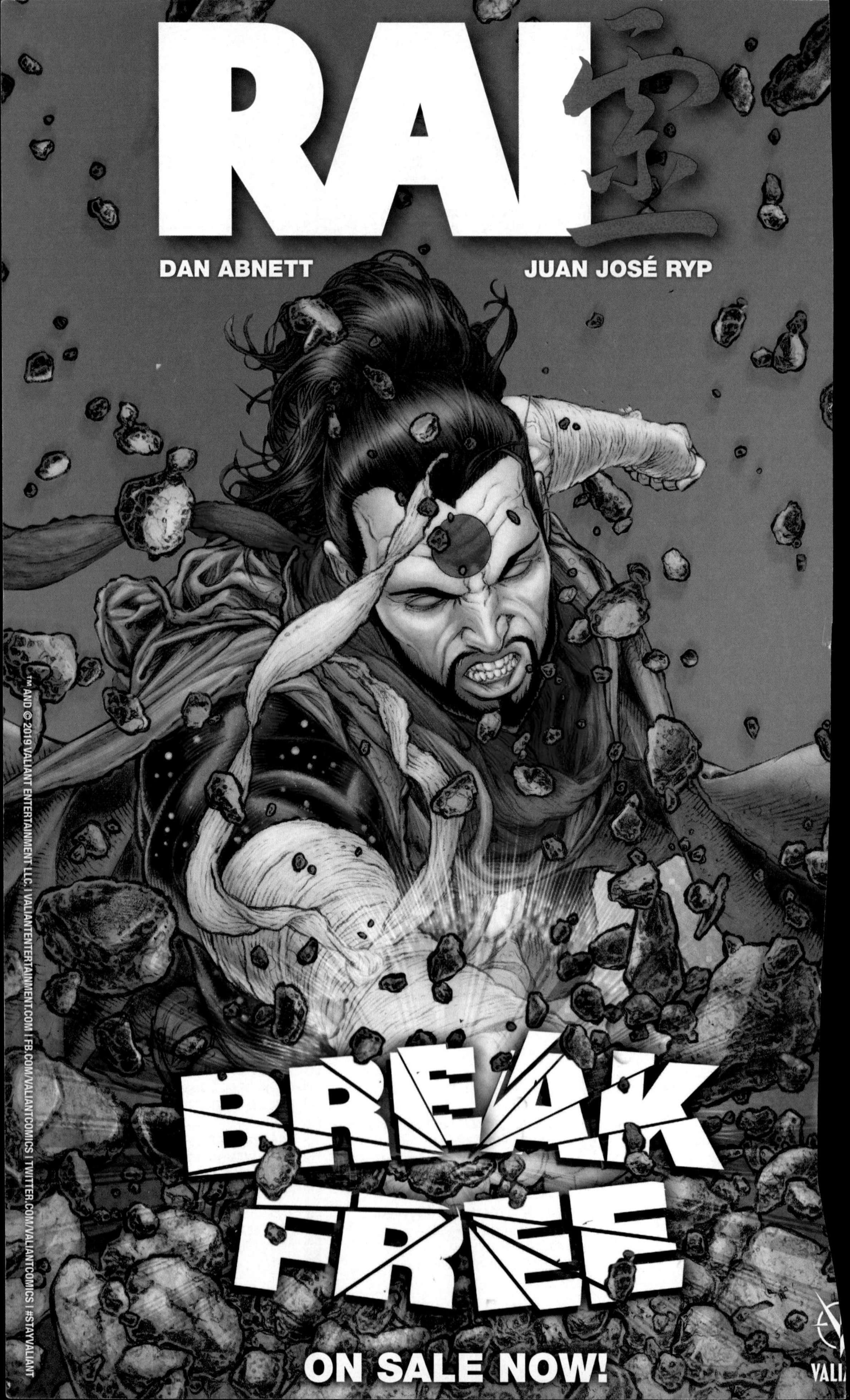
RAI
DAN ABNETT
JUAN JOSÉ RYP
BREAK FREE
ON SALE NOW!